Contents

Abacus Foundation

Since the introduction of the Foundation Stage and the publication of the related *Curriculum Guidance* in May 2000, teachers in playgroups, nurseries and reception classes now have both curriculum content and a set of principles to inform their teaching. The *Curriculum Guidance for the Foundation Stage* designates six areas of learning for children – 'Personal, social and emotional development', 'Communication, language and literacy', 'Mathematical development', 'Knowledge and understanding of the world', 'Physical development' and 'Creative development'. Each area is outlined in some detail and provides a series of 'stepping stones'. These are intended to help practitioners plan a progression of activities to allow children to achieve the Early Learning Goals.

The **Abacus Foundation** materials are designed and written to support teachers with planning and teaching to match the *Curriculum Guidance for the Foundation Stage*. There are two books provided at each level (F1 for 3- to 4-year-olds and F2 for 4- to 5-year-olds) – a Teachers' Resource Book and an Activity Book. The Teachers' Resource Book comprises a complete series of weekly plans, backed up by the bank of activities in the Activity Book. With the 'Mathematical development' area of learning as their basis, the plans are grounded in the progression referred to in the *Curriculum Guidance* and provide a comprehensive two-year programme leading clearly to the attainment of the Early Learning Goals for mathematics.

Teachers' Resource Book

The **Abacus Foundation F2** materials are intended for all those teaching the second year of the Foundation Stage in nurseries, playgroups or infant schools. The Teachers' Resource Book comprises the following:

- **Yearly plans for F1 and F2**
- **Weekly plans to cover each term**
- **Activities for daily 'On the rug' sessions**
- **'At home' activities and advice for parents**
- **Recipe Bank**
- **Curriculum matching charts**
- **Record-keeping grids**
- **Rhyme and storybook references**

At the heart of the materials are the weekly plans, around which we have structured the materials and support offered. In our experience, all over the country teachers, nursery nurses, playgroup leaders and others are replicating each other's planning on an almost daily basis. Consultation with many professionals has led us to believe that a more efficient and effective scenario involves planning from agreed starting points. Therefore, the **Abacus Foundation** Teachers' Resource Book provides these in the form of weekly plans, which practitioners can adapt to use in their own settings.

The weekly plans include both a variety of teaching contexts and all the different types of activity vital for effective early years education. They offer suggestions for daily 'on the rug' large group teacher-led activities, and outlines of differentiated ideas for teacher-initiated small group or paired activities (which are expanded in detail in the Activity Book). As well as this they make explicit reference to opportunities for learning through structured play activities. Mathematical ideas, skills and knowledge are introduced both in the wider context of everyday activity and also in the course of specifically mathematical endeavours. Using the weekly plans as a starting point means that it is no longer necessary to continually re-invent the wheel – which has to be good news for all of us!

Weekly plans

The weekly plan is at the heart of every professional's preparation for effective teaching and learning in the early years. It should indicate that teaching will take place in at least three contexts – large group, small group, and as individuals/pairs. It should make clear that informal and formal activities to support learning are envisaged, and recognise where maths skills or knowledge are likely to form an aspect of a play activity. Possessing a clear, focused, balanced and appropriate plan for the children in each specific setting is the first and most essential step towards delivering an effective curriculum. In addition, it is important that the weekly plans give clear evidence of progression and coherence over a period of time, as well as of curriculum coverage.

Teacher-led activities

This is a short session consisting of 5 to 10 minutes of focused demonstrative activity. It commonly starts with a number rhyme, song or a small counting exercise as a warm up. The teacher then demonstrates a mathematical operation or performs a mathematical activity, often using a role-play or narrative element, in a context which will make sense to the children and also be memorable. This 'on the rug' element in the day's activities can be a very powerful catalyst in developing children's knowledge, understanding and skills in mathematics.

Teacher-initiated activities

These are intended for use by a practitioner working with small groups of three to four children. This means that the adult involved is in an excellent position to teach to each child's specific needs. Comparisons with, and connections to, topics of individual interest can be created and sustained. The activities are differentiated so that each child can be encouraged to take part in an activity of an appropriate level, and are described in detail in the Activity Book, which also provides a bank of extra activities. A child would not normally be expected to engage in more than one, or at most two, of these activities over the course of the week.

Objective

This is the focus of the teaching in mathematics for the week. It always relates to an aspect of the 'Mathematical development' strand in the *Curriculum Guidance for the Foundation Stage*.

Independent activities

Young children sometimes require both direction and focus to enable a play activity to take off and go well. Contexts for supported play are outlined on the plan, some for independent and some for semi-independent activities. Teachers can choose which, if any, to use during the week. The structure can be altered or activities rearranged to suit particular topics or circumstances.

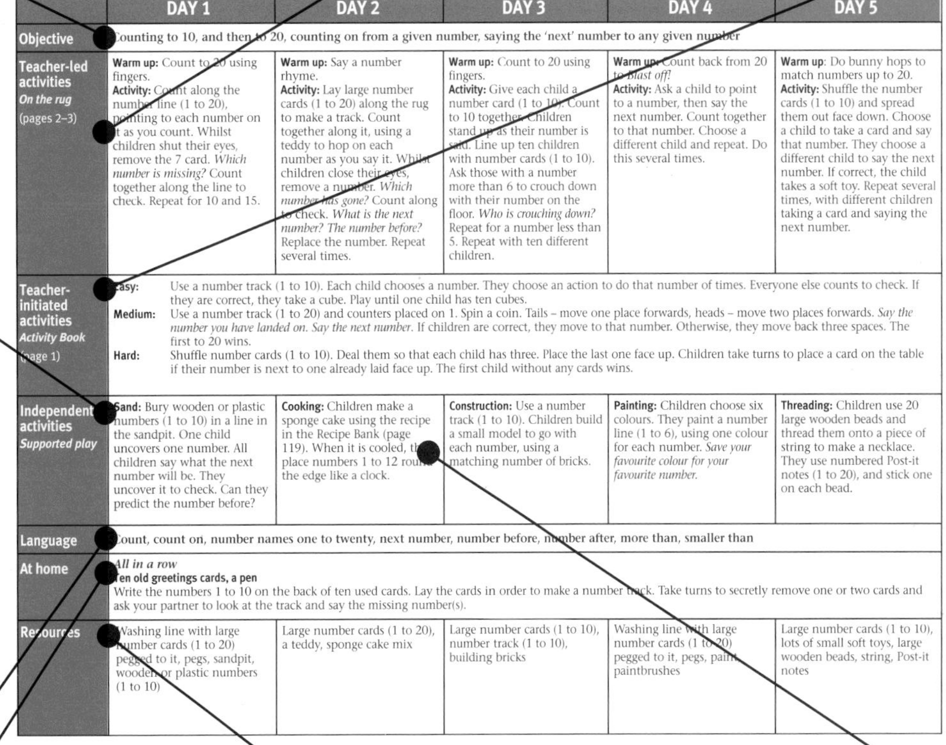

	DAY 1	DAY 2	DAY 3	DAY 4	DAY 5
Objective	Counting to 10, and then to 20, counting on from a given number, saying the 'next' number to any given number				
Teacher-led activities *On the rug* (pages 2–3)	**Warm up:** Count to 20 using fingers. **Activity:** Count along the number line (1 to 20), pointing to each number on it as you count. Whilst children shut their eyes, remove the 7 card. *Which number is missing?* Count together along the line to check. Repeat for 10 and 15.	**Warm up:** Say a number rhyme. **Activity:** Lay large number cards (1 to 20) along the rug to make a track. Count together along it, using a teddy to hop on each number as you say it. Whilst children close their eyes, remove a number. *Which number has gone?* Count along to check. *What is the next number? The number before?* Replace the number. Repeat several times.	**Warm up:** Count to 20 using fingers. **Activity:** Give each child a number card (1 to 10). Count to 10 together. Children stand up as their number is said. Line up ten children with number cards (1 to 10). Ask those with a number more than 6 to crouch down with their number on the floor. *Who is crouching down?* Repeat for a number less than 5. Repeat with ten different children.	**Warm up:** Count back from 20 to *Blast off!* **Activity:** Ask a child to point to a number, then say the next number. Count together to that number. Choose a different child and repeat. Do this several times.	**Warm up**: Do bunny hops to match numbers up to 20. **Activity:** Shuffle the number cards (1 to 10) and spread them out face down. Choose a child to take a card and say that number. They choose a different child to say the next number. If correct, the child takes a soft toy. Repeat several times, with different children taking a card and saying the next number.
Teacher-initiated activities *Activity Book* (page 1)	**Easy:** Use a number track (1 to 10). Each child chooses a number. They choose an action to do that number of times. Everyone else counts to check. If they are correct, they take a cube. Play until one child has ten cubes. **Medium:** Use a number track (1 to 20) and counters placed on 1. Spin a coin. Tails – move one place forwards, heads – move two places forwards. *Say the number you have landed on. Say the next number.* If children are correct, they move to that number. Otherwise, they move back three spaces. The first to 20 wins. **Hard:** Shuffle number cards (1 to 10). Deal them so that each child has three. Place the last one face up. Children take turns to place a card on the table if their number is next to one already laid face up. The first child without any cards wins.				
Independent activities *Supported play*	**Sand:** Bury wooden or plastic numbers (1 to 10) in a line in the sandpit. One child uncovers one number. All children say what the next number will be. They uncover it to check. Can they predict the number before?	**Cooking:** Children make a sponge cake using the recipe in the Recipe Bank (page 119). When it is cooled, they place numbers 1 to 12 round the edge like a clock.	**Construction:** Use a number track (1 to 10). Children build a small model to go with each number, using a matching number of bricks.	**Painting:** Children choose six colours. They paint a number line (1 to 6), using one colour for each number. *Save your favourite colour for your favourite number.*	**Threading:** Children use 20 large wooden beads and thread them onto a piece of string to make a necklace. They use numbered Post-it notes (1 to 20), and stick one on each bead.
Language	**Count, count on, number names one to twenty, next number, number before, number after, more than, smaller than**				
At home	***All in a row*** **Ten old greetings cards, a pen** Write the numbers 1 to 10 on the back of ten used cards. Lay the cards in order to make a number track. Take turns to secretly remove one or two cards and ask your partner to look at the track and say the missing number(s).				
Resources	Washing line with large number cards (1 to 20) pegged to it, pegs, sandpit, wooden or plastic numbers (1 to 10)	Large number cards (1 to 20), a teddy, sponge cake mix	Large number cards (1 to 10), number track (1 to 10), building bricks	Washing line with large number cards (1 to 20) pegged to it, pegs, paint, paintbrushes	Large number cards (1 to 10), lots of small soft toys, large wooden beads, string, Post-it notes

Language

This section lists some of the terms and vocabulary that teachers may want to stress as they teach a particular objective. The words and phrases could be displayed around the nursery or classroom during the week, so that they become the focus of the children's interest as well as being used in the teaching. This will also ensure that all the adults working with the children are aware of the importance of using appropriate mathematical vocabulary.

'At home' activities

A suggested letter to parents is provided on page 118 to explain what the children are working on. This can be sent home or displayed on the noticeboard with a simple instruction sheet for the 'At home' activity, which will enable parents to share the activity with their child and take part in their mathematical development. The activities are also suitable for a small group activity in the nursery/playgroup, so can be followed up or repeated in the classroom.

Resources

This section lists the resources needed for that day's 'on the rug' teacher-led activity as well as the suggested independent play activity. This enables the teacher to ensure that they have all the necessary materials available before organising the children.

Cooking

Cooking with children is an excellent way to use mathematical skills in a practical, useful and enjoyable way. A cooking activity is therefore included on most of the weekly plans. Whilst cooking to a recipe, children are following a procedure, measuring, counting, estimating, discussing amounts and quantities, and using a host of other skills. The recipes for all the cooking activities are provided in the Recipe Bank on page 119.

Teaching

The two pages following each weekly plan provide a more detailed description of the teacher-led activity for each day's 'on the rug' session. The teaching for each week is expanded into a more comprehensive explanation and offers a 'script' for teachers to adapt as they wish. For simplicity it is categorised by day. Suggested questions and vocabulary are given in italics.

Classroom management

Good early years practice involves the setting up of a wide variety of informal learning situations, and also some direct teaching in several different contexts. Play is crucial and so is demonstrating or modelling how to do something. Young children's development relies upon the regular supply of a varied diet of educational activity. The most successful – and also the most appealing – educational settings are those which provide both free play as well as short sessions of direct teaching. 'On the rug' time of teacher-led activities with a large group, or teacher-initiated activities with a small group, allows teachers to demonstrate particular skills very effectively. Equally, becoming an 'expert play partner' helps the practitioner offer specific learning opportunities, e.g. recognising colours or comparing and sorting when playing in the water tray or sand pit. In any of these contexts, children will learn not only the maths in question, but also how to persevere, concentrate and work with others.

In accordance with the principles of the *Curriculum Guidance for the Foundation Stage*, the **Abacus Foundation** materials allow for children to be taught and learn in a variety of contexts. Some areas of mathematics are best taught directly, to a large group. Others are better suited to teaching to a small group, but some skills, such as writing numerals, require attention on an individual level. A variety of all these teaching – and learning – methods can be used at different times for most skills. Some, however, cannot be directly taught, and are best acquired in the course of an informal activity, i.e. a structured play activity that is initiated or led by the child. The following table categorises the mathematical skills in the Foundation Stage into suitable learning situations.

	Large group	Small group	Individuals or pairs
Taught directly	• Counting • Chanting the number names in order • Counting objects/ events/movements • Number rhymes • Days of the week • Shape names	• Counting objects • Matching a spoken numeral to quantity • Adding 1 or 2 more • Partitioning a set • Comparing lengths	• Matching numerals to sets • Writing numerals • Matching days of the week to special events
Learned informally	• Sorting shapes • Recognising large numbers	• Colours • Positions	

Progression

Throughout the Foundation Stage, children progress in two ways. They acquire mathematical skills, knowledge and understanding, and they also progress in terms of their ability to learn effectively in a variety of different contexts. Thus, in F1, in the playgroup or nursery, children can be expected to work as part of a large group only for quite short periods of time – perhaps 10 to 15 minutes at most. By the end of F2 or Reception, it is reasonable to expect that the children can focus in the same situation for up to half an hour. Similarly, at the start of F1, it is impossible for a group of children to complete an independent and focused mathematical activity without an adult present to support them. However, by the end of the Reception year, children need to be comfortable working with two or three others with no adult directly participating in the activity. This progression in terms of how children learn is every bit as important as the progression in terms of what they have learned. Children entering Year 1 who have not learned to pay attention as part of a large group, or to persevere with an independent activity, are much more likely to experience or develop learning difficulties at that stage. The Foundation Stage is just that – a foundation or grounding of what is to come, both in terms of how children learn and of what they learn.

The **Foundation F2** materials have been written to run alongside or in conjunction with **Abacus Reception**. Since the Early Learning Goals in the *Curriculum Guidance for the Foundation Stage* are identical to the Key Objectives for Reception in the National Numeracy Strategy *Framework for Teaching Mathematics*, **Abacus Reception** and **Abacus Foundation F2** cover the same content. However, the new resources have clearly been written to dovetail with the *Curriculum Guidance*, which has arrived since **Abacus Reception** was published. References to the appropriate **Abacus Reception** Teacher Card are included on the F2 yearly plan.

	Term 1	Term 2	Term 3
Week 1	Numbers to 10: counting to 6 and then to 10, using a number track	Counting to 10 and then to 20, using a number track, recognising numbers to 6	Counting to 10, and then to 20, counting on from a given number less than 6 and saying the 'next' number
Week 2	Numbers to 10: counting to 10, and counting up to four objects	Numbers to 10: counting to 10, counting up to 6 objects	Numbers to 20: counting to 20 and counting up to 10 objects
Week 3	Matching similar 2-d shapes, recognising circles, squares and triangles	Beginning to use the vocabulary of position	Beginning to use the language of direction
Week 4	Beginning to use the language of adding, placing one more into a small set	Beginning to understand that adding is increasing a set by one, two or three	Understanding that adding is increasing a set by a given number, counting on 1 or 2 to find the total
Week 5	Rearranging a small set of objects and showing that there are still the same number	Rearranging a small set of objects and partitioning in different ways	Adding by partitioning a set
Week 6	Comparing objects by size, categoris-ing into 'big' and 'small'	Comparing objects by size, and starting to distinguish tall and long objects	Comparing objects by size, distinguishing between tall and wide and long and short
Week 7	Comparing objects by weight, and sorting things into 'too heavy to pick up' and 'light enough to pick up'	Comparing objects by weight, and talking about heavy and light	Comparing full and empty with regard to different containers
Week 8	Talking about 'big' numbers and 'small' numbers	Comparing two quantities, who has less, who has more, discussing 'big' numbers	Comparing two numbers, recognising the larger and the smaller
Week 9	Counting to 10, recognising numbers to 6	Counting to 10, counting backwards from 5, beginning to recognise numbers to 10	Counting forwards and backwards to/from 10, recognising numbers to 10
Week 10	Matching similar 3-d shapes (e.g. spheres to spheres, cubes to cubes)	Sorting 3-d shapes by shape, beginning to recognise cubes and spheres	Sorting 3-d shapes by shape, beginning to discuss flat and curved faces
Week 11	Looking at coins, recognising that things are bought and sold using these	Looking at coins, recognising £1 and £2 coins will buy a lot	Looking at coins, recognising that £1 and £2 coins will buy lots and that pennies do not buy much
Week 12	Talking about day and night, recognising the difference	Recognising the concept of several days as after two 'sleeps' or after three 'sleeps'	Recognising that there are different days in the week, beginning to distinguish weekdays from weekends
Week 13	Counting to 10, recognising numbers to 6, counting sounds and movements	Counting to 10, estimating a small number of objects and matching these to a numeral	Counting to 20, estimating small numbers of objects and checking by counting

F2 Yearly Plan

	Term 1	Term 2	Term 3
Week 1	Counting to 10, and then to 20, counting on from a given number, saying the 'next' number to any given number N1	Counting to 20 and then to 100, saying the 'next' number to any given number N9	Counting to 100, counting on from a given number, saying the 'next' number to any given number N17
Week 2	Numbers to 20: counting up to 10 objects, beginning to record numbers to mark the number in a set N2	Numbers to 20: counting up to 20 objects, estimating, starting to record numbers to mark the number in a set N10	Numbers to 20: counting up to 20 objects, estimating, recording numbers to mark the number in a set N18
Week 3	Sorting 2-d shapes by shape, naming squares and circles, beginning to name other 2-d shapes S1	Using the language of position, and placing things in given positions in relation to each other S3	Using the language of direction, moving in given directions in relation to a starting point S4
Week 4	Adding 1 to a number up to 10, finding a total by counting on one when that object is hidden N3	Adding 2 or 3 to a number up to 10, finding a total by counting on when that object is hidden N11	Adding by counting on, subtracting by counting back, beginning to know the number 1 more or 1 less N19
Week 5	Adding by partitioning a set or by combining two sets N4	Understanding addition as a combination of two sets, relating this to counting on and the partitioning of a set N12	Understanding addition as counting on and as the combination of two sets/partitioning of a set N22
Week 6	Comparing the lengths of two or three objects, and using the language of length comparison M1	Comparing the lengths of two/three objects, and beginning to measure lengths using a non-standard unit M7	Beginning to estimate a length/ height, measuring a length/height using a non-standard unit M8
Week 7	Comparing tall and short and beginning to understand the language associated with height M2	Comparing heavy and light objects and beginning to measure weights on scales using non-standard units M4	Comparing the capacities of two containers, beginning to understand the language of capacity M5
Week 8	Comparing two numbers, comparing two quantities, recognising who has less and who has more N5	Comparing numbers up to 20, ordering numbers to 20 N14	Recognising a set of numbers more or less than a given number, recognising the numbers between given numbers N21
Week 9	Counting forwards and backwards to and from 10, recognising numbers to 10 N6	Counting forwards and backwards to/from 20, recognising numbers up to 15 N16	Removing a small number of objects from a larger number, counting back to find the remainder N24
Week 10	Sorting 2-d shapes by shape, beginning to name rectangles and triangles, rehearsing naming squares and circles S5	Sorting 3-d shapes by shape, recognising and naming a cube, beginning to recognise a cuboid S2	Sorting 3-d shapes, recognising and naming cubes and cuboids, beginning to name pyramids and cones S6
Week 11	Recognising coins, counting up to ten coins N8	Recognising coins, beginning to match each coin to its appropriate number of 1p coins N13	Recognising coins, solving simple addition and subtraction problems using money N20
Week 12	Understanding we can measure time, recognising a minute as a unit of time, counting how many times a thing happens in one minute M3	Recognising the hours on an analogue clock, and reading and setting the time to the hour M6	Recognising the days of the week, ordering the days of the week, beginning to understand today, tomorrow and yesterday M9
Week 13	Counting to 20, recognising numbers to 20, counting sounds and movements, estimating quantities N7	Counting to 20, recognising numbers to 20, counting sounds and movements, estimating quantities N15	Counting to 100, recognising larger numbers, beginning to count in tens, estimating quantities N23

The icons, e.g. N1 show the equivalent unit in **Abacus Reception.**

	DAY 1	DAY 2	DAY 3	DAY 4	DAY 5
Objective	Counting to 10, and then to 20, counting on from a given number, saying the 'next' number to any given number				
Teacher-led activities *On the rug* (pages 2–3)	**Warm up:** Count to 20 using fingers. **Activity:** Count along the number line (1 to 20), pointing to each number on it as you count. Whilst children shut their eyes, remove the 7 card. *Which number is missing?* Count together along the line to check. Repeat for 10 and 15.	**Warm up:** Say a number rhyme. **Activity:** Lay large number cards (1 to 20) along the rug to make a track. Count together along it, using a teddy to hop on each number as you say it. Whilst children close their eyes, remove a number. *Which number has gone?* Count along to check. *What is the next number? The number before?* Replace the number. Repeat several times.	**Warm up:** Count to 20 using fingers. **Activity:** Give each child a number card (1 to 10). Count to 10 together. Children stand up as their number is said. Line up ten children with number cards (1 to 10). Ask those with a number more than 6 to crouch down with their number on the floor. *Who is crouching down?* Repeat for a number less than 5. Repeat with ten different children.	**Warm up:** Count back from 20 to *Blast off!* **Activity:** Ask a child to point to a number, then say the next number. Count together to that number. Choose a different child and repeat. Do this several times.	**Warm up**: Do bunny hops to match numbers up to 20. **Activity:** Shuffle the number cards (1 to 10) and spread them out face down. Choose a child to take a card and say that number. They choose a different child to say the next number. If correct, the child takes a soft toy. Repeat several times, with different children taking a card and saying the next number.
Teacher-initiated activities *Activity Book* (page 1)	**Easy:** Use a number track (1 to 10). Each child chooses a number. They choose an action to do that number of times. Everyone else counts to check. If they are correct, they take a cube. Play until one child has ten cubes. **Medium:** Use a number track (1 to 20) and counters placed on 1. Spin a coin. Tails – move one place forwards, heads – move two places forwards. *Say the number you have landed on. Say the next number.* If children are correct, they move to that number. Otherwise, they move back three spaces. The first to 20 wins. **Hard:** Shuffle number cards (1 to 10). Deal them so that each child has three. Place the last one face up. Children take turns to place a card on the table if their number is next to one already laid face up. The first child without any cards wins.				
Independent activities *Supported play*	**Sand:** Bury wooden or plastic numbers (1 to 10) in a line in the sandpit. One child uncovers one number. All children say what the next number will be. They uncover it to check. Can they predict the number before?	**Cooking:** Children make a sponge cake using the recipe in the Recipe Bank (page 119). When it is cooled, they place numbers 1 to 12 round the edge like a clock.	**Construction:** Use a number track (1 to 10). Children build a small model to go with each number, using a matching number of bricks.	**Painting:** Children choose six colours. They paint a number line (1 to 6), using one colour for each number. *Save your favourite colour for your favourite number.*	**Threading:** Children use 20 large wooden beads and thread them onto a piece of string to make a necklace. They use numbered Post-it notes (1 to 20), and stick one on each bead.
Language	Count, count on, number names one to twenty, next number, number before, number after, more than, smaller than				
At home	*All in a row* **Ten old greetings cards, a pen** Write the numbers 1 to 10 on the back of ten used cards. Lay the cards in order to make a number track. Take turns to secretly remove one or two cards and ask your partner to look at the track and say the missing number(s).				
Resources	Washing line with large number cards (1 to 20) pegged to it, pegs, sandpit, wooden or plastic numbers (1 to 10)	Large number cards (1 to 20), a teddy, sponge cake mix	Large number cards (1 to 10), number track (1 to 10), building bricks	Washing line with large number cards (1 to 20) pegged to it, pegs, paint, paintbrushes	Large number cards (1 to 10), lots of small soft toys, large wooden beads, string, Post-it notes

- Count together to 20, using fingers to mark the units. Stress the whole hand at *Five* by waving it in the air. Stress the whole hands at *Ten* by waving both hands in the air.
- Say a number rhyme together.
- Count together to 20, using fingers to mark the units. Encourage the children to jump up and wave one hand in the air at *Five*. At *Ten* jump up and wave both hands in the air.
- Count backwards from 20 to 1, then shout *Blast off!* together. Help with the 'teen' numbers by stressing the first part of the word each time. Then hold up ten fingers and turn down one on each number to help mark the number of units.
- Make sure all the children have room to move. Say a number between 1 and 20. *Five*. The children all do five bunny hops while counting together. Repeat for wing flaps, hand claps, etc.

DAY 1

- *Counting to 20*
- *Saying the next number*

A washing line with large number cards (1 to 20) pegged to it, pegs

- Count along the number line, pointing to each number as you count. Count slowly and deliberately, stressing each number.
- Whilst children shut their eyes, remove the number 7. *Which number is missing?* Count along the line from 1, pointing to each number as you say it. *What number do we say when we reach the gap? Seven.*
- Choose a child to replace the 7, talking about the numbers before and after. *The number before seven is six. The number after seven is eight.*
- Repeat, removing the 10 and the 15.

DAY 2

- *Counting to 20*
- *Saying the next number*

Large number cards (1 to 20), a teddy

- Lay the numbers along the middle of the rug to make a number track.
- Count slowly along it, using the teddy to hop onto each number as you count together. Count slowly and deliberately, stressing each number.
- Make the teddy shut its eyes, covering them with its paws. Whilst children shut their eyes, remove one of the numbers.
- *Which number has gone?* Make the teddy say the wrong number. *Is the teddy right?* Count along the track. *What number do we say when we reach the gap? What is the next number?* Count on 1 to check. *Is this the right number?*
- Replace the number, and repeat with a different number, stressing the number before it and the number after it. *Nine comes after eight. Nine comes before ten.*
- Repeat several times.

DAY 3 • *Counting to 10*

Large number cards (1 to 10)

- Give each child a number card.
- Count to 10 together. Children stand up as their number is said.
- Line up ten children, holding cards 1 to 10. Ask those with a number more than 6 to crouch down and to hold their number by their feet. *Who is crouching down?* Point out that all the children with numbers further up the line than 6 are crouching down. Stress the 'further up the line'. *These numbers are **more than** six.*
- Repeat for children with a number less than 5. Stress the 'further down the line'. *These numbers are **smaller than** five.*
- Repeat with ten different children holding the numbers in the line, with a number more than 8, then less than 4.

DAY 4 • *Counting to 20.*

• *Saying the next number.*

A washing line with large number cards (1 to 20) pegged to it, pegs

- Count along the number line, pointing to each number.
- Choose a child to point to a number and to say the next number, e.g. 6. *What number comes after six?* Count to that number to check. *One, two, three, four, five, six and what comes next? Seven.* Point to 7.
- Repeat several times with different children. Always count to check, as well as pointing on the line, to give oral/aural stimulation, which will be stronger than visual stimulation (numeral recognition) for many children.

DAY 5 • *Saying the next number*

Large number cards (1 to 10), lots of small soft toys

- Shuffle the number cards and spread them out face down. Choose a child to take a card and say that number. She shows the class. Do they agree?
- If the child is correct, she chooses a different child to say the next number. If he is correct, he takes a soft toy.
- Repeat several times, with different children taking a card and saying the next number.
- Continue until all the children have a toy each.

	DAY 1	DAY 2	DAY 3	DAY 4	DAY 5
Objective	Numbers to 20: counting up to 10 objects, beginning to record numbers to mark the number in a set				
Teacher-led activities *On the rug* (pages 5–6)	**Warm up:** Count to 20 using fingers. **Activity:** Whilst children close their eyes, put ten small soft toys into the bag. Show children the bag. *How many?* Write sensible guesses on the board. Take the toys out one by one, counting as you do so. Write the total on the board. Repeat with four, five and seven toys.	**Warm up:** Count to 20 using fingers. **Activity:** Use the skipping rope to make a river down the middle of the rug, with the class in two equal teams on each side. Give each side ten teddies. Teams take turns to throw a spotty dice, and pass that number of teddies across the river. After each turn, ask *Which side has more teddies?* The first team to get all its teddies across the river wins.	**Warm up:** Count back from 20 to *Blast off!* **Activity:** Look at the pictures drawn on the board. Shuffle the number cards (1 to 10) and place them in a pile face down. Choose a child to take a card, e.g. 4. *Which picture shall we add four to?* E.g. draw four legs on the dog. *Some cards haven't been used. Which things have this number of legs/arms/wheels?*	**Warm up:** Count to 20 using fingers. **Activity:** Choose three children to stand at the front. Each player needs to collect exactly ten bricks. Choose another child to take a card. They count out that many bricks and give them to the first player. Repeat, choosing a different child to take a new card and give bricks to the next player. *Who gets to exactly ten first?*	**Warm up:** Show fingers to match numbers up to 10. **Activity:** Hold up the mug with some pencils in it. *How many pencils?* Encourage children to guess. Write sensible guesses on the board. Demonstrate how to form the numerals. Count the pencils. Use the number line to see how close they were. Repeat.
Teacher-initiated activities *Activity Book* (page 2)	**Easy:** The children choose a jigsaw, count the number of pieces and then assemble it. They draw a picture on card and cut it into jigsaw-shaped pieces. **Medium:** One child puts a handful of pencils in a mug. The others guess how many. Help them to record their guesses. Count to check, taking each pencil out as you count it. The child who guessed closest takes a cube. Repeat. **Hard:** Shuffle number cards (1 to 10). The children take a card each and count that number of cubes. *Whose number is largest? Who can make the tallest tower?* The child with most cubes takes a counter. Replace the card on the bottom of the pile. Repeat, continuing like this until a child has collected five counters.				
Independent activities *Supported play*	**Sand:** Children build a road in the sand. They take a number card (1 to 10) and place that number of cars on the road. Smooth out the sand and start again.	**Cooking:** Children make biscuits using the recipe in the Recipe Bank (page 119). Before baking, they press currants into the cut shapes. When baked and cooled, they count the currants on each biscuit.	**Playhouse:** Children decide how many toys to invite for tea. They count out plates, cups, etc. They use the telephone and say the numerals when phoning the toys to invite them.	**Drawing:** Children choose their favourite number. Write a large numeral and the children draw that number of animals, cars, cartoon characters, etc.	**Cutting and sticking:** Children make a nest from strips of paper. *How many eggs shall we place in each nest?* They count beads into the nest as eggs.
Language	Count, how many, number names one to twenty, more				
At home	*Collecting bricks* **A dice, building bricks/buttons** Take turns to roll the dice and collect that number of bricks or buttons. The first to collect twenty items is the winner.				
Resources	A cloth bag, ten small soft toys, washing line with large number cards (1 to 10) pegged to it, pegs, sandpit, toy cars, number cards (1 to 10)	Skipping rope, 20 teddies, spotty dice (1 to 6), biscuit mix, currants	Large number cards (1 to 10), six incomplete pictures drawn on the board, toys, tea party crockery, telephone	Large number cards (1 to 9), 30 large building bricks, crayons, colouring pencils	A mug, ten pencils, washing line with large number cards (1 to 10) pegged to it, pegs, strips of paper, scissors, glue, beads

- Count together to 20, using fingers to mark the units. Stress the whole hand at *Five* by waving it in the air. Stress the whole hands at *Ten* by waving both hands in the air.
- Count backwards from 20 to 1, then shout *Blast off!* together. Help with the 'teen' numbers by stressing the first part of the word each time. Then hold up ten fingers and turn down one on each number to help mark the number of units.
- Count together to 20, using fingers to mark the units. Encourage the children to jump up and wave one hand in the air at *Five*. At *Ten* jump up and wave both hands in the air.
- Say a number between 1 and 10. *Five*. Ask the children to hold up that number of fingers. Who has to count and who just 'knows'? Repeat for other numbers.

WARM UPS

DAY 1

- *Counting up to 10 objects*
- *Beginning to record numbers*

A cloth bag, ten small soft toys, a washing line with large number cards (1 to 10) pegged to it, pegs

- Whilst children close their eyes, put the soft toys into the bag.
- Show children the bag. *How many toys?* Take guesses, writing each sensible guess on the board. As you write, stress how to write each numeral.
- *How will we find out the right number? We will count.* Count the toys together, taking one soft toy out of the bag for each number spoken. Write the total on the board.
- Compare the actual number with their guesses. Use the number line help you compare. *Which guesses were closest?*
- Repeat with four, five and seven toys, asking children to guess, then count.

DAY 2

- *Counting up to 10 objects*

A skipping rope, 20 teddies, a spotty dice (1 to 6)

- Use the skipping rope to make a 'river' running down the middle of the rug, with the class divided into two equal teams, one on each side. *There is a river down the middle of this rug – be careful not to fall in!*
- Give each team ten teddies. Each side counts them. *The first team to get all its teddies across the river, wins.*
- Give one team the spotty dice. Choose a child on that side to throw the dice. *What number has she thrown? How many spots?* Count the spots, pointing to each spot as you count it.
- That team counts out a matching number of teddies and passes them across the river.
- Pass the spotty dice to the other team, who repeat the process.
- After each turn, ask which side has more teddies.

DAY 3

- *Counting up to 10 objects*

Large number cards (1 to 10), six incomplete pictures drawn on the board (a teddy with no ears, a tricycle with no wheels, a dog with no legs, a starfish with no arms, a beetle with no legs and an octopus with no legs)

- Shuffle the number cards and place them in a pile face down. Choose a child to take a card, e.g. 4.
- Point to the board. *Each picture has things missing. Which picture has four things missing? Does a tricycle have four wheels? Does an octopus have four legs?* Take suggestions, adding carefully to the correct picture, i.e. draw four legs on the dog. Count the legs as you draw them.
- Some cards cannot be used, e.g. 1, 7, 9 and 10. Put these to one side. When each picture has been completed, look at the the numbers that are left. *Can you think of things that have this number of legs, arms or wheels? A unicycle would have one wheel.*

DAY 4

- *Counting up to 10 objects*

Large number cards (1 to 9), 30 large building bricks

- Shuffle the number cards and spread them out face down. Choose three children to stand in a row at the front.
- *In this game each player is going to collect exactly ten bricks.*
- Choose another child to take a number card. He shows the class. *What number has he taken?* Count together to help him count that many bricks. He gives the bricks to the first player in the row.
- Repeat, choosing a different child to take a card. *What number has she taken?* She counts out that many bricks and gives them to the second player in the row at the front.
- Continue. Which player gets to exactly 10 first?

DAY 5

- *Counting up to 10 objects*
- *Beginning to record numbers*

A mug, ten pencils, a washing line with large number cards (1 to 10) pegged to it, pegs

- Hold up the mug with up to ten pencils in it. *How many pencils?* Take some guesses, writing each sensible guess on the board. As you write, stress how to write each numeral.
- Count the pencils, taking each one out of the mug as you count it. Write the total on the board, demonstrating how to form each numeral.
- Compare the total with their guesses. Use the number line to see how close they were.
- Repeat, starting with a different number of pencils.

	DAY 1	DAY 2	DAY 3	DAY 4	DAY 5
Objective	**Sorting 2-d shapes, naming squares and circles, and beginning to name other 2-d shapes**				
Teacher-led activities *On the rug* (pages 8–9)	**Warm up:** Count to 20 using fingers. **Activity:** Show the class a square. Discuss its properties. Show a rectangle. Point out the differences. Show a triangle and point out differences. Show a circle and discuss its properties. Show an oval. Point out differences. Choose a child. Blu-tack a shape to her back and show the class, who describe it to her. Can she guess the shape?	**Warm up:** Sing number song. **Activity:** Gradually reveal a shape from behind the wall. Children guess what the shape is. *How much of the shape do you need to see to be sure?* Repeat several times, using different shapes. Name the circles and the squares.	**Warm up:** Show fingers to match numbers up to 10. **Activity:** Stick one of each shape on the board. Talk about them. Whilst children close their eyes, place a shape in the bag. Choose two or three children to feel the shape. They describe it to the class, who guess what the shape is by naming it or pointing to the matching shape on the board. Repeat.	**Warm up:** Say a number rhyme. **Activity:** Give each pair of children a shape. *I am looking for a shape with four corners.* Any pair holding a shape with four corners, holds it up. Discuss the differences between squares and oblongs or rectangles. Repeat, using a different property, e.g. curved sides.	**Warm up:** Count to 20 using fingers. **Activity:** Place two hoops on the rug. Label one 'squares', the other 'circles'. Choose a child to take a shape from the bag. Point to the 'squares' hoop. The class shows 'thumbs up' if the shape belongs in this hoop and 'thumbs down', if not. *If it isn't a square, does it belong in the 'circles' hoop?* If neither, discuss what shape it is and put it outside the hoops. Repeat.
Teacher-initiated activities *Activity Book* (pages 2–3)	**Easy:** Have shapes and pictures of matching shapes. Use a book as a wall. One child reveals a shape gradually. The others try to guess what shape it is by pointing to the matching picture. Repeat, choosing a different child to reveal the shape. **Medium:** Make a line of shapes. Children repeat the pattern, discussing and, if possible, naming each shape as they do so. *Remove all the squares.* Can they do this? Replace these. Repeat for circles. Repeat for four-sided shapes, etc. **Hard:** Line up some different plastic shapes. Each child selects a shape and draws round it, using Blu-tack to hold the shape in place. Children can try drawing the shapes for themselves. Discuss the properties of each shape as children try to draw it.				
Independent activities *Supported play*	**Toys:** Children arrange or draw fields of different shapes to make a farm for the toys. They place cows in the square field, sheep in the circle field, etc.	**Cooking:** Children make flapjacks, using the recipe in the Recipe Bank (page 119). They cut them into different shapes, using cutters and a knife. *What shape do you get if you cut a rectangle in half? A triangle.*	**Construction:** Children arrange building bricks to make different-shaped car parks, e.g. circle, square or triangle, and drive toy cars into these.	**Painting:** Children paint brightly-coloured shapes, e.g. square, circle or triangle, using several colours for each. Mount their shapes on matching shaped paper, i.e. triangle on a triangle of paper.	**Cutting and sticking:** Fold cardboard to make greetings cards. Children use three or four cut-out shapes, e.g. square, triangle and circle, to make a picture to stick on the front of the card. They sign their cards and take them home.
Language	**Circle, square, rectangle, oblong, triangle, oval, flat, curved, edge, side, corner, same size**				
At home	*Drawing shapes* **Coloured pencils/crayons, paper** Ask your child to find three different shaped items – a circle, a square and a triangle. Encourage them to draw around each one and then colour each shape. Remind them to take the shapes to show in class.				
Resources	Plastic 2-d shapes (square, rectangle, triangle, circle, oval), Blu-tack, toy animals, building bricks or paper and crayons	Plastic 2-d shapes (square, rectangle, triangle, circle, oval), flipchart or large sheet of card, flapjack mix, different-shaped cutters, a knife	Two sets of plastic 2-d shapes, (circle, square, triangle), Blu-tack, a cloth bag, building bricks, toy cars	Plastic 2-d shapes (squares, rectangles, triangles, circles, ovals), paint, paintbrushes, paper, scissors	Two hoops, two labels ('squares', 'circles'), plastic 2-d shapes (squares, rectangles, triangles, circles, ovals), a cloth bag, cardboard, cut-out shapes, glue

- Count together to 20, using fingers to mark the units. Stress the whole hand at *Five* by waving it in the air. Stress the whole hands at *Ten* by waving both hands in the air.
- Sing a number song, which involves counting down.
- Say a number between 1 and 10. *Four*. Ask the children to hold up that number of fingers. Who has to count and who just 'knows'? Repeat for other numbers.
- Together say a number rhyme, which involves counting back.
- Count together to 20, using fingers to mark the units. Encourage the children to jump up and wave one hand in the air at *Five*. At *Ten* jump up and wave both hands in the air.

WARM UPS

DAY 1

- *Sorting 2-d shapes*
- *Naming squares and circles*
- *Beginning to name other 2-d shapes*

Plastic 2-d shapes (square, rectangle, triangle, circle, oval), Blu-tack

- Show the class a square. *This is a* ***square*** *shape. It has four sides, one, two, three, four. All the sides are the same length. How many corners does it have?* Point to each corner as you count. *One, two, three, four. The square has four sides, all the same length, and four corners all the same.* Pass round the square. Stress its shape.
- Show how rectangle is different from a square. *This shape has four sides.* Count them, pointing to each one. *But they are not all the same length.* Point out that two of the sides are long and two are short. *How many corners?* Point to each corner as you count it. *One, two, three, four. Like the square, it has four corners and four sides. But it is not the same shape because two sides are longer than the other two. It is called a rectangle or an oblong.*
- Show a triangle. *This is a triangle. It has three sides and three corners.*
- Show a circle. *This is a circle. It has just one curved side and no corners.*
- Show an oval, and point out how it is different from a circle. *The* ***oval*** *has one curved side, but it is long and thin and not round.*
- Choose a child. Blu-tack a shape to her back without her seeing, and show the class. Encourage children to describe the shape. *It has four corners and four sides. Two of the sides are longer than the other two.* Can she guess the shape?
- Repeat with different children and different shapes.

DAY 2

- *Sorting 2-d shapes*
- *Naming squares and circles*

Plastic 2-d shapes (square, rectangle, triangle, circle, oval), flipchart or large sheet of card

- Use the flipchart as a 'wall'. Hold a shape behind it so that part of it is hidden. Gradually show more of the shape.
- *What shape do you think this is?* Encourage children to make sensible guesses, based on what they can see. *We can see a corner – it can't be a circle.*
- *How much of the shape do you need to see to be sure?* Show the whole shape and discuss its properties.
- Repeat several times, using different shapes, asking children to name them if they can. Check that they can name circles and squares.

DAY 3
- *Sorting 2-d shapes*
- *Naming squares and circles*

Two sets of plastic 2-d shapes (circle, square, triangle), Blu-tack, a cloth bag

- Blu-tack one of each shape onto the board. Talk about the shapes. *The square has four sides, all the same length. It has four corners. The rectangle also has four sides and four corners. Its sides are different lengths, two are longer.*
- Whilst children close their eyes, place a shape in the bag. Choose two or three children to feel the shape. Children can ask questions. *How many sides and how many corners? It has four corners and four sides. Are all the sides the same length?*
- Children guess what the shape is. They can do this either by naming the shape or by pointing to the matching shape on the board.
- Repeat several times.

DAY 4
- *Naming squares and circles*
- *Beginning to name other 2-d shapes*

Plastic 2-d shapes (squares, rectangles, triangles, circles, ovals)

- Give each pair of children a shape.
- Describe a property of a shape. *I am looking for a shape with four corners.* Any pair with a shape with four corners holds it up. Discuss the differences. *Squares have four sides that are the same. Oblongs or rectangles have two long sides and two short sides.*
- Repeat, using a different property. *I am looking for a shape with curved sides.* All children with ovals or circles wave them. Discuss the differences.
- Repeat for other shapes.

DAY 5
- *Sorting 2-d shapes*
- *Naming squares and circles*
- *Beginning to name other 2-d shapes*

Two hoops, two labels ('squares', 'circles'), plastic 2-d shapes (squares, rectangles, triangles, circles, ovals), a cloth bag

- Place the hoops on the rug. Label one 'squares' and the other 'circles'.
- Place lots of shapes in a cloth bag. Choose a child to take one out. *What shape is that? It has three corners and three sides. It is a triangle.*
- Point to the 'squares' hoop. *Does it belong in this hoop?* The children show 'thumbs up' if they think the shape belongs in it, or 'thumbs down' if they think it does not belong in the 'squares' hoop. If it does not fit in the hoop, ask if it fits in the 'circles' hoop. If the shape is neither a square nor a circle, it should be placed outside both hoops. Discuss what shape it is.
- Repeat with a different child choosing a shape.

	DAY 1	DAY 2	DAY 3	DAY 4	DAY 5
Objective	Adding 1 to a number up to 10, finding a total by counting on 1 when that object is hidden				
Teacher-led activities *On the rug* (pages 11–12)	**Warm up:** Sing a number song. **Activity:** Lay large number cards (1 to 12) along the rug to make a track. A child throws a dice (numbered 5 to 10). Another child jumps that many spaces along the track. Write the number, e.g. '5', on the board. *What number will he be on if he jumps to the next space?* Write '+ 1 ='. Ask him to jump to the next space. Write '6'. Say the number sentence. Repeat.	**Warm up:** Count to 20 using fingers. **Activity:** Choose a child. Show six fingers. She holds up one hand and one finger. Everyone copies. *Hold up one more finger.* Point to the fingers, *Six*, and count on, pointing to next finger, ... *Seven. Six and one more is seven.* Write '6 + 1 = 7' on the board. Repeat with different numbers.	**Warm up:** Show fingers to match numbers up to 10. **Activity:** Use stickers to number each rung on the ladder (1 to 12). Throw a dice (5 to 10) and help the teddy climb up the ladder to the number thrown. *What number will the teddy be on if he climbs another rung?* Write the number sentence, e.g. '7 + 1 ='. Ask the children to suggest answers. Write '8'. Repeat.	**Warm up:** Count to 20 using fingers. **Activity:** Arrange 12 chairs in rows of two to make a bus. Show children the number 7 card. *This is how many passengers are on the bus.* Choose a conductor. Choose seven children. Count them onto the bus. The conductor gives each a ticket. Write '7' on the board. *How many if another passenger gets on?* Count on from 7. Write '+ 1 = 8'.	**Warm up:** Show fingers to match numbers up to 10. **Activity:** Lay large number cards (1 to 12) along the rug to make a track. Count eight biscuits into the tin. *How many?* Find '8' on the number track. Place a counter on that number. *How many biscuits if we add one more?* Place another biscuit in the tin. *How many now?* Move the counter on one space. Repeat. Say and write the sum.
Teacher-initiated activities *Activity Book* (page 3)	**Easy:** Use a number track (1 to 12) and building bricks. Each child chooses a number on the track and matches that number to bricks. They say how many they will have if they take one more. If they are correct, they keep the bricks. They have six turns. *Build a model with your bricks.* **Medium:** Use a number dice (5 to 10). Children take turns to throw the dice and count that many pebbles. *Each make a line of your pebbles. How many will you have if you take one more?* If they are correct, they keep one pebble and put the rest back. Continue until one child has six pebbles. **Hard:** Use a number track (1 to 20) and counters placed on 1. Spin a coin. Heads – move one place forwards, tails – move two places forwards. *Take the number of bricks that matches the number you landed on, plus one. So, if you land on three, take four bricks.* If children are not correct, they replace their bricks. They continue to the end of the track. How many bricks do they have?				
Independent activities *Supported play*	**Toys:** Line up some toy cars. Children find a matching number card. Add another car to the line. *How many cars now?* Children find the matching number card.	**Cooking:** Children make sugar mice using the recipe in the Recipe Bank (page 119). *How many mice? How many if we make two more?*	**Construction:** Children make towers to match each number along a number track (1 to 10). Discuss how many bricks to add to make the next number each time.	**Role play:** Children go shopping to buy cans of food. They buy five cans. Then they buy two more. *How many now?* They pay with 10p or £1 coins. *How many coins?*	**Papier mâché:** Children make two numerals each, one number 1 more than the other. They attach a thread to each numeral and hang the appropriate number of beads from it.
Language	Number names one to twenty, add, and, more, makes, equals, how many?, count, count on				
At home	*How many buttons?* **Ten buttons/counters** Ask your child to count out some buttons into your hand. Close your hand. Can your child remember how many were counted? If not, ask them to count the buttons into your other hand. *If I put one more button into my hand how many will I have?* Repeat with other numbers and for taking away one button.				
Resources	Large number cards (1 to 12), a large dice numbered 5 to 10 with stickers (opposite sides add to 15), toy cars, number cards (1 to 10)	Sugar mice mix	A home-made ladder with 12 rungs, a large dice numbered 5 to 10 with stickers (opposite sides add to 15), a teddy, building bricks, a number track (1 to 10)	Large number cards (1 to 10), tickets, washing line with large number cards (1 to 10) pegged to it, pegs, cans of food, 10p or £1 coins	Large number cards (1 to 12), biscuits, an empty tin, a counter, papier mâché mix, thread, beads

- Sing a number song together.
- Count together to 20, using fingers to mark the units. Stress the whole hand at *Five* by waving it in the air. Stress the whole hands at *Ten* by waving both hands in the air.
- Say a number between 1 and 10. *Six.* Ask the children to hold up that number of fingers. Who has to count and who just 'knows'? Repeat for other numbers.
- Count together to 20, using fingers to mark the units. Encourage the children to jump up and wave one hand in the air at *Five.* At *Ten* jump up and wave both hands in the air.
- Say a number between 1 and 10. *Eight.* Ask the children to hold up that number of fingers. Who has to count and who just 'knows'? Repeat for other numbers.

WARM UPS

DAY 1

- *Adding 1 to a number up to 10*

Large number cards (1 to 12), a large dice numbered 5 to 10 with stickers (opposite sides add to 15)

- Lay the numbers along the rug to make a track.
- Choose a child to throw the dice. *What number has she thrown?*
- Choose another child to jump that many spaces along the track. The class counts with him. Write that number, e.g. '5', on the board.
- *What number will he be on if he jumps to the next space?* Write '+ 1 =' on the board. Read the sentence. *Five and one more makes?*
- Ask the child to jump to the next space. *What number has he landed on? Six.* Write '6' to complete the sentence. *Five and one more makes six. Five and one equals six.*
- Repeat with a different child and different numbers.

DAY 2

- *Adding 1 to a number up to 10*
- Choose a child. Ask her to show six fingers. She holds up one hand and one more finger. Everyone copies. *Six fingers.* Demonstrate yourself.
- *I want you all to hold up one more finger.* Point to the original fingers and then count on, pointing to the next finger. *Six, seven. Six and one more is seven.*
- Write the matching addition on the board. *Six,* write '6', show fingers, *and one more,* write '+ 1', show fingers, *makes seven,* write '= 7'. Read the whole sentence. *Six and one equals seven.*
- Repeat, starting with different numbers.

DAY 3

- *Adding 1 to a number up to 10*

A home-made ladder with twelve rungs, stickers, a large dice numbered 5 to 10 with stickers (opposite sides add to 15), a teddy

- *How many steps on this ladder?* Use stickers to number each rung (1 to 12). Count the rungs as you number them.
- Throw the dice. *What number have I thrown?*
- Choose a child to help the teddy climb up the ladder to match the number thrown, counting the rungs as he climbs.
- *What number will the teddy be on if he climbs another rung?* Write the number sentence, e.g. '7 + 1 =', and read it together. *The teddy is on seven and he climbs another rung. Seven and one more is?*
- Ask the class to suggest answers. Move the teddy up one more rung. *Seven, eight.* Write the answer, '8'.
- Repeat, throwing the dice again and moving the teddy up from the bottom of the ladder. Write a matching addition.

DAY 4 • *Adding 1 to a number up to 10*

Large number cards (1 to 10), tickets, a washing line with large number cards (1 to 10) pegged to it, pegs

- Arrange 12 chairs in rows of two to make a 'bus'. Choose a child to be the conductor.
- Take the number 7 card. *What number is this? Seven. This is how many passengers I have on my bus.*
- Choose seven children and count them onto the bus. The conductor gives each passenger a ticket, counting as she does so. *One, two, ... seven tickets.* Write '7' on the board.
- *How many will there be if another passenger gets on?* Encourage children to estimate. Point to the number line to help them.
- Let another passenger on to the bus, and count on from 7. If necessary, start at 1, count to 7, and then count on 1 more.
- Complete the matching addition on the board as '+ 1 = 8'. Read this together, relating it to the event. *Seven passengers and one more makes eight passengers.*
- Repeat with different children, and starting with nine passengers.

DAY 5 • *Adding 1 to a number up to 10*

Large number cards (1 to 12), biscuits, an empty tin, a counter

- Lay the numbers along the rug to make a number track. Count along the track.
- Count eight biscuits into the tin. *How many biscuits?* Find '8' on the number track and place a counter on that number. *Eight biscuits in the tin.*
- *How many if we add one more?* Place another biscuit in the tin. *How many now?* Encourage children to see where the counter will be if it is moved one space along the track.
- Write the matching sum on the board. *Eight,* write '8', *biscuits in the tin and one more,* write '+ 1', *makes nine biscuits,* write '= 9'. *Eight and one more equals nine.*
- Repeat, starting with five biscuits, then ten.
- Eat the biscuits.

	DAY 1	DAY 2	DAY 3	DAY 4	DAY 5
Objective	Adding by partitioning a set or by combining two sets				
Teacher-led activities *On the rug* (pages 14–15)	**Warm up:** Sing a number song. **Activity:** Arrange six chairs in a line. Choose six children to sit on them. Give three children a red scarf and three a blue scarf. *How many children?* Write '6' on the board. *How many red scarves? How many blue scarves?* Write '3 + 3 ='. Read this together. Replace one blue scarf with a red scarf and repeat to show 4 + 2 = 6. Repeat, to show 5 + 1 = 6.	**Warm up:** Count to 30 using fingers. **Activity:** Peg seven blue beanbags on the washing line. *How many?* Count them. Choose a child to hold the number 7 card. Replace one blue beanbag with a red one. *How many blue beanbags now?* Choose a child to hold number 6 card. *How many red?* Choose a child to hold number 1. Say the addition. *Six and one make seven.* Repeat for 5 + 2 and 4 + 3.	**Warm up:** Say a number rhyme. **Activity:** Draw two clouds on the board. Blu-tack four birds on one cloud. *How many birds here? Four.* Blu-tack three birds on the other cloud. *How many here? Three. How many altogether?* Encourage children to remember from the previous day. *Four and three make seven.* Remove the birds and repeat for 5 + 2 and 6 + 1.	**Warm up:** Count to 30 using fingers. **Activity:** Ask children to show you three fingers. *How many? Three.* Ask for three more. *And three more makes? Six.* Repeat, matching fingers to teddies. Start again with four fingers. *How many?* Children show two more. *Four and two more make?* Repeat, matching to teddies. Repeat for 5 + 1. Write the additions. Read them together.	**Warm up:** Do eye winks to match numbers up to 20. **Activity:** Peg four socks on the line. *How many?* Encourage children to match this number to fingers, holding up four fingers. Peg up three more socks. *How many now?* Hold up three more fingers. *Four and three make? Seven.* Count the socks to check. Write '3 + 4 = 7' and read it together. Repeat for 5 + 2 and 6 + 1.
Teacher-initiated activities *Activity Book* (pages 3–4)	**Easy:** Give children a pile of yellow and red building bricks. Each child has to make a tower of seven. They make as many different towers as they can. They count the numbers of red and yellow bricks in each tower and say the sum. *Six and one make seven.* **Medium:** Use two cardboard or mirror 'ponds' and seven plastic ducks. One child finds a way of distributing the ducks. Record this, e.g. '5 + 2 = 7'. Another child finds another way. Record this. Continue until there are no new ways. Repeat for six or eight ducks. **Hard:** Use 1p coins to work out all the different ways of distributing 8p between two purses. *Suppose we use 2p and 5p coins as well?*				
Independent activities *Supported play*	**Toys:** Use six toy animals and place them in two 'fields' in different ways. Do the same with cars and car parks, or dolls and 'rooms'.	**Cooking:** Give each child in the group six crackers. Each child puts cheese on some crackers and honey on others. *How many different ways can you do it?* Encourage them to find all the different combinations.	**Construction:** Children build as many different shapes as they can, using only ten bricks in two colours. They count the number of bricks in each colour in their shapes.	**Sand:** Draw a line to divide the sandpit into two halves. Children create two 'towns', one in each half. They build seven sand castles to be distributed between the two towns. Compare the two towns. *Which town has more castles? How many castles altogether?*	**Painting:** Use sugar solution to paint children's paper. They paint over the wet paper using two colours to create a marbled raised effect. *How many parts of each colour? How many in all?*
Language	Number names one to ten, and, more, how many?, makes, altogether				
At home	*Making totals* **Two plates, sultanas/buttons/counters** Ask your child to count out six small items and place them all on one plate. Ask them to say the number sentence. *Six sultanas and no sultanas is still six.* Move one item onto the empty plate. Ask your child to count again. *Five and one more make six.* Continue until the first plate is empty and all six items are on the second plate. *No raisins and six raisins make six.* Repeat with different numbers of items up to ten.				
Resources	Twelve scarves (six red, six blue), toy animals, toy cars, dolls	Eleven beanbags (seven blue, four red), washing line, pegs, large number cards (1 to 10), crackers, cheese, honey	Seven card 'flying' birds, Blu-tack, building bricks	Six teddies, sandpit, buckets, scoops	Seven socks, washing line, pegs, paint, paintbrushes, sugar solution

WARM UPS

- Sing a number song together.
- Count together to 30, using fingers to mark the units. Help the children with the 'decade' numbers. *Twenty-nine, thirty* is particularly hard.
- Together say a number rhyme, which involves counting back.
- Count together to 30, using fingers to mark the units. Help the children with the 'decade' numbers. Encourage them to jump up and wave both hands at *Ten, Twenty* and *Thirty*.
- Make sure all the children have room to move. Say a number between 1 and 20. *Seven*. The children all do seven eye winks while counting together. Repeat for hops, wing flaps, touching toes, etc.

DAY 1

- *Adding by partitioning a set*

Twelve scarves (six red, six blue)

- Place six chairs in a line at the front, and choose six children to sit on them.
- Give three children a red scarf each and three children a blue scarf each. *How many children? Six*. Write '6' on the board.
- *How many children are wearing a red scarf? Three. How many are wearing a blue scarf? Three.*
- Point to the three children in the red scarves and the three in the blue scarves. Write '3 + 3 =' to complete the number sentence. Read this together. *Three and three make six.*
- Choose a child wearing a blue scarf and give her a red scarf instead. *How many children? Six*. Write '6' on the board.
- *How many children are wearing a red scarf? Four. How many are wearing a blue scarf? Two.*
- Point to the four children in the red scarves and the two in the blue scarves. Write '4 + 2 =' to complete the number sentence. Read this together. *Four and two make six.*
- Repeat to show 5 + 1 = 6.

DAY 2

- *Adding by partitioning a set*

Eleven beanbags (seven blue, four red), a washing line, pegs, large number cards (1 to 10)

- Peg seven blue beanbags on the washing line.
- How many beanbags? Count them together. *Seven.*
- Choose a child to hold the number 7 card.
- Replace one blue beanbag with a red beanbag. *Count the beanbags. There are still seven beanbags.*
- *How many blue beanbags now?* Choose a child to hold the number 6 card. *How many red beanbags?* Choose another child to hold the number 1 card. Say the addition. *Six and one make seven.*
- Repeat for 5 + 2 and 4 + 3.

DAY 3 • *Adding by combining two sets*

Seven card 'flying' birds, Blu-tack

- Draw two clouds on the board.
- Blu-tack four birds on one cloud. *How many birds are flying here? Four.* Write '4' on the board.
- Blu-tack three birds on the other cloud. *How many birds are flying here? Three.* Write '+ 3' next to '4' on the board.
- Point to '4 + 3' and write '='. *Four and three. How many birds in all?* Encourage children to remember the lesson on Day 2. *Four and three make seven.* Demonstrate by pointing to the cloud with four birds. *Four.* Count on, pointing to each bird on the other cloud. *Five, six, seven. Four and three make seven.*
- Write '7' to complete the addition. Read it, pointing to the numbers as you say them. *Four and three make seven altogether.*
- Remove the birds and repeat for 5 + 2 and 6 + 1.

DAY 4 • *Adding by combining two sets*

Six teddies

- Ask children to show you three fingers. *How many fingers? Three.*
- Ask them to show you three more fingers. *And three more makes? Six.* Encourage those who do not know to count on as they hold up the three more fingers. *Three, ... four, five, six. That's six fingers in all.*
- Repeat, matching each set of three fingers to three teddies. *Three and three make six.*
- Start again with four fingers. *How many? Four.* Ask children to show you two more. *Four and two more make? Six.*
- Repeat, matching to teddies.
- Repeat to show 5 + 1.
- Write '3 + 3 = 6' on the board. Underneath write '4 + 2 = 6'. Underneath that write '5 + 1 = 6'. Read all the additions together.

DAY 5 • *Adding by combining two sets*

Seven socks, a washing line, pegs

- Peg four socks on the line. *How many socks?* Encourage children to match this number to fingers, holding up four fingers.
- Peg three more socks on the line. *How many socks now?* Hold up three more fingers. *Four and three make? Seven.* Count the socks to check.
- Write '4 + 3 = 7' on the board and read it together.
- Repeat, pegging up five socks and then another two. Write '5 + 2 = 7' below the first addition and read it together.
- Repeat to show 6 + 1 = 7.

	DAY 1	DAY 2	DAY 3	DAY 4	DAY 5
Objective	Comparing the lengths of two or three objects, and using the language of length comparison				
Teacher-led activities *On the rug* (pages 17–18)	**Warm up:** Sing a number song. **Activity:** Show children the two snakes. *Which of these snakes is longer? Which is shorter?* Hold the snakes next to each other. Show children the longer snake. *This is a long snake.* Repeat for the short snake. Show children the two ribbons and repeat. Repeat for the two pencils.	**Warm up:** Count to 30 using fingers. **Activity:** Choose two children. Give one a pair of long socks to put on. Give the other the short pair. *Who is wearing the longer/shorter socks?* Stand the children next to each other. Choose another child. Give her the medium-length socks. Compare her with the 'long socks' child. Repeat, with the 'short socks' child. Stand the children in order.	**Warm up:** Say a number rhyme. **Activity:** Give each pair of children a long and a short straw. Choose a pair. *Who has the longer straw? The shorter?* Each pair decides. Ask those with the short straw to stand up. Repeat for each child with the longer straw. Choose two children with 'long' straws and compare their straws. Compare two with 'short' straws.	**Warm up:** Count back from 20 to *Blast off!* **Activity:** Stick three paper fish on the board. *Which fish is the longest? Which is the shortest?* Show children how to line up the fish, using ends of tails or heads in a line. Give another fish to a child. Ask her to describe her fish. *Is it long or short?* Compare it with the fish on the board. Repeat with three more fish.	**Warm up:** Show fingers to match numbers up to 10. **Activity:** Choose three children to choose a book each. *Who has the longest book?* Demonstrate how to compare the length of two of the books, and then the third book. Repeat for the shortest book. Choose a child to find a book that is longer than the longest book. Choose another child to find a book shorter than the shortest book.
Teacher-initiated activities *Activity Book* (pages 4–5)	**Easy:** Paste three strips of paper horizontally across the door. Choose children who are not as tall as the bottom strip and stick their names below this. Choose children who are taller than the bottom strip but less tall than the middle and paste their names in that space. Continue, using adults who are taller than the top strip. **Medium:** Use a pile of paper fish of different lengths. Each child chooses a long fish, a short fish and a middle-length fish and sticks them in order on a sheet of paper painted to look like the sea. **Hard:** Use pictures of insects of different lengths and paste them in order from the longest to shortest on a sheet of paper painted to look like grass.				
Independent activities *Supported play*	**Water:** Use a short, fat container and a tall, thin container. *Which holds more?* Tip water from one to the other to check. Show that taller containers don't always hold more.	**Cooking:** Children make cheese straws using the recipe in the Recipe Bank (page 119). They cut the pastry into long and short straws before baking. When cool, they line up the straws in order of length.	**Construction:** Children use construction straws to make a long structure and a short structure.	**Sand:** Children build a short trench in the sand. Now try to make a long trench. *How long can we make it? How many cars long is it?*	**Cutting and sticking:** Cut gummed paper squares into long and short strips. Children stick the strips of paper to make a pattern.
Language	Long, short, tall, shorter, longer, taller, longest, shortest, tallest, middle-sized, medium				
At home	*A leaf collection* **Long, short and medium-length leaves, glue** Encourage your child to find three leaves in the garden or while out on a walk – one short, one long and one in between. Let your child stick all the leaves onto a sheet of paper to take into class.				
Resources	Two card snakes (one long, one short), two ribbons (one long, one short), two pencils (one long, one short), water containers, water	Three pairs of socks (one long, one short, one medium-length), cheese straw mix	Straws (one long and one short for each pair), construction straws	Eight paper fish (some long, some short, but all different lengths), Blu-tack, sandpit, toy cars	Books (various sizes), strips cut from gummed paper squares

- Sing a number song together.
- Count together to 30, using fingers to mark the units. Help the children with the 'decade' numbers.
- Say a number rhyme together.
- Count backwards from 20 to 1, then shout *Blast off!* together. Help with the 'teen' numbers by stressing the first part of the word each time. Then hold up ten fingers and turn down one on each number to help mark the number of units.
- Say a number between 1 and 10. *Three.* Ask the children to hold up that number of fingers. Who has to count and who just 'knows'? Repeat for other numbers.

WARM UPS

DAY 1

- *Comparing the length of two objects*

Two card snakes (one long, one short), two ribbons (one long, one short), two pencils (one long, one short)

- Show children the two snakes. *Which of these snakes is longer? Which is shorter?* Let children look at and discuss these.
- Show children the longer snake. *This is a long snake. It is longer than its friend.* Demonstrate by holding the longer snake next to the shorter snake.
- Show children the shorter snake. *This is the short snake. It is shorter than its friend.* Demonstrate by holding the shorter snake next to the longer snake.
- Repeat to compare the ribbons and then the pencils. *Which is longer? Which is shorter?*

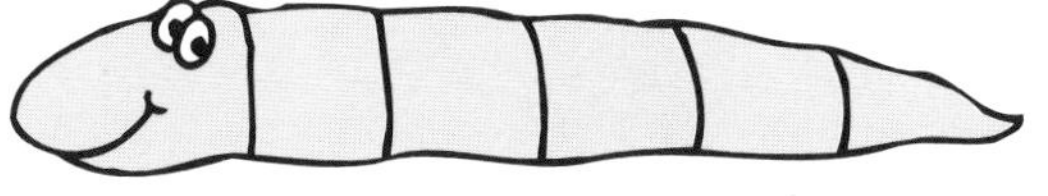

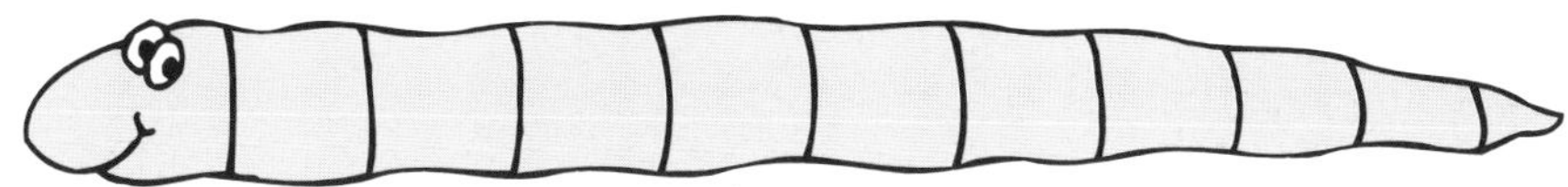

DAY 2

- *Comparing the length of three objects*

Three pairs of socks (one long, one short, one medium length)

- Choose two children and give one the pair of long socks and the other the pair of short socks to put on.
- *Who is wearing the longer socks? Who is wearing the shorter socks?* Compare the two children's socks. Discuss which are short and which are long.
- Stand the two children next to each other. *Which socks are longer?* Choose a child to point to the longer socks. *These socks are longer.* Repeat for the shorter socks.
- Choose another child. Give her the medium-length socks. Compare her with the 'long socks' child. *Who has longer socks?* Point to the longer socks. *These socks are longer.*
- Repeat to compare her with the 'short socks' child.
- Finally stand children in order – from the child wearing the longest socks to the child wearing the shortest socks.

DAY 3

- *Comparing the length of two objects*
- *Using the language of length*

Straws (one long and one short for each pair)

- Give each pair of children a long and a short straw. Children compare straws. Encourage them to use the language of length as they do so.
- Choose a pair. *Who has the longer straw? Who has the shorter?* Demonstrate that one child in the pair has the longer straw, and one has the shorter straw.
- Each pair directly compares their straws. Help them to hold the straws so that they are lined up at one end. *Who has the longer straw? Who has the shorter straw?*
- Ask children with the short straws to stand up. Ask children with the long straws to stand up.
- Choose two children with a 'long' straw and compare their straws. *Whose is longer?*
- Repeat, choosing two children with 'short' straws.

DAY 4

- *Comparing the length of three objects*
- *Using the language of length*

Eight paper fish (some long, some short, but all different lengths), Blu-tack

- Blu-tack three of the fish to the board. *Which fish is the longest? Which is the shortest?* Show how they can be directly compared by lining them up with the ends of the tails, or the heads, in a line down the board. *Which fish is the longest? Which is the shortest?* Line up the fish down the board from shortest to longest.
- Give another fish to a child. Ask her to describe her fish. *Is it long or short? Where do you think it will go on the board?*

- Hold her fish below the longest fish on the board. *Is your fish longer or shorter than this fish?* Compare her fish directly with the other two fish on the board. Stick it on the board in the correct position.
- Repeat, sticking three new fish on the board.

DAY 5

- *Comparing the length of three objects*
- *Using the language of length*

Books (various sizes)

- Ask three children to choose a book each. *Who has the longest book?* Show how to compare the length of two of the books by holding one book against the other. Then compare the longer of those two with the third book. *Which is the longest of all?*
- *Who has the shortest book?* Compare two of the books directly to find out which is the shorter. Then compare the shorter book with the third book. *Which is the shortest book of all?*
- Choose a child to find a book that is longer than the longest book. *Is he right?*
- Choose another child to find a book that is shorter than the shortest book.

	DAY 1	DAY 2	DAY 3	DAY 4	DAY 5
Objective	Comparing tall and short and beginning to understand the language associated with height				
Teacher-led activities *On the rug* (pages 20–21)	**Warm up:** Show fingers to match numbers up to 10. **Activity:** Choose two children of different heights. *Who is taller? Who is shorter?* Illustrate with your hand the difference in height. Compare two other children. Ask the taller child to stretch up and the shorter to crouch down. In pairs, ask children to find who is taller and who is shorter, and to stretch or crouch, as applicable.	**Warm up:** Count to 40 using fingers. **Activity:** Give interlocking cubes to each pair. Ask one child to build a tall tower and another to build a short tower. Compare the two towers. Choose a short tower from two different pairs. *Which is shorter?* Choose a tall tower from two different pairs. *Which is taller?* Compare three towers and place them in height order.	**Warm up:** Say a number rhyme. **Activity:** Put a tall hat and a short hat on a table. *Which hat is taller?* Point to the short hat. Show children a still shorter hat. *Which hat is taller? Which is shorter?* Use all five hats and arrange them in order of height by comparing hats until you find the shortest, then the tallest, then those in between.	**Warm up:** Count back from 20 to *Blast off!* **Activity:** Choose a child. Stand him beside a cupboard. *Is he taller or shorter than the cupboard?* Ask children if he is taller or shorter than something at a different height, e.g. shelves. Before comparing him directly, ask children to predict. Stand him beside the shelves. Use a hand to show different heights. *Am I taller/shorter than the door?* Stand by the door to check.	**Warm up:** Count to 50 using fingers. **Activity:** Show children the two jars. Place them on a table. *Which is taller? Which is shorter?* Show a third jar. *Is it shorter or taller?* Use a puppet to arrange the jars in order of size but make it do it incorrectly. Can children correct his order? Discuss how to compare for height, lining up the bottom of the jars and using hands to compare.
Teacher-initiated activities *Activity Book* (page 5)	**Easy:** Use different-sized boxes. Pick one that is fairly tall and one that is fairly short. Compare the two and ask children to point to the taller. Point to the tallest box. Point to the shortest. Each child compares two boxes to say which is taller. **Medium:** Use pictures of buildings. Sort these into tall and short buildings. Each child draws a tall building and a short building. **Hard:** Use nets of cuboids to help children make and decorate a tall box and a short box each.				
Independent activities *Supported play*	**Construction:** Children build a tall, thin building and a short, flat building using large building bricks. Discuss the difference in heights.	**Cooking:** Children make a milkshake using the recipe in the Recipe Bank (page 119). Fill some glasses. Talk about tall and short glasses.	**Cutting and sticking:** Children make cylindrical containers using tubes of card. *Do the tall thin cylinders hold more than the short fat cylinders?* The children fill them, e.g. with lentils, to compare.	**Sand:** Children build the tallest sand castle they can. *Whose sand castle is tallest? How do you make a tall castle?*	**Cutting and sticking:** Children roll card to make conical hats. They make a tall hat and a short hat, decorate them and put a bobble on top.
Language	Long, short, tall, shorter, longer, taller, longest, shortest, shortest, middle-sized				
At home	*Comparing packets* **Containers or packets, paper, a pen** Encourage your child to find two containers or packets, one taller than the other. Help them to draw round each packet. Write the name of the contents on each one. Remind your child to take the drawings into class.				
Resources	Building bricks	Interlocking cubes, milkshake mix, tall and short glasses	Five hats (varying heights), card, glue	Sandpit, buckets, scoops	Three transparent plastic jars (different heights), a puppet, card, glue, bobbles

- Say a number between 1 and 10. *Seven.* Ask the children to hold up that number of fingers. Who has to count and who just 'knows'? Repeat for other numbers.
- Count together to 40, using fingers to mark the units. Help the children with the 'decade' numbers.
- Together say a number rhyme, which involves counting up.
- Count backwards from 20 to 1, then shout *Blast off!* together. Help with the 'teen' numbers, if they find these difficult.
- Count together to 50, using fingers to mark the units. Help the children with the 'decade' numbers, especially *Twenty-nine, thirty ..., Thirty-nine, forty ...,* and *Forty-nine, fifty.*

WARM UPS

DAY 1

- *Comparing tall and short*
- Choose two children of different heights. They stand up in front of the class. *Who is taller? Who is shorter?* Illustrate the difference in height with your hand.
- Choose two different children and compare them by standing them back to back and showing the difference in height with your hand. Ask the taller child to stretch their arms up high and the shorter to crouch down low.
- Ask children to work in pairs. Explain that you want them to compare their heights. *If you are taller, stretch up high. If you are shorter, crouch down low.*
- Watch children as they do this. What sort of judgements are they making? How accurate are they about their heights? Are they right about who is taller and who is shorter?

DAY 2

- *Comparing tall and short*

Interlocking cubes

- Give a generous handful of cubes to each pair of children. Ask one child to build a tall tower and another to build a short tower.
- Choose a pair and compare their two towers. *Which is the taller? Which is the shorter?*
- Repeat with another pair's towers.
- Choose a short tower from two different pairs. *Which of these short towers is shorter?* Compare the two towers directly, standing them next to each other. *Which is shorter?* Hold up the shorter tower. *This is the shorter tower.*
- Choose a tall tower from two different pairs. Compare the two towers directly, standing them next to each other. *Which is taller?*
- Compare three towers, and place them in height order.

DAY 3
- *Comparing tall and short*

Five hats (varying heights)

- Show children a tall hat and a short hat. *Which hat is taller?*
- Compare the two hats directly. *We have to stand these hats on something to make sure we can see which hat is actually the tallest. Otherwise it might be the person wearing it who is the tallest.* Stand the hats on the table. *Which hat is the taller?*
- Take the shorter hat and show children an even shorter hat. *Which hat is the taller?* Compare these directly, placing them both on the table.
- *Which hat is the shortest?* Use all five hats. Continue comparing two hats, putting the taller aside each time until you have found the shortest hat.
- Repeat to find the tallest hat.
- Arrange the other three hats in order of height. Line up all five in order of height.

DAY 4
- *Comparing tall and short*
- Choose a child. Stand him beside a cupboard. *Is he taller or shorter than the cupboard?* Choose a child to demonstrate why he is shorter (or taller).
- Now ask children if he is taller or shorter than something at a different height, e.g. shelves. Before you compare him directly, ask children to predict.
- Now stand him beside the shelves to compare him directly. Use your hand to indicate the different heights. *Who is taller?*
- *Am I taller or shorter than the door?* Ask children to predict. Stand by the door and encourage children to see how much taller the door is. *I am shorter than the door.*

DAY 5
- *Comparing tall and short*

Three transparent plastic jars (different heights), a puppet

- Show children two jars. *Which jar is taller? Which jar is shorter?* Agree which is taller and which is shorter by comparing the jars directly, by placing them on a table.
- Show a third jar. *Is this jar shorter or taller?* Use a puppet to arrange the jars in order of size, but ensure he makes mistakes. Can children correct his order?
- Discuss how to compare the jars for height by lining them up next to each other with the bases of the jars at the same height and using hands to compare heights. *Which jar is shortest?* Put it first. *Which jar is next shortest?* Continue until the jars are lined up in order.

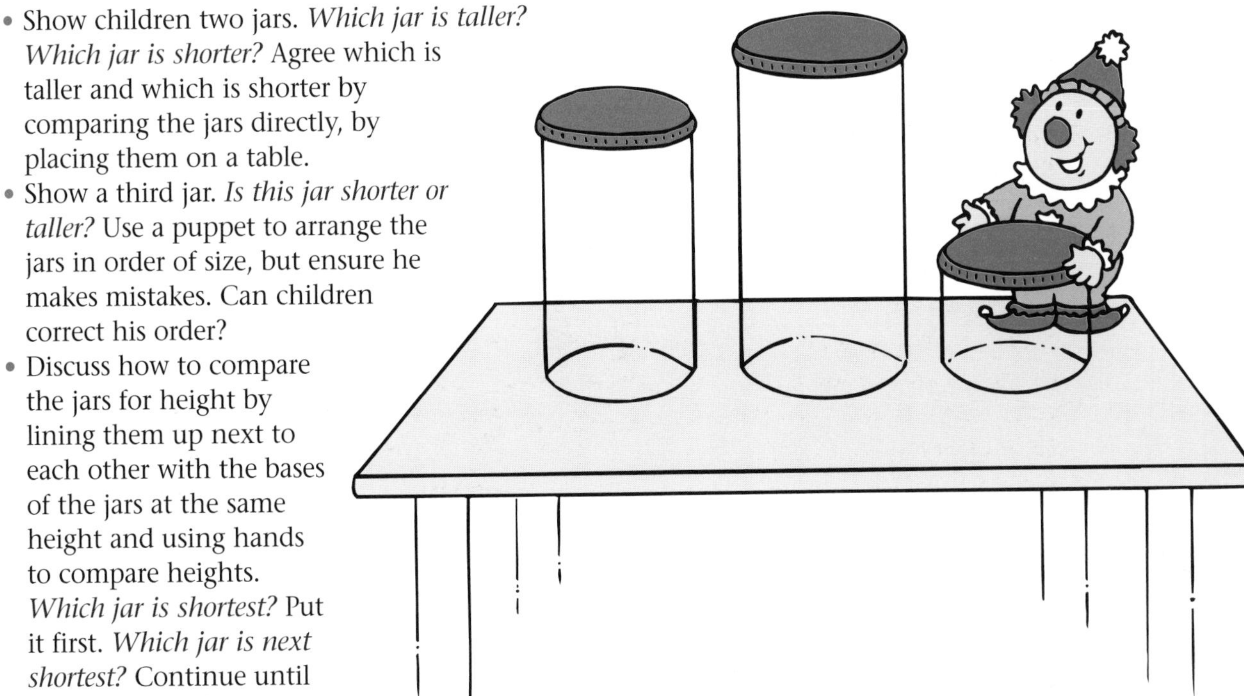

	DAY 1	DAY 2	DAY 3	DAY 4	DAY 5
Objective	Comparing two numbers, comparing two quantities, recognising who has less and who has more				
Teacher-led activities *On the rug* (pages 23–24)	**Warm up:** Sing a number song. **Activity:** Count along the number line to 20. Choose one of the younger children in the class. *How old are you?* Ask her to point to her number on the line. Choose one of the older children to point to his number. *Who is older? Which number is larger?* Repeat, using the ages of brothers or sisters. The further along the line, the larger the number and the older the child.	**Warm up:** Count to 50 using fingers. **Activity:** Spread out the spotty cards, face up. Ask a child to find the card with one spot and peg it to the line. Continue to 12 spots. Point to the 5 and 3 spotty cards. *This card has more spots than this one.* Repeat for two other cards.	**Warm up:** Show fingers to match numbers up to 10. **Activity:** Give one number card to each pair of children. Choose two pairs. Each pair points to their number on the line. *Whose number is further along the line?* Each pair builds a tower of building bricks to match their number. *Whose tower is taller? Whose number is larger?* Repeat with different pairs. *The numbers further along the line are larger.*	**Warm up:** Count to 30 then back from 10 to *Blast off!* **Activity:** Put crackers on the two plates. *Which has more crackers on it?* Count the crackers on each plate. Match each one to a number card. *Which plate has more? Which number is larger?* Repeat with different numbers of crackers and different children. Share out the crackers.	**Warm up:** say a number rhyme. **Activity:** Lay large number cards (1 to 20) along the rug to make a track. Play a track game against the class. Spin a coin. Heads – move two spaces forwards, tails – move one space forwards. After each turn, look at the two numbers and decide who is further ahead. *Whose counter is on the larger number?* First to 20 wins.
Teacher-initiated activities *Activity Book* (pages 5–6)	**Easy:** Use a large pile of building bricks. Each child takes 20 bricks. They see what these look and feel like, then return them to the pile. Each child then takes a handful. *Who has most?* They build each set into a tower to check. They count the number in each tower. **Medium:** Use a number track (1 to 20) and counters placed on 1. Spin a coin. Tails – move two spaces forwards, heads – move three spaces forwards. After each turn, pause and compare. *Who is on the largest number? Who is furthest along the track?* The child on the largest number takes a cube. Continue to 20. The child with most cubes wins. **Hard:** Use number cards (1 to 30). Each child takes a card. They compare numbers. The child with the largest number takes a cube. Continue until all the cards have been used. The child with most cubes wins.				
Independent activities *Supported play*	**Playhouse:** Give each child a 3-digit telephone number to remember for one of the toys. *What is the teddy's telephone number? What is the largest digit in teddy's phone number?*	**Cooking:** Children make sponge buns using the recipe in the Recipe Bank (page 119). They decorate the cooled buns by sticking on cherries – one on the first bun, two on the second, etc. They arrange the cakes in order and count up and down. Compare two buns. *Which has more cherries?*	**Play dough:** Roll out the play dough. Children make name plaques. They decorate them with beads or small shells. *How many beads did you use? Who used the most?* Display the plaques.	**Sand:** Bury eight red bricks, ten blue bricks and five yellow bricks. Children guess which colour there are most of. They dig up the bricks and count to check.	**Cutting and sticking:** Children use different shapes cut from sticky paper to create a picture. *Which colour is there most of? Which colour is there least of?* Count to check.
Language	Number names one to twenty, how many?, more, less, larger, smaller, further along, near, close, largest, smallest				
At home	***Who has the largest number?*** **A set of playing cards, sultanas** Remove the picture cards from the set. Explain that the ace cards are number 1. Play in a small group. Deal out a card to each player. The person with the largest number keeps the card. The others are placed at the bottom of the pack. Continue until one player has five cards. Give the winner a handful of sultanas.				
Resources	Washing line with large number cards (1 to 20) pegged to it, pegs, toys	Washing line, pegs, spotty number cards (1 to 12), sponge buns mix, cherries	Two sets large number cards (1 to 10), washing line with large number cards (1 to 10) pegged to it, large building bricks, pegs, play dough, beads or small shells	Two plates, crackers (up to 20), large number cards (1 to 10 – two sets), building bricks (red, blue and yellow), sandpit	Large number cards (1 to 20), a coin, two counters, sticky paper

- Together sing a number song.
- Count together to 50, using fingers to mark the units. Help the children with the 'decade' numbers.
- Say a number between 1 and 10. *Five.* Ask the children to hold up that number of fingers. Who has to count and who just 'knows'? Repeat for other numbers.
- Count together to 30, then backwards from 10 to 1, shouting *Blast off!* together at the end.
- Say a number rhyme together.

DAY 1

- *Comparing two numbers*

A washing line with large number cards (1 to 20) pegged to it, pegs

- Count together along the number line to 20, pointing to each number as you say it.
- Choose one of the younger children. *How old are you?* Ask her to point to her number on the line.
- Choose one of the older children. *Can you find your number on the line?* He points to his number.
- Point to the two numbers, e.g. 4 and 5. *Who is older? Which number is larger?* Remind children that the further along the line the numbers are, the larger they are. *Who is older? Tom. Your number is further along the line than Annie's because you*

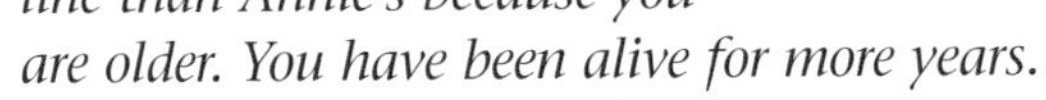

are older. You have been alive for more years.

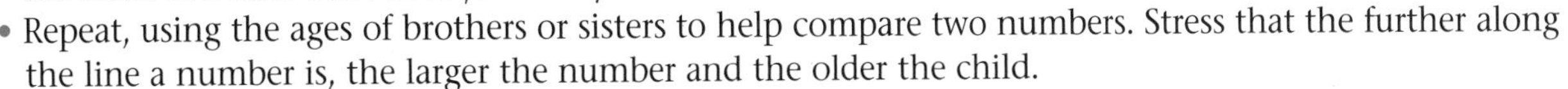

- Repeat, using the ages of brothers or sisters to help compare two numbers. Stress that the further along the line a number is, the larger the number and the older the child.

DAY 2

- *Comparing two quantities*
- *Recognising which has less and which has more*

A washing line, pegs, spotty number cards (1 to 12)

- Spread out the spotty number cards, face up. Ask a child to find the card with one spot and peg it to the line. Point to the card. *One spot.*
- Ask another child to find the card with two spots and peg it to the line. Point to the two cards in turn. *One, two.*
- Continue to 12 spots. Count along the line from 1 to 12, pointing to each card in turn.
- Point to the five spot and three spot cards. *This card has more spots than this one.* Show that the five spots is more than the three spots. *Five is bigger than three. Five is further along the line because it is a larger number. There are more spots on the five card than there are on the three card.*
- Repeat for two other cards.

DAY 3 • *Comparing two numbers*

Two sets of large number cards (1 to 10), a washing line with large number cards (1 to 10) pegged to it, large building bricks, pegs

- Give one number card to each pair of children, making sure they recognise their own number.
- Choose two pairs. Each pair points to their number on the number line. Compare the two numbers. *Whose number is further along the line?*
- Each pair builds a tower of large bricks to match their number. *Whose tower is taller? Whose number is larger? This number is further along the line. It is a larger number.*
- Repeat using different pairs.

DAY 4 • *Comparing two quantities*

• *Recognising which has less and which has more*

Two plates, crackers (up to 20), large number cards (1 to 10 – two sets)

- Put some of the crackers on each plate. *Which plate has more crackers on it?*
- Point to the first plate and count the crackers. Count together and touch each cracker to show you have counted it. Choose a child to select the matching number card and place it on the plate, e.g. 7.
- Point to the second plate and count the crackers. Choose another child to match the total to a number card.
- Look at the two plates. *Which plate has more? Which number is larger?*
- Repeat with different numbers of crackers and different children.
- Share out the crackers.

DAY 5 • *Comparing two numbers*

Large number cards (1 to 20), a coin, two counters

- Lay the number cards along the rug to make a number track.
- *We are going to play a track game, me against all of you.* Each side has a counter, placed on 1.
- Take turns to spin a coin. Heads – move two spaces forwards, tails – move one space forwards. *Which number am I on? Which number are you on?*
- After each turn, look at the two counters and decide who is further ahead. *Whose counter is on the larger number?* Discuss where the two counters are.
- The first side to reach 20 wins.

	DAY 1	DAY 2	DAY 3	DAY 4	DAY 5
Objective	Counting forwards and backwards to and from 10, recognising numbers to 10				
Teacher-led activities *On the rug* (pages 26–27)	**Warm up:** Count to 50 using fingers. **Activity:** Give one number card (1 to 10), to each pair. Give interlocking cubes to children without cards. Point to the last peg on the washing line. *What number comes here? Ten.* The pair with the 10 card peg it on the line. Choose a child to make a tower of 10 cubes. Continue, working down from 10 to 1.	**Warm up:** Show fingers to match numbers up to 10. **Activity:** Lay large number cards (1 to 10) along the rug to make a track. Select a soft toy and count the beads on its necklace together. *How many?* Encourage children to find the matching number on the track. Place the toy on that number. Talk about the number before. Repeat, putting each toy on its matching number.	**Warm up:** Say a number rhyme. **Activity:** Children count back from 10 to 1 using the number line. Choose a child to select an animal toy. She makes the noise of that animal. Then, in an animal voice, she counts back from 10 to 1, using the toy to point to each number on the line. Repeat, until several children have counted back from 10 to 1.	**Warm up:** Count to 50 using fingers. **Activity:** Stand ten children in a line. Count along, giving each child a card to match their number. Ask a child to choose one of the ten and say her number. She kneels, holding up her number. Build a tower to match her number. *What is the number before?* Remove a brick. *How many? The number one less is the number before.* Repeat.	**Warm up:** Sing a number song. **Activity:** Use the puppet. Choose a child to point to a number on the line. The puppet says the number. Make the puppet say the wrong number. Children correct it. *What is the number before?* Point to the number before. Build a tower of building bricks to match the first number and then remove one. Show that this is the number before. Repeat.
Teacher-initiated activities *Activity Book* (pages 6–7)	**Easy:** Each child threads ten beads on string. They find the 10 card from the number line and place it on the table. Children each remove one bead. They count the remaining beads on their strings and find the matching number card. Continue, until the line of cards goes from 10 to 1. **Medium:** Shuffle number cards (1 to 10) and place them in a pile face down. Children take turns to take a card. They count down to 1 from that number. If they are correct, they take a 1p coin. They replace the card on the bottom of the pile. First to collect 10p wins. **Hard:** Use a number track (1 to 20) and counters, placed on 20. Spin a coin. Tails – move one place backwards, heads – move two places backwards. *Say the number you will land on* ***before*** *you move.* If they are correct, they take a 1p coin. They stop when their counter reaches 1. *Who has collected most?*				
Independent activities *Supported play*	**Construction:** Each child builds a small Lego car. *How many pieces have you each used? Who has used the most?* The children count their Lego pieces then count back from that number to 1.	**Cooking:** Children put a dollop of honey on pieces of cut apple. Line up the pieces. *How many pieces? Eat one. How many are there now? Say the number before you count and eat.*	**Water:** Fill a teapot. *How many cups will it fill?* Ask children to estimate, then check by counting. Pour away one cup. *How many cups now?*	**Sand:** Children build eight sand castles. *How many sand castles?* Knock one down. *How many sand castles now?*	**Colouring:** Each child draws a rainbow with seven colours. They draw a building below their rainbow, using one less colour. *How many colours?*
Language	**Number names one to twenty, how many?, more, less, the number before, the number after**				
At home	*Jumping around* **Old greetings cards, a pen** Write the numbers from 1 to 12 (or up to the number of stairs in your house) on the back of old greetings cards. Place each card on the side of a stair. Taking care, encourage your child to jump up and down the stairs, saying the numbers as they jump. Alternatively, lay the cards along a garden path.				
Resources	Washing line with ten pegs on, large number cards (1 to 20), interlocking cubes, Lego	Large number cards (1 to 10), ten soft toys each with a necklace (first toy has one bead, second has two, ...), apples, honey	Washing line with large number cards (1 to 10) pegged to it, animal soft toys, pegs, teapot, cups, water	Large number cards (1 to 10), large building bricks, sandpit, buckets, scoops	Washing line with large number cards (1 to 10) pegged to it, pegs, a puppet, large building bricks, crayons or colouring pencils

- Count together to 50, using fingers to mark the units. Help the children with the 'decade' numbers, especially *Twenty-nine, thirty, ... Thirty-nine, forty, ...* and *Forty-nine, fifty.*
- Say a number between 1 and 10. *Six.* Ask the children to hold up that number of fingers. Who has to count and who just 'knows'? Repeat for other numbers.
- Together say a number rhyme, which involves counting down from 10.
- Count together to 50, using fingers to mark the units. Help the children with the 'decade' numbers.
- Together sing a number song, which involves counting down from 10.

DAY 1

- *Counting backwards from 10*

A washing line with ten pegs on, large number cards (1 to 10), interlocking cubes

- Give one of the number cards to each pair, and give interlocking cubes to children without cards.
- Point to the last peg on the washing line. *Which number comes here? Ten.* The pair with the number 10 card peg it on the line. *This is ten.*
- Choose a child to make a tower of ten cubes and stand it on the table. *Here are ten cubes.* Point to the 10 card. *This is ten.*
- Continue, working down from 10 to 1, standing the towers of cubes in descending order on the table. Count down the line of cubes. *Ten, nine, eight, seven, ... one.*

DAY 2

- *Counting backwards from 10*

Large number cards (1 to 10), ten soft toys each with a necklace (first toy has one bead, second has two beads, ...),

- Lay the number cards along the rug to make a number track. Count down the track from 10 to 1.
- Choose one of the soft toys and count the beads on its necklace together. *How many beads?*
- Encourage children to find the matching number on the track. Place the toy on that number.
- *What is the number before this toy's number?* Children look at the track and say the number before. If necessary, whisper a count. *One, two, three, ...* up to the number before the card the toy is sitting on.
- Repeat, putting each toy on its matching number. Each time, talk about the number before.

DAY 3 • *Counting backwards from 10*

A washing line with large number cards (1 to 10) pegged to it, animal soft toys, pegs

- Show children the number line. Count back from 10 to 1, pointing to each number as you say it.
- Choose a child to select a soft toy. She makes the noise of that animal.
- In an animal voice, she counts back from 10 to 1, using the toy to point to each number on the line.
- Continue until several children have counted back from 10 to 1. Finally all the children count back together, using their best animal voices.

DAY 4 • *Counting forwardss to 10*

Large number cards (1 to 10), large building bricks

- Place ten children in a line. Count along the line from 1 to 10, each child saying a number.
- Give each child a card to match their number. Ask one of the class to choose a child and say their number. That child kneels down, holding up her number.
- Point to the child's number. Build a tower of building bricks to match. Show the class.
- *What is the number before this?*
- Remove one brick. *How many now?* Demonstrate that the number one less is the number before.
- Repeat several times, choosing different children to select different numbers each time.

DAY 5 • *Recognising numbers to 10*

A washing line with large number cards (1 to 10) pegged to it, pegs, a puppet, large building bricks

- Choose a child to point to a number on the line. Ask the puppet which number she is pointing to. Make the puppet say the wrong number. Ask children to correct it.
- Point to the number and say it correctly. Point to the number before. *What is the number before?*
- Build a tower of bricks to match the first number and then remove one. Show that this is the number before.
- Repeat several times, choosing different children to point to different numbers on the line.

	DAY 1	DAY 2	DAY 3	DAY 4	DAY 5
Objective	Sorting 2-d shapes by shape, beginning to name rectangles and triangles, rehearsing naming squares and circles				
Teacher-led activities *On the rug* (pages 29–30)	**Warm up:** Show fingers to match numbers up to 10. **Activity:** Give a child the 'triangle' hat. Point to the triangle. *This is a triangle.* Point to the sides and the corners. Discuss the properties of the triangle. Repeat for the 'square' hat, the 'circle' hat and the 'rectangle' hat. Give each pair a 2-d shape. They take turns to give it to the child wearing the matching hat.	**Warm up:** Count to 50 using fingers. **Activity:** Place the shapes in a line. Talk about them, looking at the number of sides, the number of corners and whether the sides are curved or straight. Whilst children close their eyes, choose a child to remove a shape from the line. Can the others say what the missing shape is? Show the shape. Were they correct? Replace the shape and repeat.	**Warm up:** Say a number rhyme. **Activity:** Give each pair of children a 2-d shape to look at carefully. Make the puppet hide a shape and describe it, focusing on the number of sides and corners, and whether the sides are curved or straight. If children think he is describing their shape, they wave it. The puppet shows his shape. Were they correct? Repeat several times.	**Warm up:** Sing a number song. **Activity:** Place the large plastic 2-d shapes in a cloth bag. Give each pair a shape card. On a count of three, bring out a shape. *What shape is this?* Any pair with that shape on their shape card, cross it out. Only **one** shape can be crossed out each time. Replace the shape and repeat. The first pair to cross out all their shapes shouts *Bingo!*	**Warm up:** Count to 50 using fingers. **Activity:** Choose a child. Blu-tack a shape on his back. Turn him round to show the class. Children describe the shape without using its name. The child tries to draw the shape on the board. Remove the shape from his back. *Has he drawn the same shape?* Discuss the properties. Repeat with a different child.
Teacher-initiated activities *Activity Book* (page 7)	**Easy:** Use a selection of shapes. Sort the shapes into four sets, labelled 'triangle', 'square', 'rectangle' and 'circle'. **Medium:** Make a line of four shapes: square, circle, triangle and rectangle. Children copy the pattern, naming the shapes as they lay them. How many times can they repeat the pattern? **Hard:** Use plastic shapes. Children draw round each shape in a different colour. Discuss each shape as they draw it. What are its properties?				
Independent activities *Supported play*	**Sand:** Bury different 2-d shapes (squares, triangles, circles and rectangles) in the sand. Children feel for them. Before they uncover a shape, they say its name.	**Cooking:** Make peppermint creams using the method in the Recipe Bank (page 119). The children roll out and cut out different shapes. They name each shape.	**Play dough:** Children make squares, triangles, circles and rectangles. They sort them into sets of each shape.	**Cutting and sticking:** Children use cut-out paper or card shapes to create a picture.	**Painting:** Children choose a shape and paint a very large one. They use bright, bold colours. Can the other children recognise the shape in their pictures?
Language	Shapes, circles, squares, rectangles, oblongs, triangles, corners, sides, curved, straight				
At home	*Collage shapes* **Strips of paper, a length of wool or ribbon, glue** With the paper and ribbon or wool, help your child to make shapes such as a square, a rectangle, a circle and a triangle. Let your child stick the shapes onto a sheet of paper to take into class.				
Resources	Four simple conical hats (each with one large shape on: square, circle, rectangle, triangle), small plastic 2-d shapes (square, circle, rectangle, triangle), sandpit	Large 2-d shapes (square, circle, rectangle, triangle), peppermint cream mix	2-d shapes (square, circle, rectangle, triangle – one for each pair), large piece of card, a puppet, play dough	Large plastic 2-d shapes (square, rectangle, circle, triangle), a cloth bag, thick pieces of card with four shapes drawn on (one card for each pair), card or paper shapes	Card 2-d shapes (square, rectangle, circle, triangle), Blu-tack, paint, paintbrushes

- Say a number between 1 and 10. *Ten*. Ask the children to hold up that number of fingers. Who has to count and who just 'knows'? Repeat for other numbers.
- Count together to 50, using fingers to mark the units. Help the children with the 'decade' numbers.
- Together say a number rhyme, which involves counting down from 10.
- Sing a number song together.
- Count together to 50, using fingers to match the count. Help the children with the 'decade' numbers.

WARM UPS

DAY 1

- *Sorting 2-d shapes by name*
- *Beginning to name rectangles and triangles*
- *Rehearsing naming squares and circles*

Four simple conical hats (each with one large shape on: square, circle, rectangle, triangle), small plastic 2-d shapes (square, circle, rectangle, triangle)

- Give the hat with the triangle on to a child. Point to the triangle. *This is a triangle*. Point to the sides and the corners. Discuss the properties of the triangle. *It has three sides. It has three corners. It is a triangle.*
- Repeat for the 'square' hat, the 'circle' hat and the 'rectangle' hat. Discuss the properties of each shape – the number of corners, the number of sides, whether the sides are the same length or different lengths, and whether the sides are curved.
- Give each pair a 2-d shape to look at and decide which shape it is. Encourage children to look at its properties, e.g. number of corners and sides.
- Choose a pair to give their shape to the child wearing the appropriate hat.
- Repeat with all the other pairs.

DAY 2

- *Sorting 2-d shapes by name*
- *Beginning to name rectangles and triangles*
- *Rehearsing naming squares and circles*

Large 2-d shapes (square, circle, rectangle, triangle)

- Place the four shapes in a line.
- Point to the rectangle. *How many sides has this shape? Four. Are all the sides the same length? No, two sides are long and two sides are short. How many corners does this shape have? It has four corners. Are the sides curved or straight? They are straight.*
- Repeat for each shape. Look at the number of sides, the number of corners and whether the sides are curved or straight.
- Whilst children close their eyes, choose a child to remove a shape from the line. Can the others say what the missing shape is? Show them the shape. Were they correct?
- Replace the shape and repeat.

DAY 3 • *Sorting 2-d shapes by shape*

2-d shapes (square, circle, rectangle, triangle – one for each pair), large piece of card, a puppet

- Give each pair of children a 2-d shape. They talk about their shape, focusing on its properties. *What shape is it?* They each name their shape.
- Make the puppet hide a shape behind the card, then describe it, focusing on the number of sides and corners and whether the sides are curved or straight.
- Children listen carefully and compare the puppet's description to their shape. If children think he is describing their shape, they wave it.
- The puppet shows his shape. Were they correct?
- Repeat several times.

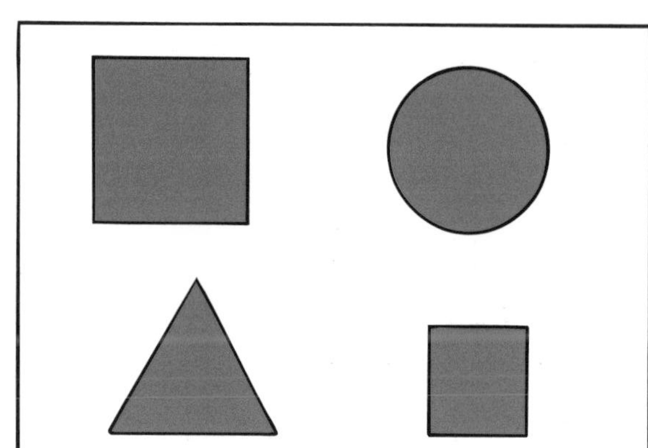

DAY 4 • *Sorting 2-d shapes by shape*

Large plastic 2-d shapes (square, rectangle, circle, triangle), a cloth bag, thick pieces of card with four shapes drawn on (one card for each pair – squares, rectangles, circles, triangles, can be more than one of the same shape and shapes can be positioned differently)

- Place the large plastic shapes in a cloth bag. Give each pair a shape card. *We are going to play a game called 'Bingo'.*
- On a count of three, take out a shape from the bag. *What shape is this?* Discuss its properties. *What is its name? Is it a circle, a square, a triangle or a rectangle?* If any pair has that shape on their card, they cross it out. Stress that only one shape can be crossed out each time.
- Replace the shape in the bag and repeat. The first pair to cross out all their shapes shouts *Bingo!* and wins.

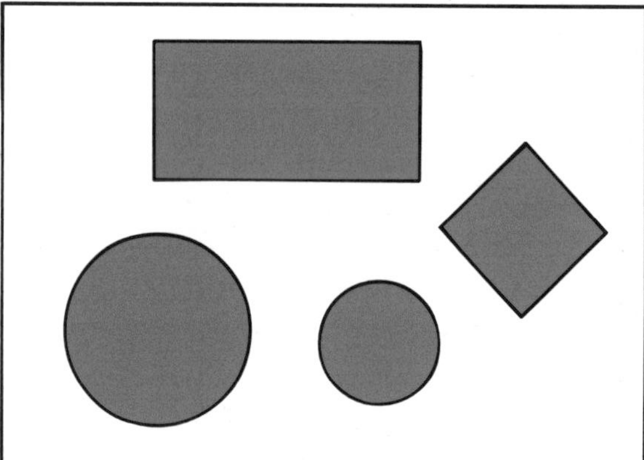

DAY 5 • *Recognising 2-d shapes*

Card 2-d shapes (square, rectangle, circle, triangle), Blu-tack

- Choose a child and Blu-tack a shape on his back.
- Turn him round to show the class. Ask children to describe the shape to him without using its name. *How many corners has it? How many sides? Are all the sides the same length?*
- The child wearing the shape tries to draw the shape on the board. Help him as appropriate.
- Remove the shape from his back and point to his drawing. *Has he drawn the same shape?* Discuss the properties of the shape.
- Repeat with a different child.

	DAY 1	DAY 2	DAY 3	DAY 4	DAY 5
Objective	Recognising coins, counting up to ten coins				
Teacher-led activities *On the rug* (pages 32–33)	**Warm up:** Show fingers to match numbers up to 10. **Activity:** Count along the number line from 1 to 10. Point to 7. *What number is this?* Count to check. *I will give the teddy seven pence.* Count out seven 1p coins and place them in the teddy's purse. *How much does he have? Seven pence.* Empty the purse and repeat for 9p. Whilst children close their eyes, put six 1p coins in the purse. *How much is in the purse?* Point to 6 on the line. Count to check. Repeat.	**Warm up:** Say a number rhyme. **Activity:** Give each pair a coin, choosing an appropriate value for the pair. They look at it carefully. Discuss different things you could buy with each coin, e.g. 10p could buy a chocolate bar. Hold up a £2 book. *Who has the coin that will buy this?* Place the coin and the book on a table. Repeat for each item.	**Warm up:** Count up to 10 then down to *Blast off!* **Activity:** Give each child a coin. Hold up a demonstration coin and say its name. Any child with a matching coin stands up to show the class their coin. Discuss how much can be bought with this coin – not much (1p, 2p, 5p), several things (10p, 20p, 50p) or quite a lot (£1, £2). Ask the standing children to sit down and repeat for each coin.	**Warm up:** Count to 50 using fingers. **Activity:** Choose a child to take out a priced object (e.g. a glass bead priced at 4p) out of the cloth bag. Show it to the class. *This bead costs four pence.* Show children the 1p coins. *We need four pennies. That's four of these, to buy it.* Choose a child to count out four 1p coins. Repeat with different children and objects.	**Warm up:** Count different numbers of jumps or claps. **Activity:** Choose a shopkeeper. Give him the apple quarters, the orange pieces and the slices of bread. Choose a child to be the shopper. Give her the 1p and 10p coins. She chooses something to buy and counts out 1p coins. *If you choose bread, we do not need to count ten 1p coins. We can use a 10p coin instead.* Repeat several times.
Teacher-initiated activities *Activity Book* (pages 7–8)	**Easy:** Use real 1p coins. Each child takes a handful of coins and counts them to find out how much they have. They match the coins to a number card. **Medium:** Use a variety of biscuits. Price each type of biscuit, e.g. chocolate 9p, raisin 6p, butter cream 7p, plain 3p. Each child chooses a biscuit and uses 1p coins to pay for it. They draw the biscuit and write its price (with help if necessary), then eat it. **Hard:** Use plastic coins (all denominations). *What can we buy with each coin?* Each child sticks each coin on a page of a small zig-zag book. They write or draw an object beside each coin.				
Independent activities *Supported play*	**Painting:** Children select a coin. They choose a side and draw or paint a picture of it, looking at it very carefully.	**Cooking:** Make shortbread using the recipe in the Recipe Bank (page 119). Cut it into different-shaped pieces and 'sell' each one for 5p or 10p, depending on the size.	**Playhouse:** Children use coins in role play, shopping in the playhouse. Encourage them to count out coins correctly.	**Cutting and sticking:** Children stick cardboard coins in order from 1p to £2 along a line. They take turns to cover one and say what it looks like.	**Jigsaws:** Children do a jigsaw. 'Pay' them 1p for every piece they do. How much do they have at the end? Encourage them to swap each lot of ten 1p coins for one 10p coin.
Language	Coin names, how much?, how many?, cost, buy, sell, more, less, pence, penny, pound, coin				
At home	*Shopping* **Toys, sticky labels, coins (1p, 2p, 5p, 10p, 20p), a pen** Using the sticky labels, price some toys using different coin values, e.g. 5p, 10p, 20p but not 11p or 12p. Ask your child to choose a toy and to give you the correct coin to pay for it. Swap roles and see whether your child knows if you have offered the correct coin. You could price the toys under 10p and ask your child to count out the appropriate number of 1p coins.				
Resources	Washing line with large number cards (1 to 10) pegged to it, pegs, a teddy, 1p coins, a purse, paint, paintbrushes	Real coins (all denominations – enough for one per pair), items labelled to match each coin, demonstration coins (all denominations), shortbread mix	Real coins (all denominations, one per child) demonstration coins (all denominations), playhouse items	Real 1p coins, a cloth bag with priced objects, e.g. glass bead (4p), pencil (8p), rubber (10p), cardboard coins	Priced items, e.g. apple quarters (3p), slices of orange (1p), slices of bread and jam (10p), real coins (1p, 10p), jigsaws

- Say a number between 1 and 10. *Seven.* Ask the children to hold up that number of fingers. Ask them to add one more finger. *How many now?* Repeat for other numbers.
- Together say a number rhyme, which involves counting down from 10.
- Count together to 10, then back down to 1, shouting *Blast off!* together at the end.
- Count together to 50, using fingers to match the count. Prompt the children with the 'decade' numbers if they find them difficult.
- Count ten jumps or claps together. Ask different children to demonstrate different numbers of actions. *Jamal, show me four claps. Slowly so we can all count.*

DAY 1

- *Recognising coins*
- *Counting up to ten coins*

A washing line with large number cards (1 to 10) pegged to it, pegs, a teddy, 1p coins, a purse

- Point to the number line and count along it from 1 to 10.
- Point to the number 7 card. *What number is this? Let's count to check. It is seven.*
- Show children the teddy. *I will give the teddy seven pence.* Count out seven 1p coins and place them in the teddy's purse. *How much does he have? Seven pence.* Empty the purse.
- Choose a child. *This time, let's give the teddy nine pence. Can you count out the pennies?* Help them to count nine 1p coins into the teddy's purse.
- Choose another child to find the matching number, 9, on the number line.
- Whilst children close their eyes, put six 1p coins in the purse. *How much is in the purse?* Point to 6 on the line. Encourage children to say the amount. *Six pence.* Count to check.
- Repeat.

DAY 2

- *Recognising coins*

Real coins (all denominations – enough for one coin per pair), items labelled to match each coin, demonstration coins (all denominations)

- Choose an appropriate coin to give to each pair.
- Each pair looks at their coin and talks about it. Look at the colour and the shape, as well as the size.
- Hold up a demonstration coin, e.g. a 10p coin, to look at together. Discuss the different things you might buy with this coin. *What could I buy with 10p?* Suggest several things, and show children a 10p chocolate bar. Repeat for the other coins.
- Hold up a £2 book. *Who has the coin that will buy this?* Any pair holding a £2 coin stands up. Discuss other things the coin will buy. *Look at its colour and shape.* Place the coin and the book on a table.
- Repeat for each item.

DAY 3

- *Recognising coins*

Real coins (all denominations – enough for one per child), demonstration coins (all denominations)

- Give each child a coin.
- Hold up a demonstration coin and say its name. Children with matching coins stand up to show the class their coin.
- Talk about what this coin looks like. *Is it round? Is it silver? How heavy is it?*
- Discuss how much can be bought with the coin – not much (1p, 2p, 5p), several things (10p, 20p, 50p) or quite a lot (£1, £2).
- Ask children who are standing to sit down.
- Repeat with each coin.

DAY 4

- *Recognising coins*
- *Counting up to ten coins*

Real 1p coins, a cloth bag with priced objects

- Choose a child to take an object out of the bag, e.g. a glass bead priced at 4p. Show it to the class. *This bead costs four pence.*
- Show children the 1p coins. *We need four one pence coins, that's four of these, to buy it.* Choose a child to count out four 1p coins. *Now she has four pence. She can buy the bead.* The child gives you the 4p and you give them the bead.
- Repeat with different children and different objects.

DAY 5

- *Recognising coins*
- *Counting up to ten coins*

Priced items, e.g. apple quarters (3p), orange pieces (1p), slices of bread and jam (10p), real coins (1p, 10p)

- Choose a shopkeeper. Give him the apple quarters, the orange pieces and the bread.
- Choose a child to be the shopper. Give her the 1p and 10p coins. *What would you like to buy?* Help the shopper choose. *How much is this?* The shopkeeper says the price. Help the shopper to count out that many 1p coins. Match the number of coins and the price.
- Choose another child to be the shopper. She chooses something to buy. Read the price to the class. Children can count with the shopper as she counts out the matching number of 1p coins. *If you choose bread, we do not need to count ten 1p coins, we can use a 10p coin instead.*
- Repeat several times.
- Share out all the food.

	DAY 1	DAY 2	DAY 3	DAY 4	DAY 5
Objective	**Understanding that we can measure time, recognising a minute as a unit of time, counting the number of times something happens in one minute**				
Teacher-led activities *On the rug* (pages 35–36)	**Warm up:** Say the days of the week. **Activity:** *This is a sand timer. How long does it take the sand to run through? One minute.* Choose a child. *One minute is not very long. How many times can you jump while the sand runs through?* Ask her to jump slowly while the class counts. Write the number of jumps on the board. Choose a child to clap for a minute. Repeat with bunny-hops.	**Warm up:** Say a number rhyme. **Activity:** Show children the pinger timer. *I use this to time my cooking. It will time one minute, like the sand timer.* Give a child the teddy. How *many children can we pass the teddy to in one minute?* Set the timer and pass the teddy round, fairly slowly. Count how many children hold the teddy. Repeat for children taking cubes from a tin in one minute.	**Warm up:** Say or sing the days of the week. **Activity:** *Can we hum for one minute?* Practise humming. *Now hum whilst the sand goes through the timer. We are going to try to hum for exactly one minute **without** watching the timer.* Hide the timer behind the book. Turn over the timer. Each child stops when they think a minute is over. Watch children and the timer. *Who was closest?*	**Warm up:** Count to 60 using fingers. **Activity:** Show children the clock. *This helps us to find out how long something takes. We will sing a song and time ourselves.* Sing several verses of 'The Wheels on the Bus'. *That took us four minutes. Every day we look at clocks to help us find out what time it is. Let's think of some of the reasons, e.g. to time cooking, to tell us when to get up, ...*	**Warm up:** Say or sing the days of the week. **Activity:** *How far can we count in one minute? To 100? More? Less?* Turn over the sand timer and start counting. Count fairly slowly, trying to get close to 60. *In one minute we can count to sixty.* Show children the clock. *The big hand moves just this much in one minute. What takes one or two minutes? Cleaning our teeth, washing our faces, ...*
Teacher-initiated activities *Activity Book* (pages 8–9)	**Easy:** Use the sand timer and time how many Lego bricks children can fix together in one minute to make a model. Display their 'one-minute models'. **Medium:** Set the pinger for one minute. Each child throws the number dice (1 to 6) and takes a matching number card. *How many times is the dice thrown in one minute? What numbers has each of you taken? Which number was thrown most often?* **Hard:** Use a large analogue clock with movable hands. Turn the hands to an 'o'clock time'. *What time is this? What might we be doing at this time?* Repeat.				
Independent activities *Supported play*	**Painting:** Children paint a picture of an activity they enjoy. *How many minutes does it normally last? Watching a favourite programme lasts 30 minutes.* Help the children write the number of minutes on their painting.	**Cooking:** Children make a milk shake using the recipe in the Recipe Bank (page 119). Pour the milk shake into different-sized glasses. *How many minutes does it take to drink each one?*	**Playhouse:** Use the sand timer to time things that are cooking. *How many minutes does it take the teddy to boil his egg?*	**Cutting and sticking:** Use pieces of gummed paper cut into shapes. *How many pieces of paper can you stick in a patterned line in one minute?* Who made the longest line?	**Toys:** Children make the toys go on journeys and outings in cars. Discuss where they could go, e.g. to the seaside, the countryside. *How long is each journey?* Encourage them to think in minutes.
Language	**Time, how long?, sand timer, pinger timer, minute, hour, clock, big hand, little hand**				
At home	***A minute's stretch*** **A timer** Set a timer, such as on a cooker or microwave, for one minute. As a family, see how many times you can stretch up and bend down in one minute. Count together as you do each stretch and bend. *How many times did we stretch before the bell rang?*				
Resources	A large one-minute sand timer, paint, paintbrushes	A pinger timer, a teddy, cubes, a tin, milk shake mix, glasses	A large one-minute sand timer, a book, a teddy, playhouse items	A working clock, gummed paper shapes	A large one-minute sand timer, a large analogue clock with movable hands, toys, toy cars

- Say the days of the week together.
- Together say a number rhyme, which involves counting back.
- Say or sing the days of the week together.
- Count together to 60, using fingers to mark the units. Help the children with the multiples of 10.
- Say or sing the days of the week together. Try starting from days other than Monday.

DAY 1

- *Understanding that we can measure time*
- *Recognising a minute as a unit of time*
- *Counting the number of times something happens in one minute*

A large one-minute sand timer

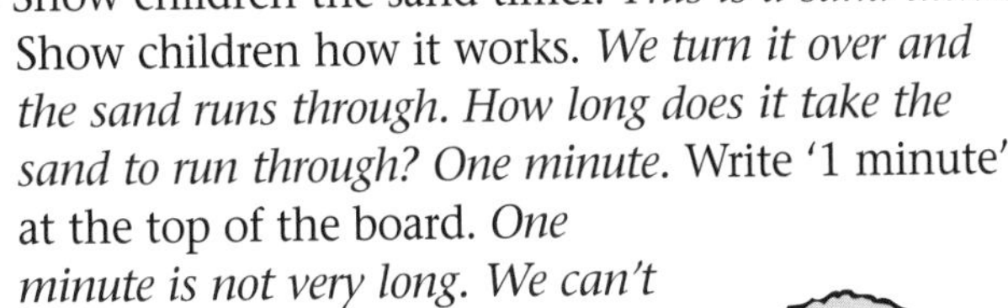

- Show children the sand timer. *This is a sand timer.* Show children how it works. *We turn it over and the sand runs through. How long does it take the sand to run through? One minute.* Write '1 minute' at the top of the board. *One minute is not very long. We can't do much in one minute.*
- *Let's find out what we can do in one minute. We will use the sand timer to time one minute. When all the sand has run through, that will be one minute.*
- Choose a child. *How many times can you jump while the sand runs through?* Ask her to jump slowly whilst everyone counts. Write the number of jumps on the board. Remind children what she can do in one minute. *She has jumped twenty times in one minute.*
- Turn the sand timer over again and choose a child to clap for one minute. Write the number of claps.
- Repeat, choosing a child to bunny-hop.

DAY 2

- *Counting the number of times something happens in one minute*

A pinger timer, a teddy, cubes, a tin

- Show children the pinger timer. *I use this to time my cooking. Sometimes, when I am making sweets, I need to time one minute. Sometimes I need to time more than one minute – for example ten minutes when I hard boil an egg.* Show children how to set the timer to time a number of minutes.
- *This timer can time one minute, just like the sand timer.* Give a child the teddy. *How many people can we pass the teddy to in one minute?* Set the timer and pass the teddy round, fairly slowly.
- Count how many children held the teddy. Write the number on the board. *This many children held the teddy in one minute.*
- Repeat, but counting how many children can take a cube from a tin in one minute.

DAY 3 • *Recognising a minute as a unit of time*

A large one-minute sand timer, a book

- Show children the sand timer. Remind them that the sand takes exactly one minute to run through. *We can time one minute.*
- *Can we hum for one minute?* Practise humming and then turn over the sand timer. Hum whilst the sand goes through. *We hummed for one minute.*
- *We are going to try to hum for exactly one minute without watching the timer.* Hide the timer behind the book. Turn over the timer as children start humming. Each child stops when they think a minute is over. Watch children and the timer.
- Notice which children stop humming at exactly one minute. *Who was closest? Who went on humming longer than one minute? Who hummed much shorter than one minute?*
- Talk about how long a minute feels.
- Repeat the humming.

DAY 4 • *Understanding that we can measure time*

A working clock

- Show children the clock. *This helps us to find out how long something takes.* Talk about when we look at clocks.
- *We are going to use this clock now. We will sing a song and time ourselves. Look at the clock. Look at where the big hand is.*
- Sing several verses of 'The Wheels on the Bus'. Look at the clock again. *The big hand has moved. That took us four minutes.*
- Every day we look at clocks to help us find out what time it is. *Let's think of some of the reasons. To time our cooking, to tell us it's time to get up, to tell us it's time for our favourite television programmes, to tell us its time to go to catch the bus or train, ...*
- Talk about clocks at school and clocks at home. Include watches.

DAY 5 • *Recognising a minute as a unit of time*
• *Counting the number of times something happens in one minute*

A large one-minute sand timer, a large analogue clock with movable hands

- *How far can we count in one minute? Do you think we could count to 100? More than 100? Less than 100?* Take some guesses and write them on the board.
- Turn over the sand timer and start counting. Count fairly slowly, trying to get as close to 60 as possible.
- *In one minute we can count to sixty.* Look at their guesses. *Which guess was closest?*
- Show children the clock. *The big hand moves just this much in one minute. Let's think of things which take one or two minutes, such as cleaning our teeth, washing our faces, putting on our shoes.* Make a list on the board.

	DAY 1	DAY 2	DAY 3	DAY 4	DAY 5
Objective	Counting to 20, recognising numbers to 20, counting sounds and movements, estimating quantities				
Teacher-led activities *On the rug* (pages 38–39)	**Warm up:** Say or sing the days of the week. **Activity:** Choose a child to unpeg number 15. *What number is this?* If necessary, help him by counting in a whisper to 15. Ask him to do 15 wing flaps. Everyone counts to check. *We can write fifteen.* Demonstrate, with children writing it on the floor with one finger. Repeat with number 13 and 13 hops, then number 18 and 18 claps.	**Warm up:** Count to 60 using fingers. **Activity:** Show children the bag of socks, rolled in pairs. *How many socks in the bag? Each 'ball' is a pair of socks – that's two socks.* Encourage children to write their guesses on the board, showing them how to form the numerals. Unroll the socks, then group them in pairs to count. Write the actual number. *Which guesses were close?*	**Warm up:** Count up to 20 then back to *Blast off!* **Activity:** Shuffle the cards and spread them out face down. Choose a child to take a card. *Which number have you taken?* Ask her to 'laugh' that many times. The rest of the class keeps a whispered count to check. Write that number on the board and children copy you, writing it on the floor. Repeat with different children, numbers and noises.	**Warm up:** Count to 60 using fingers. **Activity:** *How many beans in the jar?* Take guesses. Children write their guesses on the board. Tip out the beans and count them, grouping in twos. Count ten beans and choose a child to hold them. Repeat until you have counted all the beans, grouping in twos and then tens. Repeat with a different jar.	**Warm up:** Say or sing the days of the week. **Activity:** Hand out number cards (2 to 19). Children work out their number without showing anyone else. Choose a child to clap the number of times on their card. The other children count the claps and say the number. Check that his claps match his number. Any other children holding that number stand up. Repeat several times with different children.
Teacher-initiated activities *Activity Book* (page 9)	**Easy:** Use small soft toys. Children have three number cards in front of them. Place a number of toys in a cloth bag. Children guess the number. Tip out the toys and count. If a child has that number card, they turn it over. The first child to turn over all three cards wins. **Medium:** Use a number track (1 to 20) and counters placed on 1. Spin a coin. Heads – move two spaces forwards, tails – move one space forwards. When a child lands on a number, the others give him an action to do that many times. If he counts correctly, he takes a cube. Continue until one child's counter reaches 20. The child with the most cubes wins. **Hard:** Use a large 4 × 5 grid (1 to 20) with counters placed on 1. Spin a coin. Tails – move sideways one place (either direction), heads – move down or up one place. Children make a noise of their choice that many times. If they are correct, they take that many cubes. Children take six turns each. The child with the most cubes wins.				
Independent activities *Supported play*	**Painting:** Each child chooses a number. Paint it at the top of their page, forming the numeral carefully. Children paint a picture using a matching number of colours.	**Cooking:** Children decorate a small pizza base with slices of ham, cheese and tomato. They estimate how many slices of each, then count. Bake and eat the pizza.	**Construction:** Children make a Lego model using lots of different-coloured bricks. *How many bricks of each colour?* Encourage children to use as many bricks as possible.	**Water:** Children estimate how many small cups will fill a teapot. They check by filling it and counting. Repeat for other containers.	**Dominoes:** Use a number track (1 to 12). Children lay a domino with a matching total number of dots beside each card.
Language	Number names one to twenty, more, less, how many?, before, after, count				
At home	*Counting doors* **Paper, coloured pencils/crayons** Encourage your child to count all the doors in your house. Help them to write down the number of doors. Encourage them to draw a door and write the number of doors in the house on it.				
Resources	Washing line with large number cards (1 to 20) pegged to it, pegs, paint, paintbrushes	A shopping bag containing pairs of socks (up to ten pairs in different colours and sizes), pizza base, ham, cheese, tomatoes	Large number cards (1 to 20), washing line with large number cards (1 to 20) pegged to it, pegs, Lego	Small transparent plastic jars full of dried beans, teapot, cups, containers, water	Large number cards (2 to 19), washing line with large number cards (1 to 20) pegged to it, pegs, number track 1 to 12), dominoes

- Say or sing the days of the week together.
- Count together to 60, using fingers to mark the units. Help the children with the multiples of 10.
- Count together to 20, then back down to 1, shouting *Blast off!* together at the end.
- Count together to 60, using fingers to mark the units. Prompt the children with any numbers they find difficult.
- Say or sing the days of the week together. Try starting from days other than Monday.

DAY 1

- *Counting sounds and movements*

A washing line with large number cards (1 to 20) pegged to it, pegs

- Point to the number line. Choose a child to unpeg the number 15 card from the line. *What number is this?* If necessary, help children by counting along the line in a whisper to 15. *It is fifteen.*
- Ask the child holding 15 to do 15 wing flaps. As he does it, all the children count to check.
- *We can write fifteen.* Demonstrate how to write 15, and children write it on the floor in front of them with one finger.

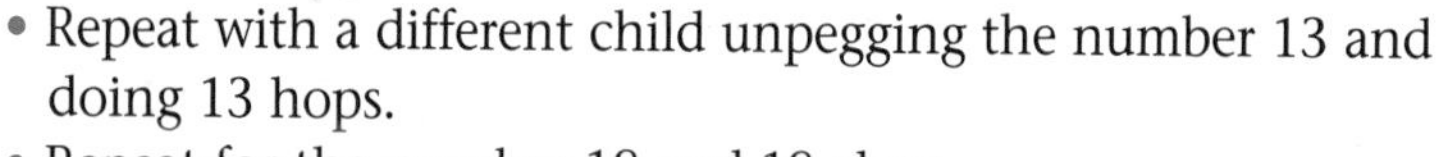

- Repeat with a different child unpegging the number 13 and doing 13 hops.
- Repeat for the number 18 and 18 claps.

DAY 2

- *Estimating quantities*

A shopping bag containing pairs of socks (up to ten pairs in different colours and sizes)

- Show children the bag of socks, rolled in pairs. *How many socks in the bag?*
- *Each 'ball' is a pair of socks. There are two socks in each ball. How many socks do you think there are?*
- Children work in pairs to guess. Encourage them to write their guess on the board, showing them how to form each of the numerals they need to write.
- Unroll the socks, then group them in pairs to help count. Write the actual number.
- Compare with children's guesses. *Which guesses were close?*

DAY 3

- *Recognising numbers to 20*
- *Counting sounds and movements*

Large number cards (1 to 20), a washing line with large number cards (1 to 20) pegged to it, pegs

- Shuffle the cards and spread them out face down.
- Choose a child to take a card. *Which number have you taken?* Point to the matching number on the number line. *Is she correct?*
- Ask the child holding the card to 'laugh' that many times. The rest of the class keeps a whispered count to check.
- Write that number on the board and children copy you, writing the number on the floor with a finger.
- Repeat with different children, number cards and noises.

DAY 4 • *Estimating quantities*

Small transparent plastic jars full of dried beans (up to 50 beans)

- Show children the jar of beans. *How many beans do you think are in the jar?* Encourage children to suggest numbers and decide on sensible estimates.
- Choose several children to write their guesses on the board, reminding them how to form the numerals.
- Tip out the beans and count them, grouping them in twos to help count. Count ten, grouped in twos, and choose a child to hold the ten beans. Repeat until you have counted all the beans, grouping in twos and then in tens. *How many beans?*
- Write the actual number on the board. Compare this total with their guesses. *Which guesses were close? Which were not?*
- Repeat the guessing game with a different jar.

DAY 5 • *Counting sounds and movements*

Large number cards (2 to 19), a washing line with large numbers cards (1 to 20) pegged to it, pegs

- Give one number card to each child. Children look at their card and work out the number without showing it to anyone else. If in doubt, they ask you.
- Choose a child. Ask him to look at his number and to clap that many times. He does this slowly and carefully with your help. Check that his number matches the claps. The other children count the claps and say the number. Point to that number on the number line.
- Any other children holding the same number stand up.
- Repeat several times, with different children.
- Line up children in order, 2 to 19.

	DAY 1	DAY 2	DAY 3	DAY 4	DAY 5
Objective	Counting to 10, and then to 20, counting on from a given number, saying the 'next' number to any given number				
Teacher-led activities *On the rug* (pages 41–42)	**Warm up:** Sing number song. **Activity:** Count together to 100, marking the units with fingers. Stress fives and tens. Help children with each multiple of ten, but then once they start that decade, e.g. *Fifty-one, fifty-two, …* they continue alone. Count again to 100, pointing to each number on the grid. Emphasise 100. Point to some numbers and say them together.	**Warm up:** Do bunny hops to match numbers to 20. **Activity:** Count to 30 on the number grid. Choose a child. Ask her to point to a number further down the grid ending in 1. Count that row, e.g. *Forty-one, forty-two, … fifty.* A boy selects a number ending in 1. Boys count that row. Repeat, with a girl. Stick a Post-it note over one of the numbers. The teddy guesses incorrectly. Children check.	**Warm up:** Count from 50 to 100 using fingers. **Activity:** Give out number cards (1 to 20), to each child. Count to 20 together. Children stand up as their number is said. Line up 20 children holding cards 1 to 20. Ask those with a number more than 16 to crouch down and hold their number by their feet. *Who is crouching down?* Repeat for a number less than 12. Repeat for other numbers.	**Warm up:** Count from 30 to 70 using fingers. **Activity:** Use the number line and count from 1 to 20, pointing to each number. Choose a child to point to a number. She writes this number in the air and says it. Show how to write it on the board. Children write it on the floor with a finger. She chooses another child to say the next number. If he is correct, he chooses a number to write. Repeat.	**Warm up:** Count back from 20 to *Blast off!* **Activity:** Point to a row on the number grid. Make the teddy count a row of the grid incorrectly. Children correct him. Cover one number in each row with a Post-it note. Count 1 to 100, passing the teddy from child to child with each number spoken. The child holding the teddy when a covered number is said takes a cube.
Teacher-initiated activities *Activity Book* (page 10)	**Easy:** Use a number track (1 to 12) and counters placed on 1. Spin a coin. Tails – move one place forwards, heads – move two places forwards. *Say the number you land on. Say the next number.* If children are correct, they move to that number. Otherwise, they move back three spaces. The first child to reach the end wins. **Medium:** Use a number track (1 to 20) and different-coloured cubes for each child. Children choose a number and say it. They cover the next number with a cube and say what it is. If they are not correct, they remove their cube. Keep playing until all the numbers are covered. Who has covered most numbers? **Hard:** Shuffle number cards (1 to 21). Place the 10 card face up. Deal out the rest so that each child has five cards. Children take turns to place a card on the table if the number shown is next to a number already laid face up. The first child to use all their cards wins.				
Independent activities *Supported play*	**Playhouse:** Children find different places to stick numbers, e.g. door numbers, telephone numbers, clockface numbers.	**Cooking:** Children make a sponge cake using the recipe in the Recipe Bank (page 119). Cut it into slices. How many slices?	**Construction:** Use a number grid (1 to 100). Each child chooses a number and builds a model with that number of building bricks. Can the others guess the number of bricks?	**Painting:** Children use large blank number tracks. They paint each space a different colour. When the paint is dry, write the numbers on their tracks.	**Threading:** Each child uses large wooden beads to make a long necklace. *Ask your friends to guess how many beads you have used.* Write their guesses. Who wins?
Language	Count, count on, number names one to one hundred, backwards, forwards, next, after, before, number grid				
At home	*Door numbers* **Paper, a pencil** Take your child for a walk to look for door numbers. Help them to write down the door numbers beginning with number 1. At home, help your child to write all the numbers from 1 to 20. Remind them to look at the number carefully before they try to write it.				
Resources	Number grid (1 to 100), playhouse items	Number grid (1 to 100), a teddy, Post-it notes, sponge cake mix, knife	Large number cards (1 to 20), number grid (1 to 100), building bricks	Washing line with large number cards (1 to 20) pegged to it, pegs, large blank number tracks, paint, paint-brushes	Number grid (1 to 100), a teddy, Post-it notes, cubes, large wooden beads, string

- Sing a number song together.
- Make sure all the children have room to move. Say a number between 1 and 20. *Twelve.* The children do the number of actions to match (e.g. bunny hops, wing flaps, toe taps, etc.) while counting together.
- Count together from 50 to 100, using fingers to mark the units.
- Count together from 30 to 70, using fingers to mark the units. Help the children with any multiples of 10 that they find difficult.
- Count backwards from 20 to 1, then shout *Blast off!* together.

DAY 1

- *Counting to 100*

Number grid (1 to 100)

- Count together to 100, using fingers to mark the units. Stress the whole hand at *Five* by waving it in the air. Stress the whole hands at *Ten* by waving both hands in the air.
- Count along the grid, pointing to each number on the first row as you count. Count slowly and deliberately, stressing each number on the top row of the grid.
- Continue counting on from 10, marking the fives and the tens, as above, by waving one and then two hands. Help children with each multiple of ten, but once they start that decade, e.g. *Fifty-one, fifty-two, ...* they continue alone.
- When they reach 100, emphasise it out on the grid. *We've reached one hundred!*
- *As we go down the grid, the numbers get larger.*
- Point to 68. *What number is this? Sixty-eight.* Pointing to the 6 and the 8 and stress ***six**ty-**eight**.*
- Repeat with 84. Stress the eight and the four.

DAY 2

- *Counting to 100*

Number grid (1 to 100), a teddy, Post-it notes

- *The teddy wants to see if we can count to 100.*
- Count to 30 on the number grid, pointing to each number. Count carefully. Keep children going by choosing different children to point to the numbers on the grid as they say them.
- Choose a child. Ask her to point to a number further down the grid ending in 1. Count that row, e.g. *Forty-one, forty-two, ... fifty.*
- Choose a boy to point to another number ending in 1. Only boys count that row. Repeat, choosing a girl to pick another number ending in 1. Only girls count that row.
- Cover the teddy's eyes and choose a child to stick a Post-it note over one of the numbers on the grid.
- Ask the class. *Which number is hidden?* Ask the teddy, making sure he gives the wrong answer. *Doesn't teddy know? Has teddy guessed wrongly?*
- Count along that row from the number ending in 1. *What number do we say when we reach the Post-it note? What is the next number?* Count on one to check.
- Remove the Post-it note and read the number.
- Repeat several times.

DAY 3

- *Counting to 20*
- *Counting on from a given number*

Large number cards (1 to 20)

- Give each child a number card.
- Count to 20 together. Children stand up as their number is said.
- Line up 20 children, holding cards 1 to 20.
- Ask those with a number more than 16 to crouch down and to hold their number by their feet. Ask the rest of the class: *Who is crouching down? All the numbers further up the line.* Stress the 'further up the line'. These numbers are more than sixteen. They are larger.
- Repeat for children with a number less than 12. Stress the 'further down the line'. *These numbers are smaller than twelve.*
- Repeat for numbers larger than 18. Continue to stress that the numbers further up the line are larger.
- Repeat with different children holding the numbers in the line and starting with a number more than 14.

DAY 4

- *Counting to 20*
- *Saying the next number*

A washing line with large number cards (1 to 20) pegged to it, pegs

- Count along the number line, pointing to each number.
- Choose a child to point to a number, e.g. 6. She says the number and writes it in the air with her finger, starting at the top.

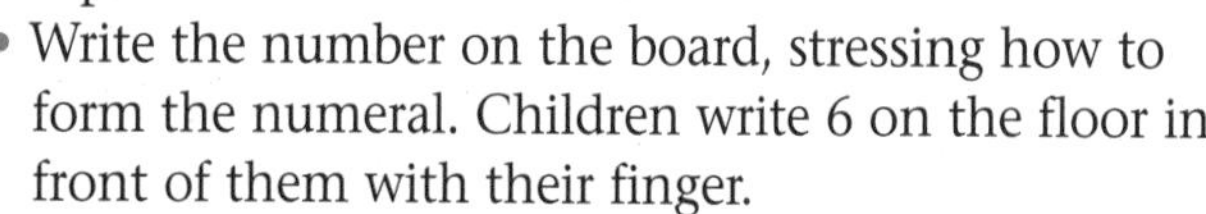

- Write the number on the board, stressing how to form the numeral. Children write 6 on the floor in front of them with their finger.
- The child who chose the first number chooses a child to say the next number. *What number comes after six?* Count along the line to that number to check. If the second child is correct, they choose a new number to write in the air.
- Repeat, allowing one child to choose another child to select the new number each time. Always count to check which number comes next, as well as pointing on the line, because the oral/aural stimulation will be stronger than the visual stimulation (numeral recognition) for many children.

DAY 5

- *Counting to 100*

Number grid (1 to 100), a teddy, Post-it notes, cubes

- Point to a row on the number grid, e.g. 61 to 70. Make the teddy count this row incorrectly. *What has teddy done wrong?* Children correct his mistake.
- Repeat for a different row.
- Cover one number in each row on the grid with a Post-it note.
- Count from 1 to 100, passing the teddy from child to child with each number spoken. The child holding the teddy when a covered number is said takes a cube.
- Repeat.

	DAY 1	DAY 2	DAY 3	DAY 4	DAY 5
Objective	Numbers to 20: counting up to 20 objects, estimating, starting to record numbers to mark the number in a set				
Teacher-led activities *On the rug* (pages 44–45)	**Warm up:** Count to 100 using fingers. **Activity:** Whilst children close their eyes, put 15 toy cars into the bag. Show children the bag. *How many cars?* Children discuss in groups. Record their guesses, encouraging them to write these on the board. Tip out the cars. Show how to count them, grouping in fives. Write the total on the board. Check on the number line. Repeat with 18 cars.	**Warm up:** Count from 40 to 80 using fingers. **Activity:** Use the skipping rope to make a river down the middle of the rug, with the class in equal teams on each side. Give each team 15 animals. Teams take turns to throw a spotty dice. They count and pass that many animals across the river. After each turn, which side has more animals? First team to get all its animals across the river wins.	**Warm up:** Count back from 20 to *Blast off!* **Activity:** Children guess how many marbles in the jar. Help them record guesses on the board. Count the marbles in fives, giving each five to a different child. Stress how to group in fives. Compare their guesses with the actual number. Which guesses were closest? Check on the number line. Point to two handfuls of five marbles. *How many?*	**Warm up:** Count from 60 to 100 using fingers. **Activity:** Choose three children. Give each a large handful of beads. *Who has most?* Children guess, with a partner. Count each handful, grouping in fives. Select a number card to match each handful. *Who had most?* Use the number line to show which number is furthest along. *This was the largest number. She had most.* Repeat.	**Warm up:** Show fingers to match numbers up to 10. **Activity:** Hold up the mug with pencils in it. *How many pencils?* Encourage children to estimate and write their guesses on the board. Count the pencils, grouping them in fives. Compare the total with their guesses. *Were you correct?* Compare their guesses, checking on the number line. *Who guessed the largest number? Smallest?*
Teacher-initiated activities *Activity Book* (pages 10–11)	**Easy:** Choose a jigsaw. Children estimate the number of pieces. *Count the pieces, grouping them in fives to help you count.* Children do the jigsaw, then count the pieces again. **Medium:** Shuffle number cards (1 to 20) and place them in a pile face down. Children take a card each. *Whose number is largest?* Children each make a tower with that number of interlocking cubes. *Who has made the tallest tower?* They write the number. Replace the card on the bottom of the pile. Continue until one child has written five numbers. **Hard:** Each child takes a large handful of beads. They each guess how many they have and take a number card to match their guess. They help each other count every handful, grouping the beads in fives. They each write the total. They compare the totals with their guesses, using a number track.				
Independent activities *Supported play*	**Sand:** Children build a road in the sand. They take a number card (1 to 20) and place that number of toy cars on the road. They smooth out the sand and start again.	**Cooking:** Make peppermint creams using the method in the Recipe Bank (page 119). Children take a number card (1 to 20) and count out a matching number of peppermint creams.	**Playhouse:** Children decide how many toys are coming for tea. They count plates, cups, etc. They use the telephone to invite the toys, and match spoken and written numerals when giving the number.	**Drawing:** Draw a large animal. Children decorate the animal with 15 spots or stripes on it. *There must be exactly 15.*	**Cutting and sticking:** Cut out circles of yellow card to make flower centres. Have ready plenty of pre-cut 'petals' in different colours. Make flowers with one centre and ten petals.
Language	**Count, how many?, number names one to twenty, less than, more than, guess, closest, most, largest, smallest**				
At home	*How many items?* **A small container, up to 30 small items, paper, a pencil** Help your child to find a small container, such as a yoghurt pot. Encourage them to count into the container up to 30 small items, such as stones or dried peas. Help them to write the number on a small piece of paper and place it inside the container. Remind your child to take the container into class so the other children can estimate how many items it holds.				
Resources	A cloth bag, 20 toy cars, washing line with large number cards (1 to 20) pegged to it, pegs, sand, toy cars	A skipping rope, 30 soft toy animals, a spotty dice (1 to 6), peppermint cream mix, number cards (1 to 20)	A transparent plastic jar full of marbles (up to 20), washing line with large number cards (1 to 20) pegged to it, pegs, toys, tea party items, telephone	Beads, washing line with large number cards (1 to 20) pegged to it, pegs, crayons or colouring pencils	A mug, 21 pencils, washing line with large number cards (1 to 30) pegged to it, pegs, card, scissors, cut-out petals, glue

- Count together up to 100, using fingers to mark the units. Help the children with any multiples of 10 that they find difficult.
- Count together from 40 to 80, using fingers to mark the units.
- Count backwards from 20 to 1, then shout *Blast off!* together.
- Count together from 60 to 100, using fingers to mark the units.
- Say a number between 1 and 10. *Five.* Ask the children to hold up that number of fingers. Who has to count and who just 'knows'? Repeat for other numbers.

WARM UPS

DAY 1

- *Counting up to 20 objects*
- *Starting to record numbers*

A cloth bag, 20 toy cars, a washing line with large number cards (1 to 20) pegged to it, pegs

- Whilst children close their eyes, put 15 toy cars into the bag.
- Show children the cars in the bag. *How many cars?* Encourage children to discuss in pairs or threes and agree a good guess.
- Encourage children to write their guesses on the board. Demonstrate how to write the numerals, starting at the top.
- Tip out the cars. Show how to count them, grouping in them in fives. Write the number on the board.
- Compare the actual number with their guesses. *Use the number line to help you compare. Which guesses were closest?*
- Repeat with 18 cars, guessing then counting, grouping in fives.

DAY 2

- *Counting up to 15 objects*

A skipping rope, 30 soft toy animals, a spotty dice (1 to 6)

- Use the skipping rope to make a 'river' running down the middle of the rug, with the class divided into two equal teams, one on each side. *There is a river down the middle of this rug – be careful not to fall in!*
- Give each team 15 toy animals. Each side counts them.
- Give one team the spotty dice. Choose a child on that side to throw the dice. *What number has she thrown? How many spots?* Count the spots, pointing to each spot as you count it. That team counts out a matching number of toy animals and passes them across the river.
- Pass the spotty dice to the other team who repeat the process.
- After each turn, ask questions. *Which side has more animals?* The first team to get all its toy animals across the river, wins.

DAY 3 • *Counting up to 20 objects*
• *Starting to record numbers*

A transparent plastic jar full of marbles (up to 20), a washing line with large number cards (1 to 20) pegged to it, pegs

- Show children the jar of marbles. *How many marbles in this jar?* Children discuss in pairs and make a sensible guess. Help children to write their guesses on the board. Demonstrate how to form the numerals.
- Count out the marbles in fives, giving each group of five marbles to a different child to hold. Stress grouping in fives.
- Write the total on the board. Compare their guesses with the actual number. *Which guesses were closest?* Check on the number line.
- Point to two handfuls of five marbles. *How many?*

DAY 4 • *Counting up to 15 objects*

Beads, a washing line with large number cards (1 to 20) pegged to it, pegs

- Choose three children to stand at the front. Give each child a large handful of beads. Ask the class. *Who is holding the most beads?* Look carefully and guess.
- Children work with a partner to guess. Record their guesses on the board.
- Count each handful, grouping in fives. Select a number card to match each handful.
- Look at the three numbers. *Who had most?* Use the number line to show which number is furthest along. *This was the largest number. She had most.*
- Repeat with three different children and three different handfuls of beads.

DAY 5 • *Counting up to 20 objects*
• *Starting to record numbers*

A mug, 21 pencils, a washing line with large number cards (1 to 30) pegged to it, pegs

- Hold up the mug with pencils in it. *How many pencils?* Encourage children to guess. They discuss it with a partner.
- Help them to write their guesses on the board. Demonstrate how to write the numerals.
- Count the pencils, grouping them in fives. Write the total.
- Compare the total with their guesses. *Were you correct?* Compare their guesses, checking on the number line. *Who guessed the largest number? Who guessed the smallest number?*

	DAY 1	DAY 2	DAY 3	DAY 4	DAY 5
Objective	Using the language of position and placing things in given positions in relation to each other				
Teacher-led activities *On the rug* (pages 47–48)	**Warm up:** Count from 1 to 50 using fingers. **Activity:** *How many spaces on the grid? Fifteen.* Children to paint a different colour in two of the spaces. *Where is the blue splodge? Above the red? Below?* Choose children to paint splodges in the rest of the spaces. Point to one of the colours in the middle. *What colour is this? Which colour is below it? Above it? To the left? To the right?*	**Warm up:** Sing a number song. **Activity:** Place the teddy on top of the wall. Choose a child to describe where he is. Place the cat in front of the wall below the teddy. *The cat is below the teddy. The teddy is above the cat.* Whilst children close their eyes, reverse the positions of the cat and the teddy. Choose children to describe their positions. Repeat for behind, in front, to the left/right of the wall.	**Warm up:** Show fingers to match numbers up to 10. **Activity:** Choose a child to Blu-tack a picture in a space on the grid. Repeat with another child. Discuss the position of the second picture in relation to the first. Choose children to position the rest of the animals. Choose an animal and describe its position. Can children guess the animal? Repeat with a child describing the position.	**Warm up:** Count from 1 to 50 using fingers. **Activity:** Place the puppet underneath the upturned box. *The puppet is hiding. Can you guess where?* Children guess, using positional words, e.g. inside, behind, underneath, on top of, ... When they have guessed, make the puppet come out. Whilst children close their eyes, choose a child to hide the puppet again in relation to the box.	**Warm up:** Count from 50 to 100 using fingers. **Activity:** Place two hats on the table with the apple under one and the orange behind the other. *I've hidden an apple and an orange.* Invite guesses. Check under, behind, on top of, beside, ... Find both fruit. Repeat for different positions. Choose a child. Ask him to hide the apple in relation to the shelf. Children say where it is and you find it.
Teacher-initiated activities *Activity Book* (pages 11–12)	**Easy:** Use a box and toy animals. One child takes an animal. Another child says a position, e.g. *Above.* The first child places it in that position in relation to the box. Continue until all the animals are placed. Then say a place, e.g. *Under the box.* Children say which animal is in this position. Repeat. **Medium:** Use a picture of a house or a tent, with cartoon stickers and cards with positions written on them, e.g. above, beneath, under, inside, outside. One child takes a position card. Read it to her. She chooses a character and places it in the appropriate position in relation to the house. **Hard:** Use a large 3 × 5 grid (1 to 15). Place three different-coloured counters on the grid. Children take turns to place new counters on the grid following instructions in relation to the existing counters. *Put a blue counter below the yellow counter.* Encourage very specific language.				
Independent activities *Supported play*	**Toy farm:** Arrange or draw a number of fields. Children place animals in them and describe their position in relation to each other. *The cows are in the field below the pigs.*	**Cooking:** Children make biscuits using the recipe in the Recipe Bank (page 119). They position chocolate drops between, on top, etc. Encourage them to use positional language.	**Construction:** Children build models and then describe the position of some components in relation to others. *The wheels are underneath, the windows are on top.*	**Painting:** Children paint pictures with some positional constraints as to colour, e.g. red at the top, blue in the middle, green at the sides and yellow at the bottom.	**Cutting and sticking:** Use gummed paper shapes. Children create a picture with a square at the top, a circle in the middle and a triangle at the bottom. They describe where they have placed other shapes.
Language	**Above, on top, over, under, beneath, below, underneath, inside, within, between, beside, alongside, outside, next to, left, right**				
At home	*Looking for teddy* **A teddy bear** Ask your child to hide a teddy bear somewhere in a room. Explain that they should use words like 'under', 'on top', 'beside', 'in front', 'above', 'below', 'between', 'on' and 'in' to describe where the teddy is so that you can find him. *Teddy is sitting on the settee but he is behind the cushion. Can you find him?* Repeat, swapping roles.				
Resources	A 3 × 5 grid (pinned on a board), paints, paintbrushes, toy animals	A wall made from large building bricks, a teddy, a toy cat, biscuit mix, chocolate drops	A 3 × 5 grid (pinned on a board), 15 different animal pictures, Blu-tack, construction materials	A large lidless box, a puppet, paint, paintbrushes	Two hats, an apple, an orange, gummed paper shapes

- Count together from 1 to 50, using fingers to mark the units. Help the children with the multiples of 10.
- Together sing a number song, which involves counting down.
- Say a number between 1 and 10. *Nine.* Ask the children to hold up that number of fingers. Who has to count and who just 'knows'? Repeat for other numbers.
- Count together from 1 to 50, using fingers to mark the units. Prompt the children with the multiples of 10, if necessary.
- Count together from 50 to 100, using fingers to mark the units. Help the children with the multiples of 10.

WARM UPS

DAY 1

- *Using the language of position*

A 3 × 5 grid (pinned on a board), paints, paintbrushes

- *How many spaces are on this grid?* Choose a child to point to each space and count. *There are fifteen spaces.*
- Choose a child to paint a red splodge in one of the spaces.
- Choose another child to paint a blue splodge in another space. *Where is the blue splodge? Is it above the red splodge? Is it below the red splodge?*
- Choose children to paint different-coloured splodges in the rest of the spaces. Discuss where each new splodge is being painted. *Is it above another colour? Is it below a colour? Is it to the left? To the right?*
- Point to one of the colours in the middle. *What colour is this? Which colour is below it? Which colour is above it? Which colour is on the left of it? What is on the right?* Identify different colours in relation to each other.

DAY 2

- *Using the language of position*

A wall made from large building bricks, a teddy, a toy cat

- Place the teddy on top of the wall. *Where is the teddy?* Choose a child to describe where he is. *He is on top of the wall.*
- Place the cat in front of the wall below the teddy. *The cat is below the teddy. The teddy is above the cat.*
- Whilst children close their eyes, reverse the positions of the cat and the teddy. *Where is the cat now? Where is the teddy now?* Choose children to describe their positions.
- Repeat for behind and in front of the wall.
- Repeat for left and right. *The teddy is to the left of the wall. The cat is to the right of the wall.* Remember to position the teddy and the cat so that they are to the left or right as children look at them.

DAY 3

- *Using the language of position*
- *Placing things in given positions in relation to each other*

A 3 × 5 grid (pinned on a board), 15 different animal pictures, Blu-tack

- *How many spaces on this grid? Fifteen.*
- Place the animal pictures in a pile. Choose a child to take an animal picture. She Blu-tacks it in one of the spaces on the grid.
- Repeat, choosing a different child to Blu-tack another picture. Discuss where he has put the second picture in relation to the first. *Is it above the first? Below the first? To the left? To the right?*
- Choose different children to Blu-tack the rest of the pictures.
- Choose an animal and describe its position. Can children guess the animal? Repeat, asking a child to choose the animal and describe its position.

DAY 4

- *Using the language of position*
- *Placing things in given positions in relation to each other*

A large lidless box, a puppet

- Turn the box upside down on a table. Place the puppet under the box without letting children see you do it.
- *The puppet is hiding. Can you guess where?* Encourage children to guess, using positional words, e.g. inside, behind, underneath, on top of, ...
- When they have guessed, make the puppet come out.
- Whilst children close their eyes, choose a child to hide the puppet again in relation to the box. Repeat.

DAY 5

- *Using the language of position*
- *Placing things in given positions in relation to each other*

Two hats, an apple, an orange

- Whilst children close their eyes, place two hats on the table with the apple under one and the orange behind the other.
- *I have hidden an apple and an orange. Where do you think they can be?* Invite guesses. Check under, behind, on top of, beside, ...
- Find both the apple and the orange. Describe where each was hidden. *The apple was under this hat. The orange was behind this hat.*
- Hide the apple and the orange in a different place in relation to the hats. Use positional language to describe where they are.
- Choose a child. Ask him to hide the apple in relation to the bookshelf, whilst you close your eyes. Children say where it is and you have to find it.

	DAY 1	DAY 2	DAY 3	DAY 4	DAY 5
Objective	Adding 2 or 3 to a number up to 10, finding a total by counting on one when that object is hidden				
Teacher-led activities *On the rug* (pages 50–51)	**Warm up:** Count from 1 to 50 using fingers. **Activity:** *How many rungs on this ladder?* Use stickers to number them. Throw the dice, e.g. 7. Write '7 + 2 =' on the board. Place the teddy on rung 7. *The teddy starts on seven. It moves up the ladder two rungs.* Move the teddy two rungs up. *What rung is it on now? Nine.* Write '9' after '7 + 2 ='. Read the sentence together. Repeat, throwing the dice and adding 3.	**Warm up:** Count from 50 to 100 using fingers. **Activity:** A child places the cat on the ladder, e.g. on 6. Choose another child to find the matching number card and Blu-tack it to the board. Write '+' and attach the 3 card. Write '='. *The cat climbs up three rungs. Six and three more make …* The child moves the cat up three rungs. *What number is the cat on?* Another child finds the card for the answer, e.g. 9. Repeat for another number.	**Warm up:** Sing a number song. **Activity:** Choose a child to take a card between 5 and 10 from the number line. Choose another child to build a tower that many bricks tall. *How tall will it be if I add two more bricks?* Children match the first number with fingers and count on, holding up two more. Write the completed addition on the board. Add two bricks to the tower. Repeat.	**Warm up:** Count from 30 to 70 using fingers. **Activity:** Arrange the chairs in rows of two to make a 'bus'. Show children the number 10 card. *This is how many passengers I have on my bus.* Choose ten children and count them onto the bus. The conductor gives each a ticket. Write '10' on the board. *How many if another two passengers get on?* Let another two on and count on from ten. Complete the sentence and read it together.	**Warm up:** Show fingers to match numbers up to 10. **Activity:** Lay large number cards (1 to 12) along the rug to make a track. Count eight biscuits into the tin. *How many?* Find 8 on the number track. Place a counter on that number. *How many if we add three more?* Place another three biscuits in the tin. *How many now?* Encourage children to count on using the number track. Record the addition. Repeat.
Teacher-initiated activities *Activity Book* (page 12)	**Easy:** Use a number track (1 to 10) and building bricks. Each child chooses a number on the track and matches that number to bricks. They say how many they will have if they take one more. If they are correct, they keep the bricks. They have six turns. *Build a model with your bricks.* **Medium:** Use a home-made ladder with ten rungs. Ask a child to put a cat on the ladder. *Where will the cat be if we move him up two rungs?* Write the number sentence on the board. Ask a child to move the cat to check. Repeat letting another child position the cat on the ladder. **Hard:** Use a number track (1 to 20) and counters placed on 1. Spin a coin. Heads – move three places forwards, tails – move two places forwards. *Take the number of bricks that match the number you land on, plus two. So if you land on three, you take five bricks.* If children are not correct, they replace their bricks. Play until children reach 20. *Who has the most bricks?*				
Independent activities *Supported play*	**Toys:** Make a line of ten chairs and put a large number card on each (1 to 10). One child places the teddy on a chair. *Which chair will he be on if he moves along two?*	**Cooking:** Make sponge buns using the recipe in the Recipe Book (page 119). Ice six of the buns. *How many if we ice three more?*	**Construction:** Children build a model using large building bricks. Count the bricks and work out how many there will be if you add three more.	**Role play:** Children play buses with chairs. *How many passengers? How many tickets are needed? How many get on? How many now?*	**Papier mâché:** Make a ladder and number the rungs. Children play track games up the ladder. First child to the top wins.
Language	Number names one to twenty, add, and, more, makes, count on, how many?				
At home	*A biscuit snake* **Ten small biscuits, a coin, paper, a pen** On a large sheet of paper, draw a snake with ten segments and number each one 1 to 10. Place two biscuits on numbers 1 and 2. Toss the coin. If it lands heads, add one more biscuit; if it lands tails, add two more biscuits. Encourage your child to say how many there will be altogether before adding them to the line.				
Resources	A home-made ladder (with at least 13 rungs), Post-it notes, a large dice (numbered 5 to 10 with stickers), a teddy, ten chairs, number cards (1 to 10)	A home-made ladder (with at least 13 rungs), a toy cat, large number cards (1 to 13), Post-it notes, Blu-tack, sponge bun mix, icing	Washing line with large number cards (1 to 10) pegged to it, pegs, large building bricks	Large number cards (1 to 12), tickets, washing line with large number cards (1 to 20) pegged to it, pegs, chairs	Large number cards (1 to 12), biscuits, empty tin, a counter, papier mâché mix

- Count together from 1 to 50, using fingers to mark the units.
- Count together from 50 to 100, using fingers to mark the units.
- Sing a number song together.
- Count together from 30 to 70, using fingers to mark the units.
- Say a number between 1 and 10. *Seven.* Ask the children to hold up that number of fingers. Who has to count and who just 'knows'? Repeat for other numbers.

DAY 1

- *Adding 2 to a number up to 10*

A home-made ladder (with at least 13 rungs), Post-it notes, a large dice (numbered 5 to 10 with stickers, opposite sides add to 15), a teddy

- Use the home-made ladder. Use Post-it notes to number each rung (1 to 13). Count the rungs as you number them.
- Throw the dice. *What number have I thrown?* Choose a child to help the teddy climb up the ladder to match the number thrown, counting the rungs as it climbs.
- *What number will the teddy be on if it climbs two more rungs?*
- Write the number sentence, '7 + 2 =' on the board. Read it together. *Seven and two more makes?*
- Point to 7. *Seven.* This is where the teddy starts on the ladder. Point to '7' in the number sentence and place the teddy on rung 7. *The teddy starts on seven.*
- Point to the '+ 2' in the sum. *Teddy moves up the ladder two more rungs.* Move the teddy two rungs up the ladder.
- *What rung is Teddy on now? Nine.* Write the answer '9'. Read the sentence together. *Seven and two more make nine. Teddy is on rung nine.*
- Repeat, throwing the dice and adding 3.

DAY 2

- *Adding 3 to a number up to 10*

A home-made ladder (with at least 13 rungs), Post-it notes, a toy cat, number cards (1 to 13), Blu-tack

- Use the home-made ladder. Use Post-it notes to number each rung (1 to 13). Count the rungs as you number them.
- Choose a child to place the cat on the ladder. *What number is the cat starting on? Six.* Choose a child to find the matching number card and Blu-tack this to the board.
- Write '+' and then stick the 3 card next to it. Write '=' after 3. *The cat climbs three more steps.* Point to the board. Read the sentence. *Six and three more make ...*
- Help a child to make the cat climb three more steps. *What number is the cat on now?* Choose a child to select the card to finish the sentence, '9'. *Six and three more make nine. The cat is on step nine.*
- Repeat, choosing another child to put the cat somewhere on the ladder. Encourage them to start the cat somewhere between 5 and 10.

DAY 3 • *Adding 2 to a number up to 10*

A washing line with large number cards (1 to 10) pegged to it, pegs, large building bricks

- Choose a child to take a number card between 5 and 10 from the line. *What number has she taken?* Encourage children to count along to see which number is missing.
- Choose another child to build a tower that number of bricks tall.
- *How tall will this tower be if I add two more bricks? Let's work it out.* Point to the missing number on the line. Ask children to hold up that number of fingers, and say the number e.g. *Six.* As you count on two along the line, encourage them to hold up two more fingers and say the numbers, e.g., ... *seven, eight.*
- Write the completed addition on the board '6 + 2 = 8'. Read this together. *Six and two more make eight.*
- Add two more bricks to the tower and check that the number of bricks matches the total on the board.
- Repeat, starting with a different number card.

DAY 4 • *Adding 2 to a number up to 10*

Large number cards (1 to 12), tickets, a washing line with large number cards (1 to 20) pegged to it, pegs

- Arrange 14 chairs in rows of two to make a 'bus'. Choose a child to be the conductor.
- Take the number 10 card. *What number is this? Ten. This is how many passengers I have on my bus.*
- Choose ten children and count them onto the bus. The conductor gives each passenger a ticket, counting as he does so. *Ten tickets.* Write '10' on the board.
- *How many will there be if two more passengers get on?* Encourage children to estimate. Help them by pointing to the number line, finding 10 and counting on 2, or by saying *Ten* and holding up two more fingers, saying ... *eleven, twelve.*
- Let another two passengers onto the bus, and count on from 10. *Eleven, twelve. There are now twelve passengers on the bus.*
- Write '+ 2 =' and then choose a child to complete the sentence by writing '12'. Read it together. *Ten and two more make twelve.*
- Repeat with different children, and starting with eight passengers and adding three more.

DAY 5 • *Adding 3 to a number up to 10*

Large number cards (1 to 12), biscuits, an empty tin, a counter

- Lay the numbers along the rug to make a number track. Count along the track.
- Count eight biscuits into the tin. *How many biscuits? Eight.* Find 8 on the number track and place a counter on that number. *Eight biscuits in the tin.*
- *How many if we add three more?* Encourage children to count on, either on their fingers or using the number track. Place three more biscuits in the tin. *How many now?* Move the counter three spaces along the track. Record the addition on the board and read it together.
- Repeat, starting at numbers less than 10 each time.

	DAY 1	DAY 2	DAY 3	DAY 4	DAY 5
Objective	Understanding addition as a combination of two sets, and relating this to counting on and the partitioning of a set				
Teacher-led activities *On the rug* (pages 53–54)	**Warm up:** Sing a number song. **Activity:** *How many spaces in this egg box?* March four egg-men into the box. *How many egg-men so far?* Write '4' on the board. *How many more do we need for a full box?* Encourage children to work it out. March two more egg-men into the spaces. Write '+ 2 = 6' on the board. Read the sentence together. Repeat for 3 + 3 = 6 and 5 + 1 = 6.	**Warm up:** Count from 50 to 100 using fingers. **Activity:** *How many flowers? Four.* Choose a child to write '4' on the board. Put the flowers in the vase. Choose another child and give him two more flowers. *If you add your flowers to the bunch, how many will we have?* Write '+ 2 =' next to '4'. Add the two flowers, one at a time. *Five, six.* Write '6'. Read the addition. Repeat for 3 + 3 and 5 + 1.	**Warm up:** Say a number rhyme. **Activity:** Show children the spider body and the eight legs. Blu-tack the spider body on the board. Put seven legs on one side and one on the other. *How many legs? How many on this side?* Blu-tack '7' on the board. *How many on this side?* Blu-tack '1' on the board. Write '+' and '= 8'. Choose a child to move a leg from one side to the other. Blu-tack '6' and '2' to create a new addition. Repeat for 5 and 3 and 4 and 4.	**Warm up:** Count from 1 to 50 using fingers. **Activity:** Show children the hanger with seven key rings. Pass round the other key ring. *How many key rings will I have on my hanger if I add this one? How many are there now?* Choose a child to write '7' on the board. Write '+ 1 ='. Help children to suggest the answer. Add the key ring and point out that 7 and 1 is 8. Write '8' on the board. Repeat for 6 + 2 and 5 + 3 and 4 + 4.	**Warm up:** Do actions to match numbers up to 20. **Activity:** Ask children to show you four fingers. *How many?* Now add four more. *How many now? Eight.* Fold down three. *How many now? Five.* Hold up the three again. *How many? Eight.* Fold down two. *How many now? Six.* Hold up the two again. *Eight.* Match each finger sum to a written sentence, e.g. 4 + 4 = 8 as you model it.
Teacher-initiated activities *Activity Book* (pages 12–13)	**Easy:** Use an egg box and six eggs (hard-boiled and painted with faces). Put six egg-men in the box. *How many are out? None.* Write '6 + 0 = 6' on the board. Take out one egg-man and make him go shopping. *How many at home? Five. How many out? One.* Write '5 + 1 = 6'. Repeat for 4 + 2 and 3 + 3. **Medium:** Use two purses and some 1p coins. Put out eight coins. Give a purse each to two pairs of children. Share the coins equally. *How much in each purse?* Write the sum '4 + 4 = 8' on the board. Now one pair gives 1p to the other. *How much in each purse now?* Write the sum. Repeat for 7p and 6p. **Hard:** Use 1p coins and two purses to work out all the different ways of distributing 10p between the two purses. *Suppose we use 2p and 5p coins as well?*				
Independent activities *Supported play*	**Toys:** Use plastic animals. Children place them in two 'fields' in different ways. Do the same with cars and car parks, or dolls and 'rooms'.	**Cooking:** Children make biscuits using the recipe in the Recipe Bank (page 119). Give each pair of children some chocolate drops and currants to decorate each biscuit with a total of seven drops and currants, in any combination. *How many of each type did you use?*	**Construction:** Children use Polydron to make shapes, using two colours. *How many of each colour have you used?* Ask a child to say and write the sum, e.g. *I used five red and twelve blue.* '5 + 12 = 17'.	**Sand:** Draw a line to divide the sandpit into two halves. Children create two 'towns', one in each half. They build eight sand castles, distributed between the two towns. Compare the towns. *Which town has more castles? How many castles altogether?*	**Painting:** Children paint hard-boiled eggs with acrylic paints and varnish them to make six egg-men. Put some egg-men in an egg box and leave some out. Say the matching sums. *Three and three make six.*
Language	Number names one to ten, and, more, how many?, makes, together				
At home	*A sum of leaves* **A saucer, leaves, glue, paper, a pencil** Encourage your child to collect seven leaves from outside. Draw two circles on a sheet of paper by drawing round a saucer. Ask your child to stick some of the leaves in each circle. Help your child to count each circle of leaves and write the number sentence, e.g. 4 + 3 = 7.				
Resources	An egg box, six egg-men (made from eggs boiled for 30 minutes, painted with acrylic paints, and varnished), plastic animals, toy cars, dolls	Six large flowers, a vase, biscuit mix, chocolate drops, currants	A large card spider body, eight pipe-cleaner legs, Blu-tack, large number cards (1 to 7), Polydron	A coat hanger, eight key rings, sandpit, buckets, scoops	Hard-boiled eggs, acrylic paint, varnish, paintbrushes, egg boxes

- Sing a number song together.
- Count together from 50 to 100, using fingers to mark the units. Help the children with the multiples of 10 if they find them difficult.
- Together say a number rhyme, which involves counting back.
- Count together from 1 to 50, using fingers to mark the units.
- Say a number between 1 and 20. *Seven.* The children do the number of actions to match, (e.g. eye winks, hand claps, toe taps, etc.) while counting together.

WARM UPS

DAY 1

- *Understanding addition as a combination of two sets*
- *Relating addition to counting on and the partitioning of a set*

An egg box, six egg-men (made from eggs boiled for 30 minutes, painted with acrylic paints, and varnished)

- Show the egg box. *How many spaces in this egg box? Six.*
- March four egg-men into the box. *How many egg-men so far? Four.* Write '4' on the board.
- *How many more egg-men do we need to have a full box?* Encourage children to work it out. They hold up six fingers (six spaces) and fold down four (four in the box already). *How many more do we need? Two.*
- March two more egg-men into the spaces. Write '+ 2 = 6' on the board. Read the sentence together. *Four and two make six.*
- Remove all the egg-men. Repeat for 3 + 3 = 6 and 5 + 1 = 6.

DAY 2

- *Understanding addition as a combination of two sets*
- *Relating addition to counting on and the partitioning of a set*

Six large flowers, a vase

- Show children four of the flowers. *How many flowers?* Choose a child to help you write '4' on the board. Demonstrate how to write the numeral. Place the four flowers in a vase.
- Choose another child and give him two flowers. *How many do you have? Two. If you added your flowers to the bunch in the vase, how many would we have then?* Encourage children to hold up four fingers and count on two more fingers.
- Write '+ 2 =' next to '4' on the board. *Four and two more make?*
- Add the two flowers to the vase, one at a time. *Five, six.*
- Write '6' on the board. Read the addition. *Four flowers and two more flowers make six flowers altogether.*
- Repeat for 3 + 3 and 5 + 1.

DAY 3
- *Understanding addition as a combination of two sets*
- *Relating addition to counting on and the partitioning of a set*

A large card spider body, eight pipe-cleaner legs, Blu-tack, large number cards (1 to 7)

- Show children the spider body and the eight legs. Blu-tack the body to the board. *How many legs does a spider have? Eight.*
- Blu-tack seven legs on one side of the spider body and one leg on the other. Point to the side with seven legs. *How many legs on this side? Seven.* Point to the side with one leg. *How many on this side? One.*
- Point to the seven legs and Blu-tack the number 7 card on the board. Point to the side with one leg and Blu-Tack the number 1 on the board. Write '+' and '= 8' to complete the addition. *Seven and one make eight. Eight legs on the spider. Seven on one side and one on the other.*
- Choose a child to move a leg from the side with seven legs to the other side.
- Point to the side with six legs. *How many on this side now?* Children may need to count, but some will see that one less than seven is six. *There are six.* Blu-tack the number 6 card to the board.

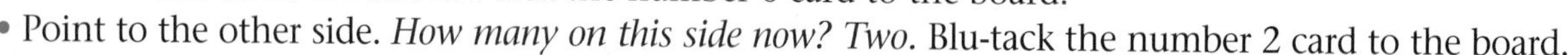

- Point to the other side. *How many on this side now? Two.* Blu-tack the number 2 card to the board.

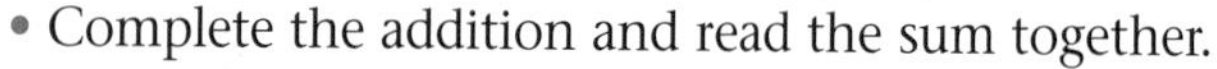

- Complete the addition and read the sum together.
- Repeat for 5 + 3 and 4 + 4.

DAY 4
- *Understanding addition as a combination of two sets*
- *Relating addition to counting on and the partitioning of a set*

A coat hanger, eight key rings

- Put seven key rings on the hanger. *How many key rings?* Encourage children to count. *Seven.*
- Pass round the other key ring. *How many key rings will I have on my hanger if I add this?*
- Add the key ring to the hanger. *How many now?* Choose a child to write '7' on the board. Write '+ 1 ='. Help children to suggest the answer, either by counting on one from seven, or by remembering from the previous day.
- Add the key ring and point out that seven and one more is eight. *We now have eight key rings on the hanger.*
- Write '8' on the board to complete the addition. Read it together. *Seven and one more make eight.*
- Repeat for 6 + 2, 5 + 3 and 4 + 4.

DAY 5
- *Understanding addition as a combination of two sets*
- *Relating addition to counting on and the partitioning of a set*

- Ask children to show four fingers. Hold up four fingers on one hand to model this. *How many fingers? Four.*
- Now add four more. Hold up four fingers on the other hand to demonstrate. *How many fingers now? Eight.*
- Write '4 + 4 = 8' on the board and read it together, modelling with fingers as you do so. *Four and four more make eight.*
- Now fold down three. *How many fingers now? Five.*
- Hold up the three again. *How many? Eight.* Write '5 + 3 = 8' on the board and read it together, modelling with fingers as you do so. *Five and three more make eight.*
- Repeat for 6 + 2 (folding down two fingers) and 7 + 1 = 8 (folding down one finger).

	DAY 1	DAY 2	DAY 3	DAY 4	DAY 5
Objective	**Comparing the lengths of two/three objects, and beginning to measure lengths using a non-standard unit**				
Teacher-led activities *On the rug* (pages 56–57)	**Warm up:** Sing a number song. **Activity:** Show two different-length snakes. *Which of these two snakes is longer? Shorter? How many crayons long do you think this snake is? How many crayons fit along it?* Record children's guesses. Lay the crayons end to end along the snake, counting. *The snake is four crayons long. Which guess is closest?* Repeat for the short snake, comparing it with the longer one.	**Warm up:** Count from 1 to 50 using fingers. **Activity:** Give two children a ribbon each. *Who has the longer ribbon? How many crayons long is this ribbon? How many crayons fit along it?* Record children's guesses. Lay the crayons end to end along the ribbon, counting. *The ribbon is ten crayons long. Which guess is closest?* Repeat for the short ribbon. Compare with the longer one.	**Warm up:** Say a number rhyme. **Activity:** Give each pair of children a straw. *How many straws will fit along this metre stick?* Write some guesses. Choose children to place straws end to end along the stick. Record its length in straws. 'The stick is 8 straws long.' Compare with guesses. *How long is this other stick? How many straws long?* Measure with straws. Compare lengths by looking at the number of straws.	**Warm up:** Count down from 20 to *Blast off!* **Activity:** Blu-tack three fish to a table. *Which fish is the longest? The shortest? Let's measure them using cubes.* Choose a pair of children to lay cubes end to end along the shortest fish. Other pairs measure the middle-sized fish and the longest fish. They lay cubes along their fish. Count the cubes. Show that the longest fish has more cubes.	**Warm up:** Show fingers to match numbers up to 10. **Activity:** Show children the two pieces of string. *Which is longer? Shorter? Let's use crayons to measure them.* Lay one piece of string on the table and choose two children to lay crayons end to end along its length. Count the crayons. Write its length. Repeat for the other piece of string. Compare lengths.
Teacher-initiated activities *Activity Book* (page 13)	**Easy:** Give each child a paper snake (all different lengths). *How many crayons can you lay along the snake? How long is your snake?* Compare the numbers of crayons. *Who has the longest snake?* **Medium:** Use a pile of paper fish of different lengths. Each child chooses a fish and measures its length using interlocking cubes. *Who has the longest fish?* Stick the fish in order of length on a sheet of paper painted to look like the sea. Write each fish's length in cubes beside it. **Hard:** Children take turns to lie on the floor with a book placed at their head and feet. The others measure their height in straws. Record each height.				
Independent activities *Supported play*	**Toys:** Children measure the height of different teddies using crayons or cubes. *Which is the tallest teddy?*	**Cooking:** Children make cheese straws using the recipe in the Recipe Bank (page 119). They cut the pastry into long and short straws before baking.	**Construction:** Build the tallest tower you can using any construction equipment available. Children guess its height, then measure using straws.	**Sand:** Children build a short trench in the sand *Now try to make a long trench. How long can we make it? How many cars long is it?*	**Cutting and sticking:** Children cut gummed paper squares into strips. *Draw a huge picture of your favourite animal on a large piece of paper. Measure its height or length in strips.*
Language	**Long, short, tall, shorter, longer, taller, longest, shortest, tallest, middle-sized, compare, how many?, measure**				
At home	*Measuring your bed* **A bed, a shoe, paper, coloured pencils/crayons** Help your child to measure the length of their bed in shoes by placing two shoes of the same length end to end and moving them along the side of the bed. *Whose shoes will you use to measure your bed?* Before they start, ask them how many shoes long they think the bed is. Encourage them to draw a picture of their bed and write how many shoes long it is.				
Resources	Two card snakes (one long, one short), same-length crayons, teddies, cubes	Two ribbons (one long, one short), same-length crayons, cheese straw mix	Straws, a metre stick, a shorter stick, construction materials	Paper fish (different lengths – enough for at least one per pair), Blu-tack, cubes, sandpit, toy cars	Two pieces of string (one long, one short), same-length crayons, gummed paper squares, scissors, colouring pencils

- Sing a number song together.
- Count together from 1 to 50, using fingers to mark the units.
- Say a number rhyme together.
- Count backwards from 20 to 1, then shout *Blast off!* together.
- Say a number between 1 and 10. *Eight.* Ask the children to hold up that number of fingers. Who has to count and who just 'knows'? Repeat for other numbers.

DAY 1

- *Comparing the lengths of two objects*
- *Beginning to measure lengths using a non-standard unit*

Two card snakes (one long, one short), same-length crayons

- Show children the two snakes. *Which snake is longer? Which is shorter?* Encourage children to answer, holding the two snakes against each other to check.
- *We can measure the snakes using crayons.* Hold up the longer snake. *How many crayons long do you think this snake is? How many crayons can we fit along the snake?* Encourage children to discuss, then guess.
- Write their guesses on the board. Lay the crayons end to end along the snake, counting each as you set it down. *The snake is four crayons long.* Write 'The snake is 4 crayons long' on the board.
- Compare the measurement with their guesses. *Which is the closest guess?*
- Repeat for the shorter snake, comparing it with the longer snake.
- *How many crayons fit along this snake? How many crayons fit along that snake? More crayons fitted along this snake than that one. This snake is longer than that snake.*

DAY 2

- *Comparing the lengths of two objects*
- *Beginning to measure lengths using a non-standard unit*

Two ribbons (one long, one short), same-length crayons

- Give two children a ribbon each. Children compare ribbons. *Who has the longer ribbon?*
- *We can measure the ribbons using these crayons.* Hold up the longer ribbon. *How many crayons long do you think this ribbon is? How many crayons can we fit along the ribbon?* Encourage children to discuss, then guess.
- Write their guesses on the board. Lay the crayons end to end along the ribbon, counting each crayon as you set it down. *The ribbon is ten crayons long.* Write 'The ribbon is 10 crayons long' on the board.
- Compare the measurement with their guesses. *Which is the closest guess?*
- Repeat for the short ribbon, comparing it with the long ribbon.
- *How many crayons fit along this ribbon? How many crayons fit along that ribbon? More crayons fitted along this ribbon than that one. This ribbon is longer than that ribbon.*

DAY 3
- *Comparing the lengths of two objects*
- *Beginning to measure lengths using a non-standard unit*

Straws, a metre stick, a shorter stick

- Give each pair of children a straw. Show children the metre stick. *How many straws do you think will fit along this?* Encourage children to discuss with a partner how many will fit along the stick.
- Write some guesses on the board. Choose some children to place straws end to end along the stick. *We are measuring the stick in straws. How many straws long is the stick?*
- Record its length in straws. 'The stick is 8 straws long'.
- Compare their guesses with the actual number. *Which is the closest guess?*
- Now show the class the shorter stick. *How long is this stick? How many straws long is it? How many straws do you think will fit along this?* Record some guesses.
- Measure the second stick with straws. Record its length and compare this with their guesses.
- Compare the lengths of the two sticks by looking at how many straws long each one is. *Which stick is longer?*

DAY 4
- *Comparing the lengths of three objects*
- *Beginning to measure lengths using a non-standard unit*

Paper fish (all different lengths – enough for at least one per pair), Blu-tack, cubes

- Blu-tack three of the fish to a table. *Which fish is the longest? Which is the shortest?*
- *We'll use cubes to measure each fish. We'll lay cubes along each fish and count how many along the whole length of the fish.*
- Encourage children to look at the shortest fish and to guess the number of cubes long it will be. Record their guesses on the board.
- Choose a pair of children to lay cubes end to end along the shortest fish. *How many cubes long is this fish?* Record its length in cubes. 'The fish is 6 cubes long'. Compare its length to their guesses.
- Choose two other pairs to measure the other two fish.
- Give each pair of children a fish to measure with cubes. Record some measurements on the board.
- Show that the longest fish has the most cubes along it.

DAY 5
- *Comparing the lengths of two objects*
- *Beginning to measure lengths using a non-standard unit*

Two pieces of string (one long, one short), crayons

- Show children the two pieces of string. *Which piece of string is longer? We shall use crayons to measure.*
- Encourage children to guess how many crayons long each piece will be. Record some guesses.
- Lay one piece of string on the table and choose two children to lay crayons end to end along its length. Count the crayons. Write its length.
- Repeat for the other piece of string.
- Compare the lengths of the two pieces in crayons. *Which measured more crayons? This one is longer. Which measured fewer crayons? This one is shorter.*

	DAY 1	DAY 2	DAY 3	DAY 4	DAY 5
Objective	Comparing heavy and light objects and beginning to measure weight on scales using non-standard units				
Teacher-led activities *On the rug* (pages 59–60)	**Warm up:** Count to 60 quickly. **Activity:** Pass round the bag of sugar so children can feel it. *This sugar is quite heavy.* Repeat with the cotton wool. *We can find out which is heavier using these scales.* Put the sugar on one side, the cotton wool on the other. Demonstrate that the sugar side goes down because it is heavier. Swap sides to show that the heavier side goes down and the lighter side up.	**Warm up:** Count from 40 to 80 using fingers. **Activity:** *Look at the kitchen roll and the smaller book. Which is larger? Which is heavier?* Pass them round for children to feel. Choose a child to put the kitchen roll on one side of the scales and the book on the other. *Which side goes down? The book side. The book is heavier.* Pass round the larger book. *Is this heavier?*	**Warm up:** Say a number rhyme. **Activity:** *Look at the large light ball and the beanbag. Which is larger? The ball. Which is heavier?* Pass round both objects. Choose a child to put the ball on one side of the scales and the beanbag on the other. *Which side goes down? This side is heavier. The beanbag is heavier. The ball is lighter.* Pass round the small heavy ball. *Is this heavier than the beanbag?* Pass round both objects. Weigh them.	**Warm up:** Count up to 20 then down to *Blast off!* **Activity:** *Which is heavier, the teddy or the car?* Pass round both. A child places the teddy on one side of the scales and the car on the other. *Which side goes down? This side is heavier. The car is heavier. The teddy is lighter.* Pass round the kilogram weight. *Is this heavier than the car?* Pass round both objects. Weigh them. *The weight is smaller than the teddy and the car, but it is heavier.*	**Warm up:** Count from 50 to 100 using fingers. **Activity:** *These jars of cotton wool and jam are both the same size. Which is heavier?* Pass them round. Weigh them. *The jar of jam is heavier because this side of the scales goes down.* Pass round the jar of beans. *Is this heavier than the jar of cotton wool? Heavier than the jar of jam?* Pass round all three jars. Use the scales to order the jars by weight.
Teacher-initiated activities *Activity Book* (page 14)	**Easy:** Use three identical boxes – one full of sand, one of dried beans and one of cotton wool. Look at all the boxes. Children choose the box they think is heaviest. Place each box on balance scales opposite another box to check. Were they correct? Repeat to find out which is lightest. **Medium:** Use one shoe from each of two children. *Which is heaviest? Which is lightest?* Check, using the scales. **Hard:** Use four tins of different sorts (e.g. beans, sweets). *Which is heaviest? Which is lightest?* Check, using the scales.				
Independent activities *Supported play*	**Toys:** Children collect several toys and decide which they think is the heaviest. They place them on balance scales to check.	**Cooking:** Children make a sponge cake using the recipe in the Recipe Bank (page 119). *Is the cooked cake heavier than the teddy?*	**Cutting and sticking:** Children make cylindrical containers using tubes of card. They fill two containers with different things and weigh them. *Which is heaviest?*	**Sand:** Place a bucket full of sand and a bucket full of water on the scales. *Which is heavier?*	**Painting:** *Paint something that you know is really heavy, using dark colours. Paint something that is really light (like a bird or a kite) using light colours.*
Language	Heavy, light, heavier, lighter, heaviest, lightest, weigh, compare, balance, scales				
At home	*Heavy and light* **Two similar envelopes, a light object, a heavy object, a pen** Give your child two similar-sized envelopes. Ask them to find a light object to put in one and a heavy object to put in the other. Write 'h' for heavy and 'l' for light on the appropriate envelope. Remind your child to take the envelopes into class to compare their weights.				
Resources	A large bag of sugar, a large bag of cotton wool, balance scales, toys	A kitchen roll, two books (one smaller but heavier than the other), balance scales, sponge cake mix	A large light ball (e.g. beach ball), bean bag, a small heavy ball (e.g. golf ball), balance scales, card, scissors, glue, items to weigh (e.g. beans, buttons, etc)	A large fluffy teddy, a heavy toy car, balance scales, a kilogram weight, buckets, sand, water	Three identical transparent plastic jars (one filled with cotton wool, one with jam, one with dried beans), balance scales, paint, paintbrushes

- Count together to 60. Encourage the children to count as fast as they can.
- Count together from 40 to 80, using fingers to mark the units.
- Say a number rhyme together.
- Count up to 20 then down to 1, shouting *Blast off!* together at the end.
- Count together from 50 using fingers to mark the units.

DAY 1

- *Comparing heavy and light objects*
- *Beginning to measure weight on scales*

A large bag of sugar, a larger bag of cotton wool, balance scales

- Show children the bag of sugar. *It is quite heavy.* Pass it round so children can feel its weight.
- Show children the bag of cotton wool. *This is a larger bag, but it is not as heavy. It is quite light.* Pass round the cotton wool so children can feel its weight.
- *We can find out which is heavier using these scales.*
- Place the sugar on one side of the balances and the cotton wool on the other. Show that the sugar side goes down. *This side goes down because it is heavier.* Point to the cotton wool side. *This side goes up because it is lighter.*
- Swap sides so it is clear that the heavier side goes down and the lighter side goes up.

DAY 2

- *Comparing heavy and light objects*
- *Beginning to measure weight on scales*

A kitchen roll, two books (one small and heavier than the kitchen roll, one large), balance scales

- Show children the kitchen roll and the smaller book. *Which is larger?* Discuss. *The kitchen roll is larger. It would take up more space in my shopping basket. The book is smaller. I could almost carry it in my pocket.*
- Show both objects again and pass them round so children can feel their weight. *Which is heavier?* Encourage children to guess.
- *We can use these scales to find which is heavier and which is lighter.* Choose a child to place the kitchen roll on one side and the book on the other. *Which side goes down? The book side goes down. The book is heavier.*
- Swap sides so that the book is on the other side. Show that the book side still goes down. *The book is heavier. The kitchen roll is lighter.*
- Pass round another book. *Is this heavier than the kitchen roll?* Place it on the scales to find out.

DAY 3
- *Comparing heavy and light objects*
- *Beginning to measure weight on scales*

A large light ball (e.g. beach ball), a beanbag, a small heavy ball (e.g. golf ball), balance scales

- Show children the large light ball and the beanbag. *Which is larger? The ball. Which do you think is heavier?* Pass round both objects for children to feel their weights.
- Choose a child to place the ball on one side of the scales and the beanbag on the other. *Which side goes down? This side goes down. The beanbag is heavier. This side goes up. The ball is lighter.*
- Pass round the small heavy ball. *Is this heavier than the large ball?* Pass round both balls.
- Choose a child to place a ball on each side of the scales.
- *Which side goes down? This ball is heavier. Which side goes up? This ball is lighter.*
- Repeat to find out whether the heavier ball is heavier than the beanbag.

DAY 4
- *Comparing heavy and light objects*
- *Beginning to measure weight on scales*

A large fluffy teddy, a heavy toy car, balance scales, a kilogram weight

- Show children the teddy and the car. *Which is heavier?* Pass round both to let children judge.
- Choose a child to place the teddy on one side of the scales and the car on the other. *Which side goes down? This side is heavier. The car is heavier. The teddy is lighter.*
- Pass round the kilogram weight. *Is this heavier than the car?* Pass round the three objects.
- Place the car and the kilogram weight on either side of the scales. *Which side goes down? This side is heavier. Which side goes up? This side is lighter.*
- Line up the three objects in order of heaviness. *The largest thing is not the heaviest. The weight is smaller than the teddy and the car, but it is heaviest.*

DAY 5
- *Comparing heavy and light objects*
- *Beginning to measure weight on scales*

Three identical transparent plastic jars (one filled with cotton wool, one with jam, one with dried beans), balance scales

- Show children the jar of cotton wool and the jar of jam. *These jars are both the same size.* Show that they are the same size by holding them beside each other.
- *Which is heavier?* Pass them round.
- Choose a child to place the jar of cotton wool on one side of the scales and the jar of jam on the other. *Which side goes down? The jar of jam. It is heavier. Which side goes up? The jar of cotton wool. It is lighter.*
- Pass round the jar of dried beans. *Is this heavier than the jar of cotton wool? Is it heavier than the jar of jam?* Pass all three jars round the class.
- Place the two jars that children think are heavier on the scales. *Which is the heaviest?*
- Place the two jars which children think are lighter on the scales. *Which is the lightest?*
- Place the jars in order by weight.

	DAY 1	DAY 2	DAY 3	DAY 4	DAY 5
Objective	Comparing up to numbers, ordering numbers to 20				
Teacher-led activities *On the rug* (pages 62–63)	**Warm up:** Sing a number song. **Activity:** Show the picture of the boy. *This is Fred. He is twelve.* Choose a child to point to 12 on the number line. Show the picture of the girl. *This is Marie. She is nineteen.* Choose a child to point to 19 on the number line. *Who is older?* Point to the two numbers. *Nineteen is further up the line than twelve. It is a larger number. Marie is older than Fred.*	**Warm up:** Count from 1 to 50 using fingers. **Activity:** Lay large number cards (1 to 20) along the rug to make a track. Place a counter on 16. *This is the teddy's counter. Which number is it on?* Point to the counter on 20. *This is the cat's counter. Which number is it on? Who is winning?* Repeat, repositioning the counters and comparing two.	**Warm up:** Show fingers to match numbers from 1 to 10, then add one more. **Activity:** Give one number card to each pair of children. Choose two pairs. They find their numbers on the line. *Whose number is further along the line?* Each pair builds a tower of building bricks to match their number. *Whose tower is taller? Whose number is larger?* Repeat with different pairs. Stress that the numbers further along the line are larger.	**Warm up:** Count from 50 to 100 using fingers. **Activity:** Blu-tack five number cards to the board in the order 3, 16, 7, 12, 9. *We will put these cards in order, smallest to largest.* Choose a child to take the 3. *Where is this on the number line?* Help her to match it to the 3 on the line. She stands by the number. Repeat for the other cards. *Who is furthest along? Sixteen is the largest number.* Blu-tack the cards back on the board in size order.	**Warm up:** Say a number rhyme. **Activity:** Lay large number cards (1 to 20) along the rug to make a track. Place five soft toy animals on the track. Choose children to build a tower of cubes to match each toy's number. *Whose tower is largest? Smallest? Which number is furthest along? This number has the tallest tower. This number is largest.* Compare each number with the others.
Teacher-initiated activities *Activity Book* (pages 14–15)	**Easy:** Use a number track (1 to 20) and counters placed on 1. Spin a coin. Tails – move two spaces forwards, heads – move three spaces forwards. After each turn, children pause. Each child builds a tower to match the number they are on. *Who is on the largest number? Who is furthest along the track?* The child on the largest number takes a cube. Continue to 20. The child with the most cubes wins. **Medium:** Use number cards (1 to 20). Each child takes a card. They compare numbers. The child with the largest number takes a cube. Continue until all the cards have been taken. The child with the most cubes wins. **Hard:** Shuffle number cards (1 to 30) and place them in a pile face down. Children take six cards and put them in order, smallest to largest. They compare their numbers with a number track. Were they right? Extend using cards 1 to 50.				
Independent activities *Supported play*	**Playhouse:** Children write an address label with a different house number to go round the arm of each toy, so they do not forget where they live. Children make one for themselves, too.	**Cooking:** Children make jam sandwiches and cut each into small circles using a pastry cutter. They count the number they make. They divide them onto two plates – one small, one large. They compare the number on each plate.	**Play dough:** Roll out the play dough. Children make door number plaques. *Who lives at the flat/house with the largest number?* They decorate the plaques with beads and small shells.	**Sand:** Bury lots of small building bricks (assorted colours). Children guess which colour there are most of. They dig up the bricks and count to check. Who was right?	**Cutting and sticking:** Children use different shapes cut from sticky paper to create a picture. *Which colour is there most of? Which colour is there least of?* Compare the number of each colour.
Language	**Number names to one to twenty, how many?, more, less, larger, smaller, further along, near, close**				
At home	*Car numbers* **Old greetings cards, scissors, glue, paper, a pencil** Use the backs of old greetings cards to make six small pieces of card. Take your child to look at the number plates of two cars and help them to write the six numbers on the plates on separate cards. At home, ask your child to read the numbers and put them in order, from smallest to largest. Help them to stick the numbers onto a sheet of paper to take into class.				
Resources	A picture of a 12-year-old boy, a picture of a 19-year-old girl, washing line with large number cards (1 to 20) pegged to it, pegs, address labels, toys	Large number cards (1 to 20), a teddy, a toy cat, counters, bread, jam, pastry cutters, plates	Large number cards (1 to 10), washing line with large number cards (1 to 10) pegged to it, pegs, large building bricks, play dough, beads, shells	Large number cards (3, 7, 9, 12, 16), Blu-tack, washing line with large number cards (1 to 20) pegged to it, pegs, building bricks, sandpit	Large number cards (1 to 20), five soft toy animals, interlocking cubes, sticky paper shapes

- Sing a number song together.
- Count together to 50, using fingers to mark the units.
- Say a number between 1 and 10. *Five.* Ask the children to hold up that number of fingers. Ask them to add one more finger. *How many now?* Repeat for other numbers.
- Count together from 50 to 100, using fingers to mark the units.
- Say a number rhyme together.

DAY 1

- *Comparing two numbers*

A picture of a 12-year-old boy, a picture of a 19-year-old girl, a washing line with large number cards (1 to 20) pegged to it, pegs

- Show children the picture of the boy. *This is Fred. He is twelve.* Choose a child to point to 12 on the number line. *Fred is twelve.*
- Show children the picture of the girl. *This is Marie. She is nineteen.* Choose a child to point to 19 on the number line. *Marie is nineteen.*
- *Who is older?* Point to the two numbers on the line. *Nineteen is further up the line than twelve. It is a larger number. Marie is older than Fred.*
- Repeat, choosing the brothers or sisters of two children in the class and comparing their ages.

DAY 2

- *Comparing two numbers*

Large number cards (1 to 20), a teddy, a toy cat, counters

- Lay the numbers along the rug to make a number track.
- *The teddy and the cat are playing a game.*
- Place a counter on 16. *This is the teddy's counter. What number is it on?* Encourage children who cannot remember the number to count in whispers up the line. *Sixteen.*
- Place a counter on 20. *This is the cat's counter. What number is it on? Twenty.*
- *Who is winning?* Point to the counter on 20. *The cat's counter is further along the track. It is winning.*
- Repeat, using two more toys and repositioning the counters, always comparing two counters to see who is winning.

DAY 3 • *Comparing two numbers*

Large number cards (1 to 10), a washing line with large number cards (1 to 10) pegged to it, large building bricks, pegs

- Give out number cards, one to each pair of children. Select carefully which card to give each pair.
- Choose two pairs of children. *Find your numbers on the line. Whose number is further along the line?*
- Each pair builds a tower of bricks to match their number. *Whose tower is taller? Whose number is larger? The taller tower matches the number that is further along the line. This number is larger.*
- Repeat, using different pairs of children and cards. Stress that the numbers further along the lines are larger.

DAY 4 • *Comparing five numbers*
• *Ordering numbers to 20*

Large number cards (3, 7, 9, 12, 16), Blu-tack, a washing line with large number cards (1 to 20) pegged to it, pegs

- Blu-tack the five number cards to the board, in the order 3, 16, 7, 12, 9.
- Point to the cards. *We are going to put these numbers in order from smallest to largest.*
- Choose a child to take the number '3'. *What number is this? Three. Can you find this on the number line?* Help her to match her card to the 3 on the line. She stands by that number.
- Repeat for the other number cards on the board. If children cannot remember the numbers, help them to count up to them in whispers.
- Look at children in the line. *Who is furthest along?* Point to 16. *She is furthest along the line. Sixteen is the largest number.*
- Look at each number's place in the line and use this to stick the numbers in order back onto the board.

DAY 5 • *Comparing five numbers, ordering numbers to 20*
• *Ordering numbers to 20*

Large number cards (1 to 20), five soft toy animals, interlocking cubes

- Lay the numbers along the rug to make a number track. Place five soft toy animals on the track.
- Point to the first soft toy. *What number is this toy on?* Choose a child to build a tower of cubes to match that number.
- Repeat for each of the soft toy's numbers.
- *Whose tower is largest? Whose is smallest? Which number is furthest along? This is the one with the tallest tower. This number is largest.*
- Compare each number with the others.

	DAY 1	DAY 2	DAY 3	DAY 4	DAY 5
Objective	Counting forwards and backwards to/from 20, recognising numbers to 15				
Teacher-led activities *On the rug* (pages 65–66)	**Warm up:** Count from 1 to 50 using fingers. **Activity:** Point to 20 on the number line. *Twenty.* Pass around the bag of twenty 1p coins. *This is twenty pennies.* Point to 19 on the number line. *Nineteen is one less than twenty.* Take the bag and remove 1p. *Now we have one less than twenty pence.* Point to 19 on the line. *We have nineteen pennies.* Repeat, until you reach 1p.	**Warm up:** Show fingers to match numbers from 1 to 10, then add one more. **Activity:** Lay large number cards (1 to 20) along the rug to make a track. Make a toy move along the track from 20 to 1, counting together. *Twenty, nineteen, eighteen, ...* Choose a child to place the toy on a number on the track, e.g. 5. *What is the number before this?* If necessary, count from 1. *The number before five is four.* Repeat several times.	**Warm up:** Sing a number song. **Activity:** Lay large number cards (1 to 20) along the rug to make a track. Count the chess pieces. Place a chess piece on each card, starting at 1. Point to the last card. *There are sixteen pieces. How many will there be if we take one away?* Children guess. Remove one piece. Point to 15. *There are fifteen now. One less than sixteen is fifteen.* Continue until one piece is left.	**Warm up:** Count from 50 to 100 using fingers. **Activity:** Place 15 children in a line. Count along the line, each child saying their number. Give each child a number card to match their number. Ask a child to choose a child in the line and say their number. *What is the number before this?* Build a tower of building bricks to match the first number. Remove one brick. *How many now?* Show that the number one less is the number before.	**Warm up:** Sing a number song. **Activity:** Show children 20 biscuits. *How many biscuits?* Put them in a pile as you count them. *Twenty biscuits.* Choose a child. Use the puppet to give her a biscuit to eat. *How many biscuits now?* Encourage children to look at the number line and see the number before 20. Repeat, taking away one biscuit each time until none are left.
Teacher-initiated activities *Activity Book* (pages 15–16)	**Easy:** Each child threads 12 beads on a string. They find the number 12 card and place it on the table. Children remove one bead each. They count the beads and find the matching number card. Continue to 1. **Medium:** Use a number track (1 to 20) and counters placed on 20. Each child takes twenty 1p coins. They take turns to play. They spin a coin. Heads – move two places backwards, tails – move one place backwards. Children remove the matching number of coins from their pile. They say how many coins are left. Continue to 1. **Hard:** Shuffle number cards (1 to 20) and place them in a pile face down. Children take turns to take a card. They count back to 1 from that number. If they are correct, they take a 1p coin. They replace the card at the bottom of the pile. *Who has the most coins?*				
Independent activities *Supported play*	**Construction:** Children each build a tall tower. *How many bricks have you each used?* Remove one brick from each tower. *How many bricks in each tower now?*	**Cooking:** Children put a dollop of honey on pieces of apple. Line up the pieces. *How many pieces?* Eat one. *How many are there now?*	**Water:** *How many cups will fill the jug?* Count as you fill it. When it is full, pour out one cup of water and throw it away. *How many cups of water left in the jug?*	**Sand:** Children build ten sandcastles. Knock down one. *How many sandcastles now?*	**Colouring:** Draw a bunch of flowers. *How many have you drawn? Colour these red. Draw another bunch with one less in. Colour these yellow.*
Language	Numbers names one to twenty, how many, more and less, one less, the number before, the number after, take away				
At home	*Toys in a row* **Ten toys, sticky labels, a pen** Use some sticky labels to number ten toys from 1 to 10. Ask your child to line up the toys in the correct order. Encourage them to say the additions. *One add another one makes two toys, two add one more makes three toys, ...* Repeat for taking away toys one at a time, starting from 10.				
Resources	Washing line with large number cards (1 to 20) pegged to it, twenty real 1p coins, a mesh bag, pegs, building bricks	Large number cards (1 to 20), a soft toy, apples, honey	Large number cards (1 to 20), 16 chess pieces, a jug, cups, water	Large number cards (1 to 15), large building bricks, sandpit, buckets, scoops	Biscuits, a plate, washing line with large number cards (1 to 20) pegged to it, a puppet, pegs, crayons or colouring pencils

- Count together to 50, using fingers to mark the units.
- Say a number between 1 and 10. *Five.* Ask the children to hold up that number of fingers. Ask them to add one more finger. *How many now?* Repeat for other numbers.
- Sing a number song together.
- Count together from 50 to 100, using fingers to mark the units.
- Together sing a number song, which involves counting down.

DAY 1

- *Counting forwardss and backwards to/from 20*

A washing line with large number cards (1 to 20) pegged to it, twenty real 1p coins, a mesh bag, pegs

- Point to 20 on the number line. *Twenty.*
- Put the coins in the bag and pass it round so that children can see the coins and feel their weight. *This is twenty pennies.*
- Point to 19 on the number line. *What number is this?* If children do not know, help them count in whispers to 19. *Nineteen.*
- Point to 20 again. *Nineteen is one less than twenty.* Take the bag and remove a 1p coin. *Now we have one less than twenty pence. We have nineteen pence.*
- Repeat, removing one coin at a time and counting back along the number line until you get to 1p.

DAY 2

- *Counting backwards from 20*

Large number cards (1 to 20), a soft toy

- Lay the numbers along the rug to make a number track. Count together along it.
- Move a toy back along the track from 20 to 1, and count in unison. *Twenty, nineteen, eighteen, ...*
- Choose a child to place the toy on a number on the track, e.g. 5. Say the number together.
- Point to the number. *What is the number before this?* If necessary, remind children by counting in whispers, stressing the number before. *One, two, three,* ***four****, five. The number before five is four.*
- Repeat several times.

DAY 3

- *Counting forwardss and backwards to/from 20*

Large number cards (1 to 20), 16 chess pieces

- Lay the numbers along the rug to make a number track. Count together along it.
- Show children the chess pieces. *How many chess pieces?* Count them together.
- Place a chess piece on each card, starting at 1. Count as you go. Point to the last piece. *There are sixteen pieces.*
- *How many will there be if we take one away?* Encourage children to work this out by counting back from 20 and noticing which number they say after 16. Remove one piece.
- Point to the card. *Fifteen. There are fifteen now. One less than sixteen is fifteen.*
- Continue until there is one piece left.

DAY 4 • *Recognising numbers to 15*

Large number cards (1 to 15), large building bricks

- Ask 15 children to stand in a line. Count along the line, each child saying their number. Give each child a number card to match their number.
- Ask one of the class to choose a child. *What is your number?* The child says her number.
- *What is the number before this?* Children point to the child before her to say his number.
- Build a tower of bricks to match the first number. Show the class and repeat the number.
- Now remove one brick. *How many now?* Count the new tower of bricks to demonstrate that the number one less is the number before.
- Repeat, choosing a different child to select a child in the line.

DAY 5 • *Counting backwards from 20*

Biscuits, a plate, a washing line with large number cards (1 to 20) pegged to it, a puppet, pegs

- Place 20 biscuits on the plate. *How many biscuits are there on this plate?* Children guess.
- *Let's count them.* Put them in a pile as you do so. *There are twenty biscuits.* Choose a child to point to 20 on the number line.
- Choose a child. Make the puppet give her a biscuit. *How many biscuits now?* Encourage children to look at the number line and read the number before 20.
- Count the remaining biscuits to check that the number left when one biscuit has been taken is 19. Demonstrate on the number line.
- Repeat, giving one biscuit each time to a child and counting down to find how many left. Give a biscuit to any child who hasn't yet received one.

	DAY 1	DAY 2	DAY 3	DAY 4	DAY 5
Objective	Sorting 3-d shapes, recognising and naming a cube, beginning to recognise a cuboid				
Teacher-led activities *On the rug* (pages 68–69)	**Warm up:** Show fingers to match numbers from 1 to 10, then add one more. **Activity:** Show children the cube. *This is a cube.* Point to one face. *This is a face.* Count the faces, putting a sticker on each face as you count it. *Look at each face. They are all the same.* Give each pair of children a cube. They count the faces. *There are six faces. How many corners?* Count the corners, putting a piece of Blu-tack on each one as you count it. *Eight corners.*	**Warm up:** Count from 1 to 50 using fingers. **Activity:** Place two cubes, the cuboid and the pyramid in a line. Talk about each shape, the number of faces and corners. *Which two shapes are the same?* Point to the two cubes. *These are cubes.* Whilst children close their eyes, choose a child to remove a shape. Children say what the missing shape is. *Look at the shape. Who was correct?* Replace the shape and repeat.	**Warm up:** Say a number rhyme. **Activity:** Give each pair of children a 3-d shape. Most should have cubes. The puppet hides a shape. He describes it, focusing on the number of faces and corners. If a pair think he is describing their shape, they wave it. The puppet then shows his shape. Were they correct? Encourage children to name the cubes. Repeat several times.	**Warm up:** Sing a number song. **Activity:** Give each group of three children a 2 × 2 grid. They place a 3-d shape in each space. Put the large shapes in a bag. On a count of three, bring out a shape. *What shape is this?* Any pair with that shape on their board remove it. (Only one shape can be removed each time.) Replace the shape in the bag and repeat. The first to remove all their shapes says *Bingo*!	**Warm up:** Count from 50 to 100 as fast as possible. **Activity:** Lay out the four shapes. Choose a child. Stick a 3-d shape on his back. Turn him to show the class. Children describe the shape without using its name. He selects a matching shape from the table. *What do we call this shape?* Remove the shape from his back. Discuss the properties. Repeat with another child.
Teacher-initiated activities *Activity Book* (page 16)	**Easy:** Use a selection of 3-d shapes. Children sort the shapes into two sets, labelled 'cubes' and 'not cubes'. **Medium:** Make a line of 3-d shapes: cube, cuboid, larger cube and cone. Children copy the pattern, naming the shapes as they lay them. *How many times can you repeat the pattern?* **Hard:** Use a net of a cuboid. Help children to decorate their net, then fold it to make a cuboid. *How many faces? What shape are they?*				
Independent activities *Supported play*	**Sand:** Bury different 3-d shapes in the sand. Children feel for them. Before they uncover a shape, they say whether or not it is a cube.	**Cooking:** Children make butter icing using the recipe in the Recipe Bank (page 119). They use the icing to stick six square plain biscuits together to make a cube.	**Play dough:** Children make spheres, cubes and cuboids. Discuss how to make the faces flat.	**Cutting and sticking:** Use small cubes made from plain card. Children decorate each face. *How many faces are there to decorate?*	**Painting:** Make a large cube from cardboard. Children paint each face a different colour. *How many colours?*
Language	Cuboid, pyramid, cone, cube, corner, face, curved, flat, square, same as				
At home	*Sorting cuboids* **A variety of cuboid boxes** Let your child look through your kitchen cupboards to find a selection of cuboid boxes. *How many boxes have you found?* Look together at the boxes. *Do they all have oblong faces or do some have square faces?* Help them to put the boxes with six oblong faces in one pile and those with some square faces in another pile. *Which pile has the most cuboid boxes?*				
Resources	A large cube, six small stickers, small cubes (one per pair), Blu-tack, 3-d shapes, sandpit	Large 3-d shapes (two cubes of different sizes, a cuboid, a pyramid), butter icing mix, square plain biscuits	3-d shapes (mostly cubes of different sizes, cuboids, pyramids), a puppet, play dough	A 2 × 2 grid on card (one for each group), large and small 3-d shapes (mostly cubes, with cuboids, pyramids and cones), a cloth bag, card, coloured pencils	3-d shapes (cube, cuboid, cone, pyramid) Blu-tack or sticky tape, cardboard, paint, paintbrushes

- Say a number between 1 and 10. *Five.* Ask the children to hold up that number of fingers. Ask them to add one more finger. *How many now?* Repeat for other numbers.
- Count together to 50, using fingers to mark the units.
- Together say a number rhyme, which involves counting back.
- Sing a number song together.
- Count together from 50 to 100. Encourage the children to count as fast as they can.

DAY 1

- *Recognising and naming a cube*

A large cube, six small stickers, small cubes (one per pair), Blu-tack

- Show children the large cube. *This is a cube.* Point to one face. *This is a face.* Count the faces, putting a sticker on each face as you count it. *There are six faces.*
- Look at each face. *Each face is the same shape. The faces are squares.* Show that each face is a square.
- Give each pair of children a cube. Count the faces. *There are six faces.*
- *How many corners?* Count the corners, putting a piece of Blu-tack on each one as you count it. *There are eight corners.*
- *How many faces has a cube? Six. How many corners? Eight. What shape are the faces? Square.*
- Rehearse the properties of a cube.

DAY 2

- *Recognising and naming a cube*

Large 3-d shapes (two cubes of different sizes, cuboid, pyramid)

- Place the two cubes, the cuboid and the pyramid in a line.
- Pick up the cube. *What shape is this?* How many faces has it? *Six. How many corners has it? Eight. Are the faces all the same shape? Yes. What shape are they? Squares. This is a cube.*
- Talk about each shape, looking at the number of faces and corners on each.
- *Which two shapes are the same?* Point to the two cubes. *These are both cubes. They are the same, although one is larger than the other.*
- Whilst the class close their eyes, choose a child to remove a shape from the line. Children say what the missing shape is.
- Look at the shape. *Which shape is it?*
- Replace the shape and repeat.

DAY 3

- *Recognising and naming a cube*

3-d shapes (mostly cubes of different sizes, cuboids, pyramids), a puppet

- Give each pair of children a 3-d shape. (Most should have cubes.)
- Make the puppet hide a shape, then describe it, focusing on the number of faces and corners. *The shape I have hidden has six faces and eight corners. All the faces are squares.*
- If a pair of children think he is describing their shape, they wave it. The puppet shows his shape. Were they correct?
- Encourage children to name the cubes.
- Repeat several times.

DAY 4 • *Beginning to recognise 3-d shapes*

A 2 × 2 grid on card (one for each group), 3-d shapes (mostly cubes, with cuboids, pyramids and cones), large 3-d shapes (mostly cubes, with cuboids, pyramids and cones), a cloth bag

- Give each group of three children a 2 × 2 grid and four 3-d shapes. (They need not have one of each shape.) They place a 3-d shape in each space.
- Place the large 3-d shapes in the bag. On a count of three, bring out a shape. *What shape is this?* Talk about its properties, e.g. number of sides, flat faces, curved faces, etc. Ask the children if they know the name of the shape. *Is it a cube, cuboid, pyramid or cone?* Check the children can recognise the shapes, even if they can't name them.
- Any group with that shape takes it off their grid. (Only one shape can be removed each time.)
- Replace the shape in the bag and repeat.
- The first group to remove all their shapes says *Bingo!*
- Play again, focusing on the properties of each shape.

DAY 5 • *Beginning to recognise 3-d shapes*

3-d shapes (cube, cuboid, cone, pyramid), Blu-tack or sticky tape

- Lay out the shapes. Choose a child. Stick a 3-d shape on his back, using Blu-tack or sticky tape. Turn him round so that the class can see the shape.
- Choose another child. *Can you describe one thing about the shape?* Encourage her to describe the number of faces or corners. Choose another child to say something else about the shape.
- The child wearing the shape tries to guess the shape and selects a matching shape.
- *Is he correct? What do we call this shape?* Encourage children to name the shape.
- Choose a different child and stick a different shape on her back.
- Repeat with two different children.

	DAY 1	DAY 2	DAY 3	DAY 4	DAY 5
Objective	Recognising coins, beginning to match each coin to its appropriate number of 1p coins				
Teacher-led activities *On the rug* (pages 71–72)	**Warm up:** Count to 100 as fast as possible. **Activity:** Show children the demonstration 1p coin. *This is one penny. It can't buy much.* Give a real 1p coin to the teddy. *Teddy is not happy.* Show children the demonstration 2p coin. *This is two pence.* Give the cat a real 2p coin. Continue with the rest of the coins. *Which toy has the most money? Which is happiest? Brown coins buy least, then the silver coins, but the gold coins buy most.*	**Warm up:** Say a number rhyme. **Activity:** Give each pair a real coin to hold. Show children the large 50p coin. *This is a silver coin. It is fifty pence. Does anyone else have a silver coin?* Talk about the other silver coins. *Which silver coin buys the most?* Repeat, showing children the 1p coin and talking about brown coins. Repeat for gold coins. *Gold coins buy most of all.*	**Warm up:** Show fingers to match numbers from 1 to 10, then add one more. **Activity:** Give each child a real coin. Hold up a demonstration coin and say its name. Any child with a matching coin stands up and shows the class their coin. Say the name of the coin. Repeat for several coins. *Stand up if you have a silver coin. Which silver coin buys most? Least?* Children sit down. Repeat for brown coins, then gold coins.	**Warm up:** Count from 1 to 50 using fingers. **Activity:** Count from 1 on the number grid. When you say a number with a matching coin, pause and choose a child to Blu-tack the matching coin on the grid. Continue counting to 100. *The larger numbers are at the bottom of the grid. One pound is one hundred pennies. It buys the most.*	**Warm up:** Count different numbers of jumps or claps. **Activity:** Blu-tack all the demonstration coins to the board. Choose a child and, whilst children close their eyes, give her a coin. Children find out which coin you gave her by asking questions. *Is it round? Is it silver? Will it buy lots?* Remove the coins it cannot be. *It is not silver, so we remove 5p, 10p, 20p and 50p.* Repeat.
Teacher-initiated activities *Activity Book* (pages 16–17)	**Easy:** Use a number track (1 to 20) and real 1p, 2p, 5p, 10p and 20p coins. Each child takes a coin and matches it to a number on the track. Discuss what could be bought with each coin. **Medium:** Use fruit and vegetables and real coins (2p, 5p, 10p,). Price each item at 10p, 5p or 2p. Each child chooses one item and uses one coin to pay for it. They talk about the shape and colour of the coins. **Hard:** Use real 1p, 2p, 5p, 10p, 20p, 50p, £1 and £2 coins. Children make coin rubbings of each coin, talking about their shapes and colours.				
Independent activities *Supported play*	**Painting:** Children choose a coin. They choose a side and draw or paint a picture of it, looking at it very carefully.	**Cooking:** Children make shortbread using the recipe in the Recipe Bank (page 119). Cut it into different-shaped pieces and 'sell' each piece for 5p or 10p, depending on the size.	**Playhouse:** Children use coins in role play, shopping in the playhouse.	**Cutting and sticking:** Stick cardboard coins in order from 1p to £2 along a line. Children take turns to cover one and say what it looks like.	**Jigsaws:** Children do a jigsaw. 'Pay' them 1p for every piece they do. How much do they have at the end? Can they swap their 1p coins for any other coins?
Language	**Coin names, penny, pence, pound, how much, how many, cost, buy, sell, more, less, brown, bronze, silver, gold, most, least**				
At home	***What can I buy?*** **Paper, coloured pencils/crayons, coins** When you are out shopping, help your child to buy something that costs a small amount of money. Encourage them to choose the correct number of coins from your purse to pay for the item. They could use only 1p coins or a variety. At home, encourage your child to draw the item they bought and the correct number of 1p coins that they used to buy it.				
Resources	Demonstration coins (all denominations), real coins (all denominations), large soft toys, paint, paintbrushes	Demonstration coins (all denominations), real coins (all denominations), shortbread mix, pastry cutters	Demonstration coins (all denominations), real coins (all denominations), play house items	Number grid (1 to 100), Blu-tack, demonstration coins (1p, 2p, 5p, 10p, 20p, 50p, £1), cardboard coins (all denominations), glue	Blu-tack, demonstration coins (all denominations), real coins (all denominations), jigsaws

- Count together to 100 very quickly. Encourage the children to count as fast as they can and give them lots of praise.
- Together say a number rhyme, which involves counting back.
- Say a number between 1 and 10. *Five.* Ask the children to hold up that number of fingers. Ask them to add one more finger. *How many now?* Repeat for other numbers.
- Count together to 50, using fingers to mark the units.
- Count ten jumps or claps together. Ask different children to demonstrate different numbers of actions. *Carly, show me thirteen hops.*

DAY 1

- *Recognising coins*

Demonstration coins (all denominations), real coins (all denominations), large soft toys

- Show children the demonstration 1p coin. *This is one penny. It can't buy much.* Give a real 1p coin to the teddy. *The teddy only has one pence. He is not very happy.*
- Show children the demonstration 2p coin. *This is two pence. It can't buy much either.* Give the cat the real 2p coin. *The cat has two pence. She has more than the teddy, but she is not very happy either.*
- Show children the demonstration 5p coin. *This is five pence. It can buy a few things – mostly sweets.* Give the dog the real 5p coin. *The dog has five pence. He has more than the cat and the teddy, but he is not very happy either.*
- Continue, with the toys becoming progressively happier.
- Point to all the toys. *Which toy has the most money? Which toy has least money?*
- Discuss how the brown coins buy least, then the silver coins, and the gold coins buy most.

DAY 2

- *Recognising coins*

Demonstration coins (all denominations), real coins (all denominations)

- Give each pair a real coin. Choose carefully which coin to give each pair.
- Show children the demonstration 50p coin. *This is a silver coin. It is fifty pence. Does anyone else have a silver coin?*
- Show children the demonstration 20p, 10p and 5p coins. *Which coin is the largest of the silver coins? The fifty pence coin. This coin will buy the most. I like this one best out of these silver coins, because I can buy the most things with it.*
- Point to the 5p coin. *This one will buy the least.* Discuss the other silver coins.
- Ask all children holding a silver coin to stand up. Compare their coins. *Who has a fifty pence coin? This will buy the most. Who has a five pence coin? This will buy very little.*
- Show children the demonstration 2p coin. Talk about the brown coins. *Which brown coin buys the most? Which buys the least?*
- Repeat, showing children the £1 and £2 coins. *The gold-coloured coins buy most of all.*

DAY 3 • *Recognising coins*

Demonstration coins (all denominations), real coins (all denominations)

- Give each child a real coin. Discuss which coins are brown, which are silver and which are gold. *Which coins will buy the most? Which coins will not buy much?*
- Hold up a demonstration coin and say its name.
- Children with a matching coin stand up to show their coin. Say the name of your coin.
- Repeat for several coins.
- *Now I want anyone with a silver coin to stand up. Which silver coin buys most? Which buys least?* Children sit down.
- Repeat for brown coins and silver coins.

DAY 4 • *Recognising coins*

• *Beginning to match each coin to 1p coins*

Number grid (1 to 100), Blu-tack, demonstration coins (1p, 2p, 5p, 10p, 20p, 50p, £1)

- Show children the grid. *This is a grid with all the numbers from one to one hundred.*
- Start counting along the grid, pointing to the numbers as you go. *One. This is a one pence coin.* Show children the demonstration 1p coin and Blu-tack it onto the grid over the number 1. *This is one pence.*
- Point to 2. *Two. This is a two pence coin.* Show children the 2p coin and Blu-tack it over 2. *This is two pence.*
- Continue, pointing to each number and counting along the grid. *Three, four, five.* Stop again, and hold up a 5p coin. *This is a five pence coin.* Blu-tack the 5p over 5. *This is five pence.*
- Continue counting along the grid to 100, choosing children to stick appropriate coins on the grid.
- Point out that the larger numbers are at the bottom of the grid. *One pound is one hundred pennies. It buys the most.*

DAY 5 • *Recognising coins*

Blu-tack, demonstration coins (all denominations), real coins (all denominations)

- Blu-tack all the demonstration coins to the board in any order. Discuss which coin is which and which buys the most.
- Whilst the class close their eyes, choose a child and give her a real coin.
- Children ask her questions to find out what coin you gave her. *Is it round? Is it silver? Will it buy lots?* Discuss the answers and then remove the coins it cannot be. *It is not silver so we remove 5p, 10p, 20p and 50p.*
- Continue, letting children ask questions until children are fairly sure which coin it is. Let them guess. Were they right?
- Repeat, giving a different child a different coin.

	DAY 1	DAY 2	DAY 3	DAY 4	DAY 5
Objective	**Recognising the hours on an analogue clock, and reading and setting the time to the hour**				
Teacher-led activities *On the rug* (pages 74–75)	**Warm up:** Count up to 20 then back to *Blast off!* **Activity:** *What time does school start? Nine o'clock.* Set the hands on the clock. *The big hand is pointing up and the little hand is pointing to nine. This is how we tell it is nine o'clock. What time does school end?* Choose a child to show 3 o'clock. Point out the position of both hands. Choose another child to set the hands to lunch time (12 o'clock). Repeat for bedtime, etc.	**Warm up:** Sing the days of the week. **Activity:** Show children the clock set to 1 o'clock. *What time does my clock say? One o'clock.* Mime what you do on a Saturday at 1 o'clock (e.g. eat lunch). Can children guess? Choose a child who guessed correuctly to be the 'lunch-time kid'. Give her a 1 o'clock sticker and the lunch plate. Repeat for 'cleaning teeth' time (7 o'clock) and getting up time (8 o'clock).	**Warm up:** Sing the days of the week. **Activity:** Shuffle the number cards and place them in a pile face down. Choose a child to take a card. *Let's make the clock say this time.* Help a child set the hands to the matching o'clock time. Discuss what we do at this time of day. Choose a child to mime the action. Repeat several times, with different children taking cards. *The big hand always points up.*	**Warm up:** Count up to 60 using fingers. **Activity:** Whilst children close their eyes, choose one child to set the clock to an o'clock time. Ask five different children what time the clock says. Do they all agree? *What would we be doing at this time of day on a weekday? At the weekend?* Repeat several times, stressing that the big hand points up to the o'clock times, and the little hand point to the hour.	**Warm up:** Say or sing the days of the week. **Activity:** Set the clock to 2 o'clock. *What time is it? Two o'clock.* Very slowly, wind the big hand, saying *Tick, tock, tick, tock.* Stop at 3 o'clock. *What time is it now?* Help children say 3 o'clock by looking at the little hand. *Two o'clock to three o'clock is one hour. The big hand goes right round the clock. One hour is quite a long time.* Talk about things you can do in one hour.
Teacher-initiated activities *Activity Book* (page 17)	**Easy:** Show pictures of objects used at certain times of the day, e.g. knife and fork, toothbrush, bed. Children match the pictures to clock faces showing the appropriate o'clock time. **Medium:** Use a large analogue clock with movable hands. Turn the hands to an 'o'clock time'. *What time is this? Think about what might happen at this time.* Repeat. **Hard:** Discuss the things we do that take an hour. Use two clock stamps to mark the beginning and end of the chosen hour. *Draw the things you might be doing.*				
Independent activities *Supported play*	**Painting:** Children paint a picture of an activity they enjoy. *How many times could you do this activity in one hour?*	**Cooking:** Children make refrigerator cake using the recipe in the Recipe Bank (page 119). *We need to leave this for one hour to set.* Look at the clock to check the times.	**Playhouse:** Set a clock on the wall to an o'clock time. Children make the toys do appropriate things for that time, e.g. get up, eat lunch, go to bed.	**Cutting and sticking:** Draw round saucers and cut out card circles to make clock faces. Children write the numbers and attach two strips of card using a paper fastener to make hands. *Set the hands to an o'clock time that you like.*	**Toys:** Children play with toy cars and go on a pretend journey. *Where are you going? To the seaside? To the country? What o'clock will you set off? What time will you arrive?*
Language	**Time, how long?, minute, hour, clock, big hand, little hand, o'clock, weekday, weekend**				
At home	*Matching clocks* **A plate, scissors, paper, a pencil** Let your child draw round a plate and cut out the circle. Help them to fold the circle twice, unfold it and write the numbers of a clock face on it. Ask your child to choose an o'clock time and help them to draw the hands for that hour on the clock face. When the actual time matches the one on your child's clock, tell them to remember what they are doing to tell the other children in class.				
Resources	A large analogue clock with movable hands, paint, paintbrushes	A large analogue clock with movable hands, Post-it notes, a lunch plate, a toothbrush, refrigerator cake mix, clock	Large number cards (1 to 12), a large analogue clock with movable hands, toys	A large analogue clock with movable hands, scissors, card, saucers, paper fasteners	A large analogue clock with movable hands, toy cars

- Count up to 20, then backwards to 1, shouting *Blast off!* together at the end.
- Sing the days of the week together.
- Sing the days of the week together. Encourage the children to remember the order by starting at days other than Monday.
- Count together to 60, using fingers to mark the units.
- Say or sing the days of the week together. Encourage the children to remember the order by starting at days other than Monday.

DAY 1

- *Recognising the hours on an analogue clock*

A large analogue clock with movable hands

- Show children the clock. *This is a clock, and we can tell the time on it.* Discuss where children regularly see clocks. *Where do you have a clock in your home? Where does your family look to tell the time?*
- *What time does school start? Nine o'clock.* Set the hands to 9 o'clock. Show that the big hand is pointing up and the little hand is pointing to 9. *This is how we tell it is nine o'clock. This is when school starts. Nine o'clock.*
- *What time does school end?* Choose a child to set the hands to 3 o'clock. Point out the position of both hands. *This is three o'clock, when school ends.*
- Choose another child to set the hands to lunch time (12 o'clock), continuing to stress the position of each hand.
- Repeat for other times, e.g. bedtime.

DAY 2

- *Recognising the hours on an analogue clock*

A large analogue clock with movable hands, Post-it notes,

a lunch plate, a toothbrush

- Set the analogue clock to 1 o'clock. *What time does my clock say?* Stress the position of the hands. *The big hand is pointing upwards. This means it is something o'clock. The little hand is pointing to one. This means it is one o'clock.*
- Mime what you might do on a Saturday at 1 o'clock, e.g. eat lunch. *On Saturday, this is what I do at one o'clock.*
- Can children guess? Choose a child who guessed correctly to be the 'lunch-time kid'. Give her a Post-it note with '1 o'clock' written on it and the lunch plate.
- Repeat for 'cleaning teeth' time (7 o'clock), miming cleaning one's teeth and setting the clock hands to 7 o'clock.
- Repeat for 'getting up' time. (8 o'clock).

DAY 3
- *Recognising the hours on an analogue clock*
- *Setting the time to the hour*

Large number cards (1 to 12), a large analogue clock with movable hands

- Shuffle the number cards and place them in a pile face down.
- Choose a child to take a card. What number is this? *Seven.*
- Show children the clock. *Let's make the clock say this time. Seven o'clock. We need to have the big hand pointing upwards and the little hand pointing to seven.* Help a child to set the hands to the matching o'clock time.
- *Seven o'clock. What do we do at this time of day?* Choose a child to mime an action.
- Repeat for other o'clock times.

DAY 4
- *Recognising the hours on an analogue clock*
- *Reading the time to the hour*

A large analogue clock with movable hands

- Whilst the class close their eyes, choose a child to set the clock to an o'clock time, e.g. 9 o'clock.
- Show the class the clock. Ask five different children what time it says. Do they all agree?
- Point to the hands. *The big hand points up to show that it is an o'clock time. The little hand points to the number of the hour. So it is nine o'clock.*
- *What would we be doing at this time of day on a weekday? What would we be doing at the weekend?*
- Repeat several times, stressing that the big hand points up to the o'clock times, and the little hand points to the hour.

DAY 5
- *Recognising the hours on an analogue clock*
- *Reading the time to the hour*

A large analogue clock with movable hands

- Set the clock hands to 2 o'clock. Point to the big hand. *The big hand is pointing upwards, so it is something o'clock. What time is it? Two o'clock.*
- Very slowly, wind the big hand saying T*ick, tock, tick, tock* as you turn the hand. Children join in. Stop at 3 o'clock.
- Point to the big hand and the little hand. *What time is it now?* Help children say 3 o'clock by looking at the little hand.
- Point to how much you turned the big hand. *It went right round the clock once. Two o'clock to three o'clock is one hour. In one hour the big hand goes right round the clock.*
- *One hour is quite a long time.* Talk about the things you can do in one hour, e.g. watch a favourite programme twice, go to the park, and so on.
- Repeat, moving the big hand another hour forwards. Discuss the new time, and the fact that the big hand travels right round the clock once in one hour.

	DAY 1	DAY 2	DAY 3	DAY 4	DAY 5
Objective	Counting to 20, recognising numbers to 20, counting sounds and movements, estimating quantities				
Teacher-led activities *On the rug* (pages 77–78)	**Warm up:** Sing the days of the week. **Activity:** Choose a child to unpeg the number 11 card from the line. *What number is this?* If necessary, help by counting in a whisper to 11. Ask another child to do 11 wing flaps. Everyone counts to check. Demonstrate how to write '11', and children write it on the floor in front of them. Choose another child to unpeg 17 and repeat, counting hops. Repeat for 14 claps.	**Warm up:** Count to 40 using fingers. **Activity:** Point to each number on a number grid. Show children a box of 18 chess pieces. *How many pieces do you think it contains?* Encourage children to write their own guess on the board, showing them how to form the numerals. Count the pieces, grouping them in twos to help count. Write the actual number. Compare with children's guesses. Who was close?	**Warm up:** Count up to 20 then down to *Blast off!* **Activity:** Shuffle the cards. Spread them out, face down. Choose a child to take a card. *What number have you taken?* Ask him to 'laugh' (ha, ha, ha, ...) that many times. The rest of the class keeps a whispered count to check. Write the number on the board and children copy, writing it on the floor. Repeat, thinking of a different noise to count each time.	**Warm up:** Count to 60 as fast as possible. **Activity:** Show children a packet of snacks. *How many snacks in this packet?* Children write guesses on the board. Tip out the snacks. Count them onto a plate, grouping in twos, up to 10. Choose a child to hold the plate. Repeat, counting onto a new plate, until the snacks are counted, grouping in twos, then tens. *How many snacks?* Repeat the game.	**Warm up:** Sing the days of the week. **Activity:** Hand out number cards (2 to 19). Children do not show each other their cards. Choose a child. Ask her to look at her number and jump that many times. The other children count the jumps. Check that her number matches her jumps. Any child also holding that number stands up. Choose another child and repeat.
Teacher-initiated activities *Activity Book* (page 18)	**Easy:** Use a number track (1 to 10) and counters placed on 1. Spin a coin. Tails – move one space forwards, heads – move two spaces forwards. When a child lands on a number, the others give him an action to do that many times. If he counts correctly, he takes a cube. Continue until one child reaches number 10. The child with most cubes wins. **Medium:** Make a large 5 × 6 grid (1 to 30) with counters placed on 1. Spin a coin. Tails – move sideways one place (either direction), heads – move down or up one space. Children make a noise of their choice that many times. If they are correct, they take a cube. When one child lands on 30, they all count their cubes. The child with the most cubes wins. **Hard:** Children estimate the number of beads in a mug. Write their estimates. Tip out and count, grouping in twos and then tens. Compare their estimates with the total.				
Independent activities *Supported play*	**Painting:** Each child chooses a number. They paint it at the top of the page, forming the numeral carefully. They paint a picture using a matching number of colours.	**Cooking:** Children decorate a small pizza base with slices of mushroom, cheese pieces and tomato slices. They estimate how many of each, then count. Bake in a preheated oven as directed.	**Construction:** Children make a large model using lots of different-coloured building bricks. *How many bricks altogether? Write your guess and then count.*	**Water:** Children estimate how many small cups will fill a teapot. They check by filling it with water and counting. Repeat for other containers.	**Dominoes:** Make a line of number cards (1 to 12). Beside each card, children lay a domino with a matching total number of dots. They continue until all the dominoes have been used.
Language	**Number names one to twenty, more, less, how many?, before, after, count**				
At home	***How many steps?*** Select a distance of about no more than 15 steps in your garden, along a path or between two shops. *About how many steps will it be from the front door to the gate?* Remember your child's estimate and then ask them to walk the distance and count their steps. *How close were you to your guess?* Repeat for other short distances.				
Resources	Washing line with large number cards (1 to 20) pegged to it, pegs, paint, paintbrushes	A box of chess pieces, washing line with large number cards (1 to 20) pegged to it, pegs, pizza base, toppings	Large number cards (1 to 20), washing line with large number cards (1 to 20) pegged to it, pegs, building bricks	Small packets of snacks, plates, number track (1 to 20), number grid (1 to 100), teapot, cups, containers, water	Large number cards (2 to 19 – enough for one for each child), dominoes

- Sing the days of the week together.
- Count together to 40, using fingers to mark the units. Point to each number on a 1 to 100 number grid as it is said.
- Count up to 20 then back to 1, shouting *Blast off!* together at the end.
- Count together to 60. Encourage the children to count as fast as they can.
- Sing the days of the week together. Encourage the children to remember the order by starting at days other than Monday.

DAY 1
- *Counting to 20*
- *Counting sounds and movements*

A washing line with large number cards (1 to 20) pegged to it, pegs

- Count along the number line to 20.
- Choose a child to unpeg the number 11 from the line. *What number is this?* If children do not know, help by counting in a whisper to 11. *It is eleven.*
- Ask another child to do 11 wing flaps. Everyone counts to check.
- *We can write eleven.* Demonstrate how to write '11', starting each numeral at the top. Ask children to write it on the floor in front of them with their finger.
- Repeat with two different children for 17 hops, then 14 claps.

DAY 2
- *Counting to 20*
- *Estimating quantities*

A box of chess pieces, a washing line with large number cards (1 to 20) pegged to it, pegs

- Show children the box of 18 chess pieces. *How many pieces in this box?* Choose a child. Help him to write his guess on the board, forming the numeral correctly.
- Encourage other children to write their guesses on the board, each time showing them how to form the numerals.
- Count the chess pieces together, taking them out of the box as you count each one, and grouping them in twos to help count.
- Write the actual number. Compare this number with the guesses. *Which was the closest guess?* Look at the numbers on the number line to check.

DAY 3
- *Counting sounds and movements*

Large number cards (1 to 20), a washing line with large number cards (1 to 20) pegged to it, pegs

- Shuffle the number cards. Spread them out face down.
- Choose a child to take a card. *Which number have you taken?* Find that number on the number line.
- Ask him to laugh (ha, ha, ha, ...) a matching number of times. The rest of the class keeps a whispered count to check.
- Write the number on the board, demonstrating how to write the numeral. Children copy this, writing it on the floor with a finger.
- Repeat, thinking of a different noise to count each time.

DAY 4 • *Counting to 20*
• *Estimating quantities*

Small packets of snacks, plates, a number track (1 to 20), a number grid (1 to 100)

- Show the children a packet of snacks. *How many snacks in this packet?* Choose a child to write his guess on the board. Help him to form the numeral correctly. Children copy this, writing it on the floor with a finger.
- Choose several other children to write their guesses on the board. Children copy the numerals, writing them on the floor with fingers.
- Tip out the snacks. Count them together onto a plate, grouping them in twos as you count them. Count ten onto the plate and choose a child to hold it.
- Repeat, counting onto a new plate each time, until you have counted all the snacks, grouping in twos and then tens.
- *How many snacks?* Compare the children's guesses. Look at the actual number and their guesses on the number track or grid. *Which guess was closest?*

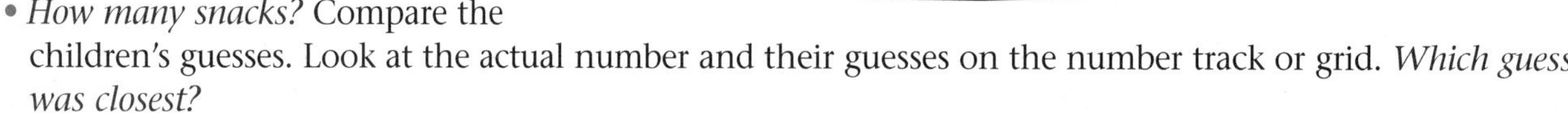

- Repeat the guessing game using another packet of snacks.

DAY 5 • *Counting sounds and movements*

Large number cards (2 to 19 – enough for one for each child)

- Give out one number card to each child. Choose carefully which card to give each child. Children do not show each other their cards.
- Choose a child. Ask her to look at her number and, very carefully and slowly, to jump that many times. The other children count the jumps. *How many jumps?* Check that her number matches the count.
- Any other children holding the same number stand up.
- Repeat several times with different children and different actions.

	DAY 1	DAY 2	DAY 3	DAY 4	DAY 5
Objective	Counting to 100, counting on from a given number, saying the 'next' number to any given number				
Teacher-led activities *On the rug* (pages 80–81)	**Warm up:** Sing a number song. **Activity:** Count together to 100, marking the units. If necessary, help children with each multiple of ten, but once they start that decade, e.g. *Fifty-one, fifty-two, …* they continue alone. Count again to 100, pointing to each number on the number grid as they say it. Point out numbers that 'say themselves', e.g **nine**ty-five and those that do not, e.g. **thir**ty-**five**.	**Warm up:** Show fingers to match numbers to 10. Show one less, then one more. **Activity:** Count slowly to 20, pointing at the numbers on the number grid as you count. Point to 1 to 10, then point to 21, 22, 23, 24 … Show that the units are the same as the numbers in the top row. Count along another row, e.g. 41, 42, 43, … Show that the units are the same. Choose a child to point to a number. *Does it say itself?* Help children work out the number.	**Warm up:** Count from 50 to 100 using fingers. **Activity:** Choose a child to unpeg the first number card from the line, choose another child to take the second number. Continue, making a line of 20 children, each holding a number. Choose a child not in the line to point to a number, e.g. 6. *What is the next number? Seven.* Ask the child holding that number to jump that many times. Repeat with different children.	**Warm up:** Count from 30 to 70 using fingers. **Activity:** Give each child a number card. They match their card with fingers and toes. Those with 'teen' numbers use both feet stretched out (ten toes) and hold up fingers. Those with numbers less than or equal to 10 use only fingers. Choose a child. *Can you find someone holding the next number?* If they succeed, they choose another child to repeat this.	**Warm up:** Count back from 20 to *Blast off!* **Activity:** Make teddy count a row of the number grid incorrectly. Children correct it. Repeat. Cover all the multiples of 10 with Post-it notes. Count to 100, all together, pointing to a different child to say each number in turn. Any child who says a multiple of 10 removes the Post-it note. Count down the multiples of 10.
Teacher-initiated activities *Activity Book* (page 19)	**Easy:** Use a number track (1 to 12) and counters placed on 1. Spin a coin. Tails – move one place forwards, heads move two places forwards. *Say the number you land on. Say the next number.* If children are correct, they move to that number. Otherwise, they move back three spaces. The first to 12 wins. **Medium:** Use a number track (1 to 20) and different-coloured cubes for each child. Children choose a number and say it. They cover the next number with a cube and say what it is. If they are not correct, they remove their cube. Keep playing until all the numbers are covered. *Who has covered most numbers?* **Hard:** Shuffle number cards (1 to 100) and place them in a pile, face down. Children take turns to take a card and order them all in a line.				
Independent activities *Supported play*	**Playhouse:** Children find different places to stick numbers, e.g. door numbers, telephone numbers, clock face numbers.	**Cooking:** Children make milkshakes using the recipe in the Recipe Bank (page 119). Stick numbers on the straws and place them in the milkshake. Children take a straw and say the number.	**Construction:** Use a number grid (1 to 100). Each child chooses a number and builds a model with that number of building bricks. Can the others guess the number of bricks?	**Painting:** Children choose a multiple of 10. They Blu-tack a matching number of 10p coins to the page and paint over them. When the paint is dry, remove the coins and paint the spaces silver. Write the amount. Wash the coins to clean them.	**Threading:** Each child uses large wooden beads to make a long necklace. They ask others in their group to guess how many beads. They write the guesses and say who is closest.
Language	Count, count on, number names one to one hundred, backwards, forwards, next, after, before				
At home	*Counting leaves* **Leaves** When you are out on a walk or in the garden, encourage your child to collect lots of leaves that have fallen on the ground. Help your child to count the leaves. How far can they count? *How many leaves have you collected?*				
Resources	Large number grid (1 to 100)	Large number grid (1 to 100), Post-it notes, milkshake mix, straws	Washing line with large number cards (1 to 20) pegged to it, pegs, number grid (1 to 100), building bricks	Large number cards (1 to 20 – enough for one per child), 10p coins, Blu-tack, paint, paintbrushes	A teddy, large number cards (1 to 100), Post-it notes, large wooden beads, string

- Sing a number song together.
- Say a number between 1 and 10. *Six*. The children hold up that number of fingers. Ask them to fold down one finger to show one less. *How many now? Stretch out that finger again. How many now?*
- Count together from 50 to 100, using fingers to mark the units. Help the children with the multiples of 10 if they are unsure.
- Count together from 30 to 70, using fingers to mark the units.
- Count backwards from 20 to 1, then shout *Blast off!* together.

WARM UPS

DAY 1

- *Counting to 100*

Large number grid (1 to 100)

- Count together to 100, using fingers to mark the units. If necessary, help children with each multiple of ten, but once they start that decade – e.g. *Fifty-one, fifty-two,* ... they continue alone.
- Count along the number grid, pointing to each number on the first row as you count. Count slowly and deliberately, stressing each number on the top row of the grid.
- Continue counting on from 10. Point to each number on the grid as you say it.
- When children reach 100, stress 100.
- Point to the numbers in the last row, 91, 92, 93, 94, ... *These numbers help us by saying themselves.* Stress ***nine***ty-***five***, pointing to the 9 and the 5. Stress how each number on this row 'says' itself.
- Point to the numbers in the third row. Count along these, pointing out that they do not say their numbers. Explain that ***thir***ty-five would really be ***three***ty-five, if it followed the rules!
- Look at different numbers, discussing whether they 'say' themselves, e.g. ***Six***ty-one, ***six***ty-two all say themselves, but ***fif***ty-one, ***fif***ty-two do not.
- Stress that as we go down the grid, the numbers get larger.

DAY 2

- *Counting to 100*

Large number grid (1 to 100), Post-it notes

- Count slowly along the top two rows of the number grid to 20. Point to the numbers on the grid as you count.
- Point to the top row, 1 to 10, then point to 21, 22, 23, ... 29. Cover the tens digit in each number in this row with a Post-it note. *The units in this row are the same as the numbers in the first row.* Demonstrate.
- Count along another row, e.g. 41, 42, 43, ... Show that the units are the same again.
- Choose a child to point to a number. Look at the tens digit. *Does it say itself? **For**ty-six does say itself, but **thir**ty-six does not.* Help children to work out which number it is.
- Repeat, looking at numbers which do say themselves and numbers which do not.

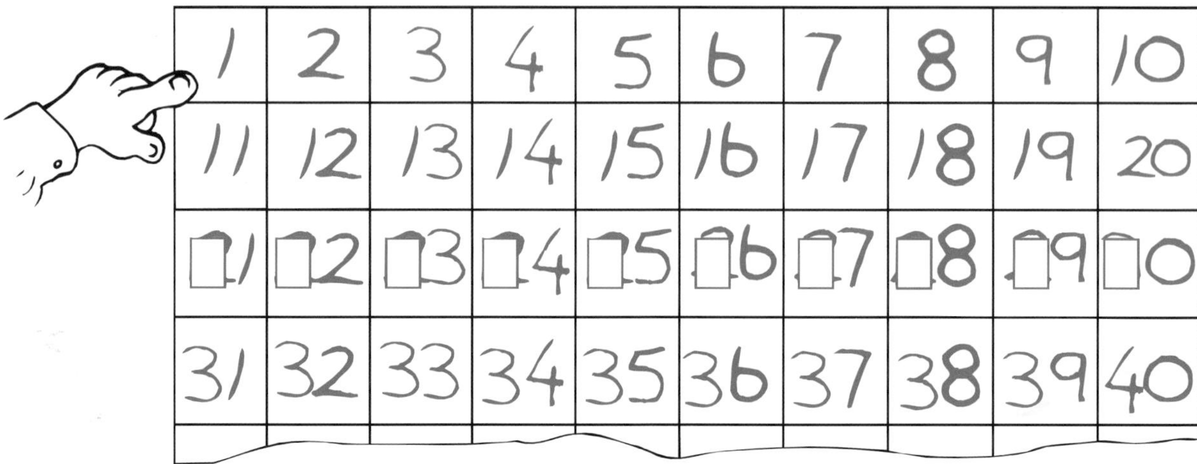

DAY 3 • *Saying the next number*

A washing line with large number cards (1 to 20) pegged to it, pegs

- Look at the number line. Choose a child to unpeg the first number card, then choose another to unpeg the second number card, and so on.
- Make a line of the 20 children, each holding a number card.
- Choose a child not in the line to point to a number, e.g. 6. *What is the next number? Seven.* Ask the child holding the next number to jump that many times.
- Repeat, asking every child not in the line to point to a number and say the next number. If they say the next number correctly, they give that child an action to do, e.g. hop, flap their arms, touch their toes.

DAY 4 • *Saying the next number*

Large number cards (1 to 20 – enough for one per child)

- Give each child a number card. They match the number on their card with fingers and toes. *We use the toes as the 'ten' and the fingers as the 'units'.* Those with 'teen' numbers use both feet stretched in front of them (ten toes) and an appropriate number of fingers held up, e.g. *Thirteen is ten toes (feet stretched out) and three fingers.* Children with numbers less than 10 just use fingers.
- Choose a child. *Can you find someone holding the next number to yours?* If they succeed, they choose another child to repeat this. Continue.
- Say a number, e.g. *Sixteen.* Hold up the card and ask all children to make this number using their fingers and toes.
- Repeat.

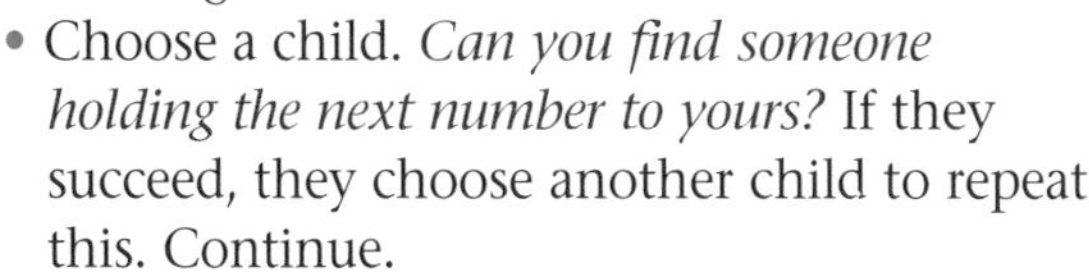

DAY 5 • *Counting to 100*

A teddy, a large number grid (1 to 100), Post-it notes

- Make the teddy count a row of the number grid incorrectly. Children correct it. Repeat.
- Cover all the multiples of 10 with Post-it notes. Count together to 100, pointing to a different child to say each number in turn (i.e. counting round the class). Point to each number on the grid as children say it.
- When you reach 10, ask the child who has to say the number to come to the grid. *What number is it?* He removes the Post-it note. Say the number together.
- Continue, counting round the class and asking children saying a multiple of 10 to remove the Post-it note.
- Count down the multiples of 10 from 100 to 10.

	DAY 1	DAY 2	DAY 3	DAY 4	DAY 5
Objective	**Numbers to 20: counting up to 20 objects, estimating, recording numbers to mark the number in a set**				
Teacher-led activities *On the rug* (pages 83–84)	**Warm up:** Count to 100 as fast as possible. **Activity:** Whilst children close their eyes, put 19 satsumas into the bag. Show children the bag. *How many satsumas?* Record their guesses, encouraging them to write these on the board. Tip out the satsumas. Show how to count them, grouping in fives. Write the number on the board. Which guess was closest? Repeat for 12 satsumas. Give out the satsumas to eat.	**Warm up:** Count from 40 to 80 using fingers. **Activity:** *How many pages in this book? Look at the pages. There are no page numbers.* Take estimates and write them on the board. Count the pages together, counting in twos as you look at each pair of pages. *How many pages?* Compare guesses. *Which guess was closest?* Count again and number the pages. Choose a child to find page 12. Repeat for other pages.	**Warm up:** Count back from 20 to *Blast off!* **Activity:** *How many spots on this ladybird?* Children write their guesses on pieces of paper. Rehearse writing the numerals, starting at the top. *How shall we count the spots so that we don't miss any or count some twice?* Take suggestions – then show how to group visually in fives when counting. Compare the total with their guesses.	**Warm up:** Say a number rhyme. **Activity:** *I have lost the box for this jigsaw.* Show children the bag of pieces. *How many pieces?* Record their guesses, encouraging children to write the numbers, starting at the top. Tip out the pieces. Remind children to group in fives as they count. Compare the total with their guesses, using the number line to see which guess was closest. Ask a few children to do the jigsaw.	**Warm up:** Show fingers to match numbers to 10. Show one less, then one more. **Activity:** *How many leaves on this twig?* Encourage children to estimate and record their guesses. Count the leaves together, grouping in twos. Compare the total with their guesses. Show children the second twig. *How many will you guess this time?* Look for estimates based on the number on the first twig. Count the number and compare the totals.
Teacher-initiated activities *Activity Book* (page 19)	**Easy:** Shuffle the number cards (1 to 20) and place them in a pile face down. Children take a card each. *Whose number is largest?* Children each make a tower with that number of cubes. *Who has made the tallest tower?* They write the number. Replace the card on the bottom of the pile. Repeat until someone has written five numbers. **Medium:** Choose a small book. Children count how many pages of story there are (not including non-story pages). They make their own small books. *How many pages?* **Hard:** Use a small box of paperclips. Children guess how many. They work out how to group them to count them accurately.				
Independent activities *Supported play*	**Sand:** Build a ziggurat (spiral castle) by smoothing a spade around the outside of a sand castle made from damp sand. Children roll marbles down the spiral. *How many can you roll before one falls off?* They guess first, then roll.	**Cooking:** Mix raisins in 150 g of melted chocolate and leave to cool in a tin. Cut into pieces. Guess how many raisins are in each piece, then count them. Enjoy the raisins.	**Playhouse:** Children decide how many toys are coming for tea. They count plates, cups, etc. They use the telephone to call each toy to invite them and match spoken and written numerals when giving the number.	**Drawing:** Children draw a large vehicle with 20 wheels. *Make your vehicle as interesting as you can.*	**Cutting and sticking:** Cut out large card ladybirds. Children stick bright spots on each. *How many spots?*
Language	**Count, how many?, number names one to twenty, less than, more than, guess, closest**				
At home	*Copying numbers* **Felt-tipped pens or coloured pencils, paper** Write the numbers from 1 to 10 in a row, leaving space below each number. Give the paper to your child and ask them to copy the numbers underneath using different-coloured pens or pencils. Encourage them to practise the numbers that they found difficult several times.				
Resources	A cloth bag, 20 satsumas, washing line with large number cards (1 to 20) pegged to it, pegs, sandpit, marbles	A picture book (with about 20 pages, not numbered), washing line with large number cards (1 to 20) pegged to it, pegs, raisins, chocolate, a tin	A large ladybird with 19 spots drawn on the board, pieces of paper, toys, tea party items, telephone	A mesh bag with a jigsaw in pieces (about 20), a tray, washing line with large numbers (1 to 20) pegged to it, pegs, crayons or colouring pencils	Two twigs with about 20 large leaves on each, washing line with large number cards (1 to 20) pegged to it, pegs, card, glue, scissors

- Count together to 100, using fingers to mark the units. Encourage the children to count as fast as they can.
- Count together from 40 to 80, using fingers to mark the units.
- Count backwards from 20 to 0, then shout *Blast off!* together.
- Together say a number rhyme, which involves counting down.
- Say a number between 1 and 10. *Eight.* The children hold up that number of fingers. Ask them to fold down one finger to show one less. *How many now? Stretch out that finger again. How many now?*

DAY 1

- *Counting up to 20 objects*
- *Estimating and recording numbers*

A cloth bag, 20 satsumas, a washing line with large number cards (1 to 20) pegged to it, pegs

- Whilst children close their eyes, put 19 satsumas into the bag.
- Show children the bag. *How many satsumas do you think are in this bag?* Encourage children to discuss in pairs and to make sensible guesses.
- Choose a child to write her guess on the board, demonstrating how to write the numerals. Help other children to record their guesses, encouraging them to write them on the board.
- Tip out the satsumas. Show how to count them, grouping in fives to make them easier to count accurately. Write the total on the board.
- Compare the actual number with their guesses. Use the number line to establish which guess was closest.
- Repeat for 12 satsumas. Record children's guesses, then count, grouping in fives.
- Share out the satsumas to eat.

DAY 2

- *Counting up to 20 objects*
- *Estimating and recording numbers*

A picture book (with about 20 pages, not numbered), a washing line with large number cards (1 to 20) pegged to it, pegs

- Show the class the book. *How many pages long is this book? Look at the pages. There are no page numbers! How many pages do you think the book has?* Flick through the book so children can estimate.
- Encourage children to discuss with a partner and make a sensible estimate. Choose a child to write their guess on the board. Demonstrate how to write the numerals. Help other children to write their estimates on the board.
- Count the pages together, counting in twos as you look at each pair of pages. *How many pages?*
- Compare the total with their guesses, using the number line to match the numbers. Which was the closest guess?
- Count the pages again and number them. Choose a child to find page 12.
- Repeat finding other pages.

DAY 3

- *Counting up to 20 objects*
- *Estimating and recording numbers*

A large ladybird with 19 spots drawn on the board, pieces of paper

- Show children the ladybird. *How many spots?* Encourage children to work in pairs to guess sensibly.
- Each pair of children agree their guess and write the number on a piece of paper. Rehearse how to write the numerals, starting at the top. If necessary, demonstrate on the board.
- Point to the ladybird. *How can we count the spots so that we know that we count each one and don't miss any or count some twice.* Take suggestions – then show them how to group visually in fives as they count.
- Compare the actual number with their guesses. Use the number line to compare numbers. *Which was the closest guess? Which guess was furthest away?*

DAY 4

- *Counting up to 20 objects*
- *Estimating and recording numbers*

A mesh bag with a jigsaw in pieces (about 20), a washing line with large number cards (1 to 20) pegged to it, pegs, a tray

- Show children the bag with the jigsaw pieces. *I have lost the box. How many pieces do you think there are?*
- Encourage children to work together to make a sensible guess. Record their guesses on the board, choosing children to come and write their number, demonstrating how to write the numerals starting at the top.
- Tip out the jigsaw pieces onto a tray. Choose a pair of children to count. Remind children to group the pieces in fives as they count.
- Compare the total with their guesses, using the number line to see which guess was closest.
- Give a few children the jigsaw to complete.

DAY 5

- *Counting up to 20 objects*
- *Estimating and recording numbers*

Two twigs with about 20 large leaves on each, a washing line with large number cards (1 to 20) pegged to it, pegs

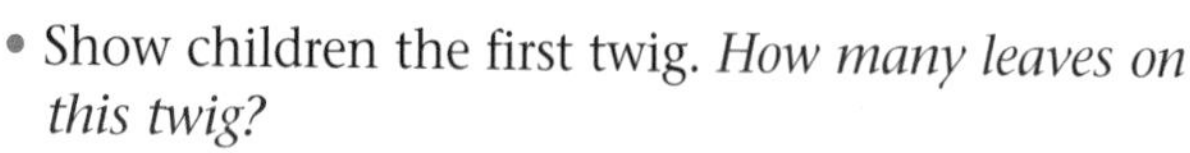

- Show children the first twig. *How many leaves on this twig?*
- Encourage children to estimate and record their guesses. If necessary, demonstrate how to write the numerals.
- Count the leaves together, grouping in twos to help count. *How many leaves altogether?* Record the total alongside their guesses.

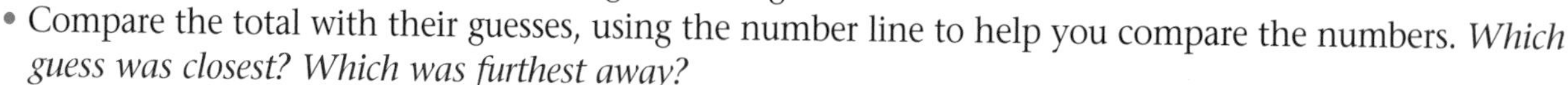

- Compare the total with their guesses, using the number line to help you compare the numbers. *Which guess was closest? Which was furthest away?*
- Show children the second twig. *How many will you guess this time?* Look for estimates based on the number on the first twig.
- Count the number on the second twig, grouping in twos again.
- Compare the total with the total number on the last twig. *Which twig had more leaves? Which had fewer?*

	DAY 1	DAY 2	DAY 3	DAY 4	DAY 5
Objective	Beginning to use the language of direction, moving in given directions in relation to a starting point				
Teacher-led activities *On the rug* (pages 86–87)	**Warm up:** Count to 60 using fingers. **Activity:** Draw a cross on the board to show four directions: up, down, left, right. Point to each direction and demonstrate it. Point to an animal in the middle of the grid. Point to another animal. *How do we get from the first animal to the second?* A child gives directions. *Up one space, left two spaces, ...* Repeat, choosing another animal as a starting point.	**Warm up:** Sing a number song. **Activity:** Blu-tack the spider onto the middle of the grid on the board. Choose a child to specify a direction for the spider. *Up four spaces.* Choose another child to move the spider in that direction. Choose another child to specify a new direction and continue like this, moving the spider around the board. Stress the direction words, 'up', 'down', 'left', 'right'.	**Warm up:** Show fingers to match numbers to 10. Show one less, then one more. **Activity:** Stand a child in front of the class and blindfold her. Choose a child to give her directions. *Walk four steps forwards.* Help the blindfolded child to do this. Choose a different child to give a new direction. *Walk three steps left.* Continue. Before you remove the blindfold, ask her where she thinks she is. Repeat with a different blindfolded child.	**Warm up:** Count to 50 as fast as possible. **Activity:** Ask four children to hold the corners of the grid flat on the rug. Put the teddy on one corner. Put the packet of biscuits on the corner diagonally opposite. Ask children to give directions to help the teddy reach the biscuits. Children use words like 'forwards', 'backwards', 'left', 'right', 'up', 'down'. Make the teddy make mistakes sometimes. The teddy shares the biscuits.	**Warm up:** Count from 50 to 100 using fingers. **Activity:** Ask children to sit on the floor with some space around them. Demonstrate the four directions: stand up, sit down, look left, look right. Use just the direction word to indicate the action, e.g. 'up' and children stand up, 'down' and they sit down. Give instructions. Who follows correctly? Repeat. Make sure that they all follow.
Teacher-initiated activities *Activity Book* (page 20)	**Easy:** Use a large 4 × 4 grid and a soft toy. One child gives directions and the other child moves the toy around the grid. Choose two other children to have a turn. Place an object on the grid and choose two more children to direct the toy to it. **Medium:** Use cartoon stickers and a large 4 × 4 grid. Choose a child to place one sticker in the middle of the grid. That child gives an instruction to the next child to place the next sticker. *Move up two spaces and left one space.* Continue with other children. **Hard:** Use a large 5 × 5 grid. Place three different-coloured counters on the grid. Children take turns to place new counters on the grid following instructions in relation to the existing counters. *Start at the red counter, move down two spaces and right three spaces.* Encourage very specific language.				
Independent activities *Supported play*	**Toy garage:** Make a grid car park. Children give directions to each other as they drive each toy car from the garage to park in the car park. *Up two and left three.*	**Cooking:** Children make biscuits using the recipe in the Recipe Bank (page 119), adding 150 g chocolate chips to the mixture. When cooled, hide the biscuits and give directions to find them.	**Construction:** Children build a complicated track, like a maze. They give directions to drive a toy car round the track.	**Painting:** Children paint a maze using short thick lines. When they have painted it, they try to direct a toy spider around it.	**Cutting and sticking:** Children stick strips on paper to divide the paper into quarters. They stick different-coloured shapes in each quadrant.
Language	**Up, down, left, right, forwards, backwards, direction**				
At home	***From room to room*** Help your child to explain how to get from one room to another in your house, using as much directional language as possible. *Walk two steps to the kitchen door, open the door, turn left, walk six steps forwards. Climb up the stairs. At the top of the stairs turn right. Walk past one door and turn left into my bedroom.* Encourage them to describe the journey in the opposite direction.				
Resources	A 4 × 4 grid with five animals drawn on it (each in a different space), toy cars, a grid car park	A 9 × 9 grid (drawn on the board) a plastic spider, Blu-tack, biscuit mix, chocolate chips	A blindfold, construction materials, toy cars	A large 5 × 5 grid (drawn on light paper or card), a teddy, a packet of biscuits, paint, paintbrushes, a toy spider	Coloured paper, shapes, scissors, glue

- Count together to 60, using fingers to mark the units.
- Together sing a number song, which involves counting down.
- Say a number between 1 and 10. *Three.* The children hold up that number of fingers. Ask them to fold down one finger to show one less. *How many now?* Stretch out that finger again. *How many now?*
- Count together from 1 to 50. Encourage the children to count as fast as they can.
- Count together from 50 to 100, using fingers to mark the units.

DAY 1

- *Beginning to use the language of direction*

A 4 × 4 grid with five animals drawn on it (each in a different space)

- Draw a vertical line and horizontal line on the board to make a cross.
- Point to the vertical line. Run your finger up the line and off the top. *This is upwards.* Run your finger down the line and off the bottom. *This is downwards.*
- Point to the horizontal line. Rub your finger along the line and off the left side. *This is going left.* Run your finger back along the line and off the right side. *This is going right.*
- Use the vertical and horizontal line to repeat the four directions, up, down, left and right. Point to each direction and demonstrate it.
- Point to an animal in the middle of the grid. Point to another animal. *How do we get from the first animal to the second?* A child gives directions. *Up one space, left two spaces, ...*
- Point to another animal. Choose a child to describe how to get from this animal to the first. They should use up or down, left or right, and count the number of spaces.
- Repeat, choosing another animal as a starting point.
- Point to an animal. Give directions to reach another animal. *What animal have I visited?*

DAY 2

- *Beginning to use the language of direction*
- *Moving in given directions in relation to a starting point*

A 9 × 9 grid (drawn on the board), a plastic spider, Blu-tack

- Point to the grid on the board. *I have divided the board into a number of spaces.*
- Blu-tack the spider onto the middle of the grid. Discuss where it is. *The spider is in the middle.*
- Choose a child to specify a direction for the spider to walk in. *Go up four spaces.* Choose another child to move the spider in that direction.
- Choose another child to tell the spider a new direction and continue, moving the spider around the grid. Stress the direction words, 'up', 'down', 'left' and 'right'.

DAY 3
- *Beginning to use the language of direction*
- *Moving in given directions in relation to a starting point*

A blindfold

- Choose a child. Stand her in front of the class and blindfold her. *She cannot see where she is going. We must give her directions.*
- Choose a child to give the blindfolded child directions. *Walk four steps forwardss.* Help the blindfolded child to do this.
- Choose a different child to give a new direction to the blindfolded child. *Walk three steps left.*
- Continue, helping the child to move. Encourage the use of directions such as forwardss, backwards, left, right. Help children remember their left from their right by holding out their hand palm down with the thumb stretched at right-angles to the rest of the hand and forming an 'L' for Left with the left hand.
- Before you remove the blindfold, ask the child where she thinks she is. *Is she right?*
- Repeat with a different child.

DAY 4
- *Beginning to use the language of direction*
- *Moving in given directions in relation to a starting point*

A large 5 x 5 grid (drawn on light card or paper), a teddy, a packet of biscuits

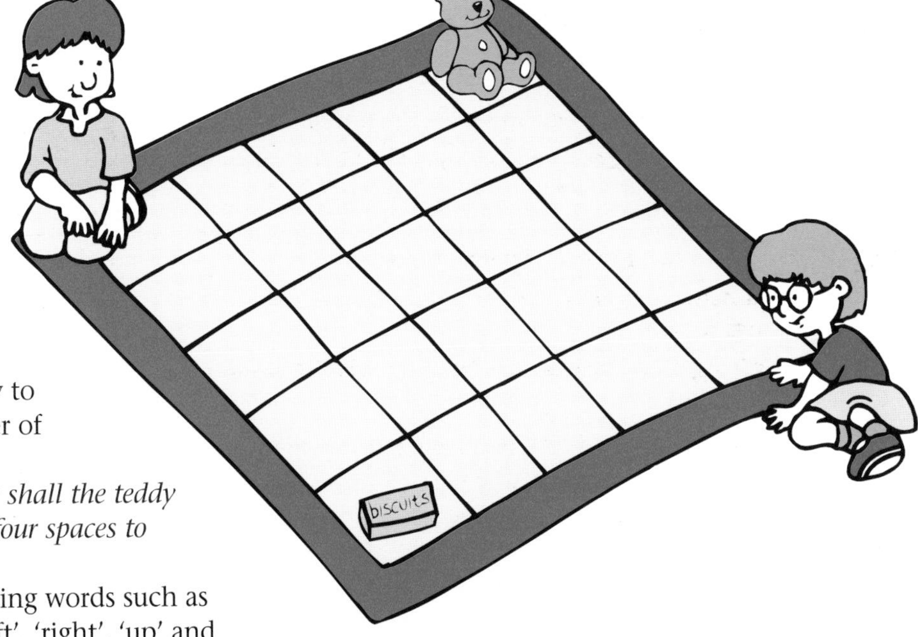

- Show children the grid. Ask four children to hold the corners of the grid flat on the rug.
- Place the teddy on one corner of the grid. Place the packet of biscuits on the corner diagonally opposite. *The teddy wants to get to the biscuits! Can we help him? We need to give him directions.*
- Ask children to suggest directions to help the teddy to move to the opposite corner of the grid.
- Choose a child. *Which way shall the teddy move first? Move the teddy four spaces to the right.*
- Children give directions, using words such as 'forwardss', 'backwards', 'left', 'right', 'up' and 'down'. Make the teddy make mistakes sometimes to check the children can correct them.

- Continue until the teddy reaches the biscuits.
- The teddy shares the biscuits between children so they get one each.

DAY 5
- *Beginning to use the language of direction*

- Ask children to sit on the floor with some space around them.
- Demonstrate the four directions: stand ***up***, sit ***down***, look ***left***, look ***right***.
- Use just the word to indicate the action, e.g. 'up' and children stand up, 'down' and they sit down, etc.
- *Up*. Children stand up. *Left*. Children look to the left.
- Continue to give a set of instructions. Who follows correctly?
- Repeat. Make sure that all children follow the instructions correctly.

	DAY 1	DAY 2	DAY 3	DAY 4	DAY 5
Objective	Adding by counting on, subtracting by counting back, beginning to know the number one more or one less				
Teacher-led activities *On the rug* (pages 89–90)	**Warm up:** Count to 50 using fingers. **Activity:** Lay large number cards (1 to 20) along the rug to make a track. Place the teddy on 7. *The teddy is on seven. He is going forwards two spaces.* Write '7 + 2 =' on the board. Choose a child to move the teddy forwards two spaces. *What number is he on now?* Write '9' and read the addition. Repeat, placing the teddy on 12 and moving it three spaces.	**Warm up:** Count from 50 to 100 using fingers. **Activity:** Lay large number cards (1 to 20) along the rug to make a track. Choose a child to stand on 11. Write '11 +' on the board. Choose another child to throw the spotty dice. Count the spots, e.g. 5. *We shall move her five spaces.* Write '5 ='. *What number will she reach?* Move the child and write '16'. Read the addition. Repeat several times with different children.	**Warm up:** Count down from 20 to *Blast off!* **Activity:** Lay large number cards (1 to 20) along the rug to make a track. Put the cat on 12. *What number is it on?* Write '12' on the board. *The cat is going to move back two down the line.* Write 'back 2 =' beside 12. *What number will it reach?* Choose a child to move the cat two spaces back. Write '10' on the board. *Twelve back two takes us to ten.* Repeat, starting on 8 and counting back 2.	**Warm up:** Count back from 20 to 0 as fast as possible. **Activity:** Arrange the chairs in rows of two to make a 'bus'. Show children the number 10 card. *I have ten passengers on my bus.* Choose ten children and count them onto the bus. Choose a conductor to give each a ticket. Write '10' on the board. *How many if two passengers get off?* Help two passengers get off and count back from 10. Write 'back 2 = 8' on the board and read it.	**Warm up:** Show fingers to match numbers to 10. Show one less, then one more. **Activity:** *Mr Red lives at number eight. Which house will he visit if he moves forwards three houses?* Encourage children to work it out. Write the matching addition, and read it together, '8 + 3 = 11'. Take Mr Red back to number 8. *What house will he visit if he goes back three houses?* Move him to find out. Repeat with a different cut-out person, starting on 6.
Teacher-initiated activities *Activity Book* (pages 20–21)	**Easy:** Use a number track (1 to 20) and building bricks. Each child chooses a number on the track and matches that number to bricks. They say how many they will have if they take three more. If they are correct, they keep the bricks. They have six turns. *Build a model with your bricks.* **Medium:** Use a home-made ladder (1 to 20). Ask a child to place a toy cat on the ladder. *Where will the cat be if we move it up three rungs?* Write the number sentence on the board. Ask a child to move the cat to check. Children who were correct take a cube. Repeat, moving the cat back three spaces. Repeat for different numbers. **Hard:** Use a number track (1 to 20) and counters placed on 10. Spin a coin. Heads – move three places forwards, tails – move two places backwards. *Say the number you will land on before you move your counter.* The first child to reach 1 or 20 wins.				
Independent activities *Supported play*	**Toys:** Make a line of ten chairs and put a large number card on each. One child places the teddy on a chair. *What chair number will the teddy sit on if it moves forwards or back two spaces? Three spaces?*	**Cooking:** Children make flapjacks using the recipe in the Recipe Bank (page 119). *How many have we made? How many will there be if we eat two?*	**Construction:** Children build a tall tower from building bricks. Ask questions. *How many bricks if you add one more? How many if you take off one? Add two? Take off two?*	**Role play:** Children play buses. *How many passengers? How many tickets are needed? How many get on? How many now?*	**Papier mâché:** Make a ladder and number the rungs. Children play track games up the ladder. First child to the top wins.
Language	Number names one to twenty, add, and, more, less, forwards, back, backwards, take away, count back, makes, leaves				
At home	***Hidden treasure*** **Two plates, ten counters/buttons/1p coins** Ask your child to count out ten small items, e.g. coins. Hide seven of them under one plate. *How many coins are under the plate?* Place the remaining coins on the other plate. *How many coins are there altogether?* Touch the plate hiding the seven coins. *Seven.* Count on the other coins, touching each one. *Eight, nine, ten.* Repeat, hiding a different number of coins.				
Resources	Large number cards (1 to 20), a teddy, chairs	Large number cards (1 to 20), a spotty dice (1 to 6), flapjack mix	Large number cards (1 to 20), a toy cat, washing line with large number cards (1 to 20) pegged to it, pegs, building bricks	Large number cards (1 to 20), tickets, chairs	A line of houses drawn on the board, cut-out people (each a different colour), Blu-tack, papier mâché mix

- Count together to 50, using fingers to mark the units. Stress the multiples of 5 by waving one hand in the air. Stress the multiples of 10 by waving both hands in the air.
- Count together from 50 to 100, using fingers to mark the units.
- Count down from 20 to 0, shouting *Blast off!* together at the end.
- Count backwards from 20 to 0. Encourage the children to count as fast as they can.
- Say a number between 1 and 10. *Seven.* The children to hold up that number of fingers. Ask them to fold down one finger to show one less. *How many now? Stretch out that finger again. How many now?*

WARM UPS

DAY 1

- *Adding by counting on*

Large number cards (1 to 20), a teddy

- Lay the numbers along the middle of the rug to make a number track.
- Place the teddy on the number 7 card. *What number is the teddy on? The teddy is on number seven.*
- Point to the teddy. *He is going forwards two spaces.* Write '7 + 2 =' on the board. Read this together, pointing to each number and sign as you say it. *Seven and two more make? The teddy moves forwards two spaces.*
- Choose a child to move the teddy forwards two spaces. *What number is he on now?* Help children to count on two from seven. *Seven, ... eight, nine.*
- Write '9' to complete the addition on the board and read it all together. *Seven and two more make nine. Seven move on two takes us to nine.*
- Repeat, placing the teddy on 12 and moving it three spaces on. Encourage children to say what number it will be on. Write the addition on the board and read it together.

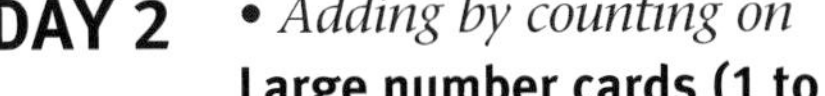

DAY 2

- *Adding by counting on*

Large number cards (1 to 20), a spotty dice (1 to 6)

- Lay the numbers along the rug to make a number track. Choose a child to stand on 11. Write '11 +' on the board.
- Choose another child to throw the spotty dice. Count the spots. *Five.* Point to the child who is standing on 11. *We shall move her this number of spaces.*
- Write more of the addition on the board, '5 ='. Read the addition together. *Eleven and five more make? What number will she reach?*
- Encourage children to work it out by counting on together 5 more from 11. Ask the child to move five spaces forwardss.
- Write the answer to complete the addition, '16'. Read it together. *Eleven and five takes us to sixteen.*
- Repeat several times, with different children moving along the track.

DAY 3 • *Subtracting by counting back*

Large number cards (1 to 20), a toy cat, a washing line with large number cards (1 to 20) pegged to it, pegs

- Lay the numbers along the rug to make a number track. Place the toy cat on 12. *What number is the cat on?* Write '12' on the board.
- *The cat is going to move back down the line.* Write 'back 2 =' beside 12. Point to 'back 2'. *Back two. The cat is going to move back two. What number will it be on?*
- Encourage children to work this out by counting back from 12. If necessary, they can use the number line to count from 20 in whispers until they reach 12.
- Choose a child to move the cat two spaces back. *Where does the cat get to? Ten.*
- Write '10' on the board to complete the addition. Read it together. *Twelve back two takes us to ten.*
- Repeat, starting on 8 and counting back 2.

DAY 4 • *Subtracting by counting back*

Large number cards (1 to 20), tickets

- Arrange the chairs in rows of two to make a 'bus'. Choose a child to be the conductor.
- Show children the number 10 card. *This is how many passengers I have on my bus.* Choose ten children and count them onto the bus. The conductor gives each passenger a ticket, counting as he does so. Write '10' on the board.
- Point to the ten children on the bus. *How many will there be if two passengers get off?* Help children to work this out by counting back from 10. *Ten, ... nine, eight.*
- Help two passengers get off the bus and count back from 10.
- Write 'back 2 = 8' on the board. Read it together. *Ten back two takes us to eight.*
- Repeat with different number cards, starting with 11 passengers and three passengers getting off.

DAY 5 • *Adding by counting on*

• *Subtracting by counting back*

A line of houses drawn on the board, cut-out people (each a different colour), Blu-tack

- Show children the line of houses. Number each house 1 to 20. Hold up the red cut-out person. *Mr Red lives at number eight.* Choose a child to point to house number 8. Blu-tack Mr Red to house number 8.
- *Which house will he visit if he moves forwardss three houses?* Encourage children to work it out by starting at 8 and counting on 3. If necessary, help children by starting at 1 and whispering to 8. Then count on 3 really loudly.
- Write the matching sum, and read it together, '8 + 3 = 11'.
- Put Mr Red back in his home at number 8. *Which house will he visit if he goes back three houses?* Encourage children to work this out by counting backwards. They can whisper the numbers from 10 to 8.

- Move Mr Red. *Eight, ... seven, six, five. Eight back three takes us to five.*
- Write the matching sentence, '8 back 3 = 5'.
- Repeat, with a different cut-out person starting on 6.

	DAY 1	DAY 2	DAY 3	DAY 4	DAY 5
Objective	Understanding addition as counting on and as the combination of two sets/partitioning of a set				
Teacher-led activities *On the rug* (pages 92–93)	**Warm up:** Sing a number song. **Activity:** Count how many teddies in the basket. Write '4' on the board. *We are going to add three more.* Remind children that there are four in the basket. Ask a child to add the three more, counting on *Five, six, seven.* Write '+ 3 = 7' on the board and read it together. Repeat, starting with five and add two more teddies. Write the addition. Repeat for 6 + 1 = 7.	**Warm up:** Count from 50 to 100 using fingers. **Activity:** *How many balloons? Seven.* Choose two children, and partition the balloons, three to one, four to the other. Count them together. Write the matching addition, '3 + 4 = 7', on the board and read it together. Count the balloons back. Repeat for 5 + 2 = 7, then 6 + 1 = 7 with different children. Stress that there are always seven balloons.	**Warm up:** Say a number rhyme. **Activity:** Put the teddy in the lift. *The teddy lives on the fourth floor of this skyscraper.* Make the lift rise to the fourth floor and Blu-tack it there. *It is four more floors to the roof garden. How tall is the building?* Write '4 + 4 =' on the board and read it together. Move the lift up four floors, counting on as you do so. Write '8' to complete the sum. Repeat for 5 + 3, 6 + 2 and 7 + 1.	**Warm up:** Count to 50 as fast as possible. **Activity:** Blu-tack the stars to the board. *How many stars? Eight.* Cover four with a cloud. *How many stars can we see? How many behind the cloud?* Point to the four visible stars. *Four.* Count on. *Five, six, seven, eight,* holding up a finger for each number. *Four hidden stars.* Write '4 + 4 = 8' on the board. Repeat, hiding three stars, then two, then one.	**Warm up:** Make animals noises to match numbers to 20. **Activity:** Ask children to show you five fingers. *How many? Now add five more. How many now? Ten.* Now fold down four. *How many now? Six.* Hold up the four again. *How many? Ten.* Now fold down three. *How many now? Seven.* Hold up the three again. *Ten.* Repeat for two folded down, then one folded. Match the finger sums to written sentences, 5 + 5 = 10, etc.
Teacher-initiated activities *Activity Book* (page 21)	**Easy:** Use a large ladybird, its back split into two sides and six movable spots. Ask a child to share out the spots equally between the sides. Write the matching sum, '3 + 3 = 6', and read it together. Ask a different child to move one spot across, and write the matching sum. Continue until all the spots are on one side. **Medium:** Use two purses and ten 1p coins. Give a purse to each of two pairs of children. Share the coins equally. *How much in each purse?* Write the addition to match. Now one pair gives 1p to the other. *How much in each purse now?* Write the sum. Continue. Repeat for other amounts. **Hard:** Create towers of ten building bricks using two colours. *How many different towers can you make? Write matching additions.*				
Independent activities *Supported play*	**Toys:** Divide eight cars between two teddies. First make it 'fair' then give one teddy a car from the other teddy's pile. *How many cars does the first teddy have now? The second teddy?* Continue until one teddy has all the cars.	**Cooking:** Children make brownies using the recipe in the Recipe Bank (page 119). Arrange eight brownies in different ways on two plates.	**Construction:** Children use construction straws to make a model. *How many straws of each colour? How many more to make ten of each colour?*	**Sand:** Use eight coins. Show the children the coins, then whilst they close their eyes, bury some of them. Show the coins you still have. *How many are buried? Can you find them?*	**Painting:** Children paint six hard-boiled eggs with acrylic paints and varnish them to make egg-men. Put some egg-men in an egg box and leave some out. Say the matching sums together.
Language	Number names one to ten, and, more, how many?, makes, together				
At home	***How many claps?*** Ask your child to show you all their fingers. *How many fingers have you got?* Tell your child to listen while you clap. *Bend down one finger for every clap you hear.* Clap up to ten times. *How many claps did you hear? How many more claps would you need to hear to make ten altogether?* Encourage your child to look at their fingers to see how many are still standing up.				
Resources	A basket, seven teddies, toy cars	Seven balloons, brownie mix, plates	An eight-floor skyscraper drawn on the board (with a lift shaft), a card lift (made from a small cardboard box open at one end), a small teddy, Blu-tack, construction straws	Eight coloured card stars, Blu-tack, a large cloud (made from black paper), coins, sandpit	Hard-boiled eggs, egg boxes, acrylic paint, varnish, paintbrushes

- Sing a number song together.
- Count together from 50 to 100, using fingers to mark the units. Encourage the children to jump up and wave both hands in the air at multiples of 10.
- Together say a number rhyme, which involves counting back.
- Count together from 1 to 50. Encourage the children to count as fast as they can.
- Choose a child to say an animal noise, e.g. *Moo*. Say a number between 1 and 20. *Seven.* Count as the children make the matching number of animal noises. Repeat for different numbers and animal noises.

WARM UPS

DAY 1

- *Understanding addition as counting on*

A basket, seven teddies

- Put four teddies in the basket. *How many teddies in the basket?* Children discuss in pairs or very small groups. *How many teddies do you think there are?*
- Count the teddies together. *There are four.* Write '4' on the board.
- Remind children that there are four teddies in the basket.
- Choose a child to add three teddies to the basket. As he adds the teddies, count **on**. *Five, six, seven. There are now seven.*
- Write '+ 3 = 7' on the board and read it together. *Four and three more make seven.*
- Repeat, starting with five and adding two more teddies. Write the addition, '5 + 2 = 7'.
- Repeat for 6 + 1 = 7.

DAY 2

- *Understanding addition as the partitioning of a set*

Seven balloons

- Blow up the balloons and show them to the children. *How many do you think there are?* Encourage children to estimate quickly and say their guesses.
- Count the balloons. *There are seven.*
- Choose two children and partition the balloons, three to one child and four to the other.
- Count the number of balloons each child is holding. Write the matching addition, '3 + 4 = 7', on the board and read it together. *Three and four make seven.*
- Count all seven back, taking three from one child and four from the other, demonstrating that there are still seven.
- Repeat with two different children and partitioning the balloons, five to one child and two to the other.
- Count all the balloons back, demonstrating that there are still seven altogether.
- Repeat, choosing two different children to demonstrate 6 + 1 = 7.

DAY 3 • *Understanding addition as counting on*

An eight-floor skyscraper drawn on the board (with a lift shaft), card lift (made from a small cardboard box open at one end), a small teddy, Blu-tack

- Point to the skyscraper on the board. Show the lift and put the teddy in it.
- *The teddy lives on the fourth floor.* Make the lift rise to the fourth floor, counting the floors as the lift goes up, and Blu-tack it there.
- Point to the roof of the skyscraper. *It is four more floors to the roof garden. How tall is the building?* Help children to work it out. They start at the floor the teddy is on – number 4 – and count on. *Five, six, seven, eight.* They can use their fingers to help, holding up four and then counting on one finger for each extra floor.
- Write '4 + 4 =' on the board and read it together. Start on the teddy's floor and move the lift, counting on as you do so. *Five, six, seven, eight.*
- Write '8' to complete the addition. Read the whole sentence. *Four and four more make eight. Four and four more floors takes us to eight.*
- Repeat, starting the teddy's lift on the fifth floor and counting on to eight. Write '5 + 3 = 8'.
- Repeat to demonstrate 6 + 2 = 8 and 7 + 1 = 8.

DAY 4 • *Understanding addition as the partitioning of a set*

Eight coloured card stars, Blu-tack, a large cloud (made from black paper)

- Blu-tack the stars randomly on the board. *How many stars can you see?* Encourage children to have a quick guess. Count the stars, grouping them visually in twos to help you count accurately. *There are eight stars.*
- Cover four of the stars with the cloud. *How many stars can we see now? How many are behind the cloud?* Point to the four visible stars. *Here are four. There are eight in all.*
- Point to the four stars. Count on. *Five* (holding up one finger), *six* (holding up a second finger), *seven* (holding up a third finger), *eight* (holding up a fourth finger). *Look at the four fingers standing up. That's four hidden stars.* Lift the cloud to check.
- Write '4 + 4 = 8' on the board and read it together. *Four and four make eight.*
- Repeat, hiding five stars behind the cloud and counting on from five, holding up one finger with each number spoken. Write '5 + 3 = 8' to match the actions.
- Repeat to demonstrate 6 + 2 = 8 and 7 + 1 = 8.

DAY 5 • *Understanding addition as the combination of two sets*

- Ask children to show you five fingers. *How many fingers? Five.*
- Now we shall add five more. Demonstrate adding another five fingers. *How many now? Ten.*
- Fold down four fingers. *How many now?* Encourage children to see that there are five on one hand and one more, making six. *Six.*
- Hold up the four fingers again. *How many? Ten.*
- Now fold down three fingers. *How many now? Seven.*
- Hold up the three again. *How many fingers? Ten.*
- Repeat, showing two folded down is eight, and that eight and two more is ten.
- Repeat for nine and one.
- Return to five and five. Show five fingers. Now show five more. *How many? Ten.* Write '5 + 5 = 10' on the board. Read this together.
- Repeat for 6 + 4 = 10, 7 + 3 = 10, 8 + 2 = 10, 9 + 1 = 10. Match the finger sums to written sentences each time.

	DAY 1	DAY 2	DAY 3	DAY 4	DAY 5
Objective	Beginning to estimate a length/height, measuring a length/height using a non-standard unit				
Teacher-led activities *On the rug* (pages 95–96)	**Warm up:** Sing a number song. Sit children in a circle. **Activity:** Choose a child to lie flat on the floor. *How many crayons fit along Annie?* Encourage guesses. Children record some on the board. Lay crayons along the child, starting at her feet. *How many crayons long is Annie?* Write the length. Compare this with the guesses. Repeat with a taller child. Help children to guess, basing their guess on the first child's length.	**Warm up:** Say a number rhyme. **Activity:** Give three children a paper fish each. *Who has the longest fish?* Compare fish. Decide which is the longest. *How many crayons long is this fish? How many crayons can we fit along it?* Help children to guess and record their guesses. Lay the crayons end to end along the fish, counting. Which guess was closest? Repeat with the other two fish. Compare the length in crayons.	**Warm up:** Count to 100 as fast as possible. **Activity:** *Which is the longest book?* We shall measure using cubes. *We shall see how many cubes we can lay along the book.* Write children's guesses. Choose a child to lay cubes along the book, counting as you go. *How many cubes long?* Write the length in cubes. Compare with their guesses. Repeat for the other two books. Compare the lengths in cubes.	**Warm up:** Count down from 20 to *Blast off!* **Activity:** *How long is the table? We shall measure it in pencils. Guess how many.* Choose a child to lay pencils along the length of the table. Count as you go. *How many pencils long is this side?* Compare with their guesses. Point to the width of the table. *How long is this side? How many pencils will fit along here?* Children guess, using their knowledge of the first side.	**Warm up:** Show fingers to match numbers to 10. Show one less, then one more. **Activity:** *How many straws tall do you think the door is?* Encourage several children to stand by the door to estimate. Choose a child to help you measure. Blu-tack straws up the side of the door. Count the straws with the children. *How many straws tall is the door? Which guess was closest?* Repeat with the width of the door.
Teacher-initiated activities *Activity Book* (page 22)	**Easy:** Give each child a paper fish (all different lengths). *How many cubes can you lay along the length of your fish? Whose is the longest fish? Whose will need the most cubes? Whose is the shortest? Whose will need the fewest cubes?* Repeat using crayons. **Medium:** Children take turns to lie on the floor. The others measure their height in crayons. Record each height. **Hard:** Each child spreads their hand on a piece of paper and marks their handspan. They measure each handspan with cubes. *Whose is longest? Shortest?*				
Independent activities *Supported play*	**Toys:** Children measure the length of different cars using beads or small cubes. *Which is the longest car? Which is the shortest?*	**Cooking:** Children make cheese straws using the recipe in the Recipe Bank (page 119). They cut the pastry into long and short straws before baking.	**Construction:** Children build the longest moving structure they can using Lego. It must have wheels and be able to move along. *How long is it in cubes?*	**Sand:** Children build a short trench in the sand. *Now try to make a long trench. How long can we make it? How many cars long is it?*	**Cutting and sticking:** Children work in pairs. One child lies on a large piece of paper whilst their partner draws round them. *Measure your height by sticking straws down the middle of your outline. How many straws?*
Language	**Long, short, tall, shorter, longer, taller, longest, shortest, tallest, middle-sized, compare, how many?, measure**				
At home	***How far can you jump?*** **Spoons, small sticks** Place a stick on the ground and ask your child to stand by it and jump forwards as far as they can. Mark the end of the jump with another stick. *How many spoons long do you think your jump is?* Remember your child's estimate and help them to lay the spoons end to end between the two sticks and count how many they used. Was your child's estimate close to the actual number of spoon lengths? Try again to see if their estimate improves.				
Resources	Lots of crayons (all the same length), toy cars, beads, cubes	Three paper fish (different lengths), lots of crayons (all the same length), cheese straw mix	Interlocking cubes, three books (different lengths), Post-it notes, Lego, cubes	Pencils (all the same length), Post-it notes, sandpit, toy cars	Straws (all the same length), Blu-tack, large pieces of paper

- Sing a number song together.
- Say a number rhyme together.
- Count together to 100. Encourage the children to count as fast as they can.
- Count backwards from 20 to 0, then shout *Blast off!* together.
- Say a number between 1 and 10. *Four.* The children hold up that number of fingers. Ask them to fold down one finger to show 1 less. *How many now? Stretch out that finger again. How many now?*

WARM UPS

DAY 1

- *Beginning to estimate a length*
- *Measuring a length using a non-standard unit*

Lots of crayons (all the same length)

- Sit children in a circle. Choose a child to lie flat on the floor. *How many crayons will fit along Annie?*
- Encourage children to talk to each other and to guess. Choose children to write their guesses on the board, reminding them how to form the numerals.
- Lay crayons along the child, starting at her feet. *How many crayons long is Annie?*
- As you lay each crayon, count. Encourage children to count with you. Write the child's length in crayons. *This number of crayons fits along Annie.*
- Compare the total with the guesses. *Which guess was closest? Which guess was furthest away?*

- Repeat with a taller child. Help children to guess, basing their guess on the first child's length.

DAY 2

- *Beginning to estimate a length*
- *Measuring a length using a non-standard unit*

Three paper fish (different lengths), lots of crayons (all the same length)

- Give three children a fish each. *Who has the longest fish?* Compare the fish by holding them up against each other. Decide which is the longest.
- Show children the longest fish. *How many crayons long is this fish? How many crayons can we fit along it?* Help children to guess and record their guesses.
- Lay the crayons end to end along the fish, counting as you do so. Write the length in the number of crayons, both on the fish and on the board.
- Compare the actual length in crayons with children's guesses. *Which guess was closest?*
- Repeat with the other two fish.
- Compare the lengths of the fish by looking at how many crayons long each fish is. *The longest fish is the most crayons long. The shortest fish is the fewest crayons long.*

DAY 3
- *Beginning to estimate a length*
- *Measuring a length using a non-standard unit*

Interlocking cubes, three books (different lengths), Post-it notes

- Show children the three books. *Which book is the longest? We shall measure how long the books are using cubes.*
- *Let's see how many cubes we can lay along each book. How many cubes do you think will fit along the length of this book?* Write some of the children's guesses on the board.
- Choose a child to help lay cubes along the book, counting as you go. *How many cubes long is the book?* Write its length in cubes on the board.
- Compare the book's length in cubes with their guesses. Write the book's length in cubes clearly on a Post-it note and stick it on the book.
- Show children the second book. *How many cubes do you think will fit along this book?* Encourage children to use their knowledge of how many cubes fitted along the first book to help them to guess sensibly how many will fit along this book.
- Measure the second book in cubes. Write the total on a Post-it note and stick it on the book. Compare the total with their guesses. How close were they?
- Repeat for the third book.
- Compare the lengths of all three books in cubes. *Which book is the longest? It measures the most cubes. Which book is the shortest? It measures the fewest cubes.*

DAY 4
- *Beginning to estimate a length*
- *Measuring a length using a non-standard unit*

Pencils (all the same length), Post-it notes

- Point to the table. *How long do you think the table is? We shall measure it in pencils.*
- Show children the pencils. *How many pencils do you think will fit along the table?* Choose children to write their guesses on the board.
- Choose a child to lay pencils along the length of the table. Count as you go. *How many pencils long is this side?* Write the total number of pencils on a Post-it note and stick it along the length of the table.
- Compare their guesses with the total. *Which guess was closest?*
- Now point to the width of the table. *How long is this side? How many pencils will fit along here?*
- Children guess, using their knowledge of the first side. Choose some children to write their guesses on the board.
- Measure the width in pencils, laying pencils along it and counting them as you go. Write the total on a Post-it note and stick it along the width of the table.
- Point to the length. *The table length is six pencils.* Point to the width. *The table width is three pencils. More pencils fit along the length than the width. The table is longer this way than this way.*

DAY 5
- *Beginning to estimate a height*
- *Measuring a length using a non-standard unit*

Straws (all the same length), Blu-tack

- Point to the door. *How many straws tall do you think the door is?* Encourage several children to stand by the door to estimate. Write some estimates on the board.
- Choose a child to help you measure. Blu-tack straws one on top of each other, up the side of the door. Count the straws with children. *How many straws tall is the door?*
- Compare the actual height in straws with their guesses. *Which guess was closest?*
- Repeat with the width.

	DAY 1	DAY 2	DAY 3	DAY 4	DAY 5
Objective	Comparing the capacity of two containers, beginning to understand the vocabulary of capacity				
Teacher-led activities *On the rug* (pages 98–99)	**Warm up:** Count to 60 as fast as possible. **Activity:** *Which holds more, the bottle or tumbler?* Find out by pouring from one to the other. Pour squash from the bottle into the tumbler. *This tumbler is half full.* Continue filling. *The tumbler is full. Some squash is left in the bottle.* Empty the bottle. Pour the squash from the tumbler into the bottle. *It does not fill the bottle. The tumbler holds less. Will two tumblers fill the bottle?*	**Warm up:** Count from 40 to 80 using fingers. **Activity:** *This flask keeps my tea hot. This is my mug. Which holds more?* Find out by filling the flask with water. Show children the flask half full, then full, stressing the vocabulary. Tip the flask into the mug. Show the half full and full mug. *There is still water in the flask. The flask holds more.* Empty the flask. Tip the mug into the flask. *The mug does not fill the flask.*	**Warm up:** Say a number rhyme. **Activity:** *Which bottle holds more shampoo?* Ask children to guess. *We can find out by tipping water from one to the other.* Fill one bottle, stressing half full and full. Tip this into the second bottle. *Does it fill it? Is there some water left in the first bottle?* Check by filling the second bottle and tipping this into the first bottle. *Which holds more? Who guessed right?*	**Warm up:** Count down from 20 to *Blast off!* **Activity:** *This jug is full of squash. How many cups do you think it will fill?* Record children's guesses. Use the jug to fill as many cups as possible. Count as you go. Show the jug when it is half empty. Show it empty. *The jug filled six cups.* Compare with their guesses. *Which guess was closest?* Show that the jug can be filled by pouring all the cups back.	**Warm up:** Count from 1 to 50 using fingers. **Activity:** *This jar is full of the teddy's honey. How many spoons do you think it will fill?* Help children to guess. Record their guesses. Use the jar to fill as many spoons as possible. Count as you go. Point out the half empty jar. *How many spoons of honey? Ten.* Compare with their guesses. Refill the jar by pouring that many spoonfuls back in.
Teacher-initiated activities *Activity Book* (pages 22–23)	**Easy:** Use two bottles of different shapes. *Which holds more water?* The children tip water from one to the other to find out. Introduce a third bottle. *Which holds most now?* They tip from one to another to order the bottles. **Medium:** *How many egg cups will fill this bottle?* Children estimate first and then fill the bottle, counting as they go. Were you right? **Hard:** Make a box using the net of a cube. *How many spoonfuls of lentils will the box hold?* Children estimate first, then count to check.				
Independent activities *Supported play*	**Toys:** Use a toy teapot. *How many toys can have a cup of tea?* Children estimate, then pour the 'tea' into cups. *Were you right?*	**Cooking:** Children make banana milkshakes using the recipe in the Recipe Bank (page 119). *How many glasses will this make?*	**Cutting and sticking:** Children make cylindrical containers using tubes of card. They fill two containers with different things, e.g. lentils or beans, and decide which holds more.	**Sand:** *How many spades will fill a large bucket? How many spoons will fill a small bucket?* Talk about 'half full', 'half empty', 'full' and 'empty'.	**Painting:** Children make a conical container out of a rolled semi-circle of card. They paint it before they roll it into a cone. *How many cups of lentils will it hold?*
Language	**Empty, full, half empty, half full, how many?, measure, fill up, nearly**				
At home	*How many cups?* **A jug, several similar cups, water** Outside, or near the kitchen sink, let your child fill a jug with water and estimate how many cups they could fill from the jug. Ask your child to set out the estimated number of cups and fill them carefully with water from the jug. *How many cups have you filled?* Was your child's estimate close to the actual number filled?				
Resources	An empty squash bottle, a large jug full of squash, two transparent plastic tumblers, a funnel, a toy teapot, water, toys	A vacuum flask, a large mug, banana milkshake mix, glasses	Two empty shampoo bottles (different sizes), shampoo mixed with water to make bubbles, card, glue, scissors, lentils, beans	Transparent plastic cups, a jug full of squash, sandpit, buckets, spades, spoons	A small honey jar (full of coloured water, a teaspoon, a teddy, card, glue, scissors, paint, paintbrushes, lentils, a cup

- Count together to 60. Encourage the children to count as fast as they can.
- Count together from 40 to 80, using fingers to mark the units. Prompt the children with the multiples of 10 if necessary.
- Say a number rhyme together.
- Count backwards from 20 to 0, shouting *Blast off!* together at the end.
- Count together from 1 to 50, using fingers to mark the units. Encourage the children to jump up and wave both hands in the air at multiples of 10.

WARM UPS

DAY 1

- *Comparing the capacity of two containers*
- *Beginning to understand the vocabulary of capacity*

An empty squash bottle, a large jug full of squash, two transparent plastic tumblers, a funnel

- Show children the bottle and a tumbler. *Which holds more?* Encourage children to express their views, for example they may point out that you can pour several tumblers from the one bottle.
- *We can find out by pouring squash from one to the other.* Fill the bottle with squash from the jug. Show children the bottle. *It is full. This tumbler is empty.* Pour some squash into the tumbler until it is half full. *This is half full.* Continue filling it until it is full. *It is full.*
- Show that some liquid is left in the bottle, but the tumbler is full. *The bottle holds more squash than the tumbler.*
- Empty the bottle into the jug. Show children. *The bottle is empty.*
- Pour the squash in the tumbler into the bottle using a funnel. *The juice does not fill the bottle. The tumbler was full, but it has not filled the bottle. The tumbler holds less squash than the bottle.*

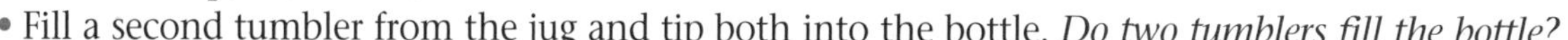

- Fill a second tumbler from the jug and tip both into the bottle. *Do two tumblers fill the bottle?*

DAY 2

- *Comparing the capacity of two containers*
- *Beginning to understand the vocabulary of capacity*

A vacuum flask, a large mug

- Show children the flask. *This flask keeps my tea hot.*
- Show the large mug. *This is my mug. Which holds more, the mug or the flask?* Ask children to peer inside the flask to see how much room there is. Ask them to look inside the mug. Encourage them to discuss how much room there is in the flask and how much in the mug.
- Find out which holds more by filling the flask with water. Show children the flask when it is half full. *The flask is half full.* Continue to fill the flask with water. Show children the flask when it is full. *The flask is full.*
- Tip water from the flask into the mug. When the mug is half full, show the children. *The mug is half full.* Continue to tip water from the flask into the mug. Show the children the full mug. *The mug is full.*
- Show children the flask. *There is still water in the flask. The flask holds more than the mug.*
- Empty the flask. Tip the contents of the mug into the empty flask and show that it does not fill it.

DAY 3
- *Comparing the capacity of two containers*
- *Beginning to understand the vocabulary of capacity*

Two empty shampoo bottles (different sizes), shampoo mixed with water to make bubbles

- Show children the two shampoo bottles. *Which holds more shampoo?* Ask children to guess. Discuss the shape of the bottles. Ask children to peer into each bottle and look at how much space there is.
- We can find out which bottle holds more by tipping water from one to the other. Show children the first, smaller empty bottle. *This bottle is empty.* Fill the larger bottle, stopping when it is half full. *This is half full.* Continue filling it and show children the bottle when it is full. *This bottle is full.*
- Show children the second bottle. *This is empty.* Tip the contents of the first bottle into the second bottle. *Does it fill it? Is there some water left in the first bottle?*
- Check by filling the second bottle and tipping it into the first bottle. *Which bottle holds more?*
- Use some shampoo to make bubbles.

DAY 4
- *Comparing the capacity of two containers*
- *Beginning to understand the vocabulary of capacity*

Transparent plastic cups, a jug full of squash

- Show children one of the cups. Show them the jug. *This jug is full of squash. How many cups do you think it will fill?* Encourage children to guess how many. Record their guesses on the board.
- Use the jug to fill as many cups as possible. Count as you go. Point out when the jug is half empty. Show children the empty jug. *The jug is empty.*
- Count the number of full cups. *The jug filled this many cups.* Compare this total with their guesses. *Which guesses were closest?*
- Show that you can fill the jug by pouring all the cups back into the jug. Count them as you pour.

DAY 5
- *Comparing the capacity of two containers*
- *Beginning to understand the vocabulary of capacity*

A small honey jar full of coloured water, a teaspoon, a teddy

- Show children the spoon. Discuss how much honey it will hold – one mouthful!
- Show them the honey jar. *This is full of the teddy's honey. How many spoons do you think it will fill?* Discuss and help children to guess. Record their guesses.
- Use the jar to fill as many spoons as possible. Count as you go. Point out the half empty jar. *How many spoons of honey? Ten.*
- Compare the total with their guesses.
- Show that we can fill the jar by pouring that number of spoonfuls back into it.

	DAY 1	DAY 2	DAY 3	DAY 4	DAY 5
Objective	Recognising a set of numbers more or less than a given number, recognising numbers between given numbers				
Teacher-led activities *On the rug* (pages 101–102)	**Warm up:** Sing a number song. **Activity:** Count quickly along the number line. Choose a child to unpeg the 7. *Which number has he taken? Seven.* Point to the numbers before 7. *These numbers are all before seven. They are less than seven.* Count from 1 to 6. Point to the numbers after 7. *These numbers come after seven. They are all more than seven.* Count on from 7. Repeat with 10.	**Warm up:** Count from 1 to 50 using fingers. **Activity:** Give 20 children a number card each. They stand in order. Count along the line. Choose a child to point to 9. *What number is this?* Children with numbers bigger than 9 hold their numbers high. Count from 10 to 20. *We say these after nine. They are bigger than nine. They are* ***more*** *than nine.* For numbers less than 9, children kneel. *We say these numbers* ***before*** *nine. They are smaller than nine. they are* ***less*** *than nine.* Repeat with 6 and 12.	**Warm up:** Show fingers to match numbers to 10. Show one less, then one more. **Activity:** Give out the number cards, one to each pair of children. Choose two pairs to find their numbers on the number line. *Whose number is further along the line?* Each pair builds a tower of building bricks to match their number. *Whose tower is taller? Whose number is larger?* Repeat with different pairs and numbers. Stress that the numbers further along the line are larger.	**Warm up:** Count from 50 to 100 as fast as possible. **Activity:** Lay large number cards (1 to 20) along the rug to make a track. Choose a child to take the 8 card. *Which number is this?* Choose a child to take the 14 card. *Which number is this? Which numbers come between eight and fourteen?* Count from 8. *Nine, ten, ... thirteen.* Point to 9 to 13. *We say these numbers when we count from eight to fourteen. They are between eight and fourteen.* Repeat with 5 and 11.	**Warm up:** Say a number rhyme. **Activity:** Choose a child to point to 6 on the number line. Children show six fingers. Point to 16. Children show ten toes (sticking out both feet) and six fingers. *Ten toes and six fingers is sixteen.* If necessary, remove a child's socks to demonstrate, counting toes and fingers. *Which numbers come between six and sixteen?* Count from 6, pointing to the number line. Repeat for 4 and 14.
Teacher-initiated activities *Activity Book* (page 23)	**Easy:** Use a number track (1 to 20). Each child has two counters placed on 1. In pairs, they spin a coin. Heads – move three spaces forwards, tails – move two spaces forwards. *Which numbers come between the two numbers you are on?* Continue to 20. **Medium:** Shuffle number cards (1 to 10). Give a card to each child. In pairs they compare numbers and the child with the smaller number holds up their card. Repeat for the larger number. **Hard:** Shuffle number cards (1 to 20) and place them in a pile face down. Reveal a card. In fours, each child takes a card to compare with the revealed number. They say which numbers come in between. They can use a number track to help. If correct, they take cubes to match the number of in-between numbers. Continue until all the cards have been taken. *Who has most cubes?*				
Independent activities *Supported play*	**Playhouse:** Children give each toy a 2-digit number as a telephone number. They compare numbers. *Which number is larger? Does this number come after or before this one?*	**Cooking:** Make chocolate-covered raisins. Stir the raisins into a bowl of melted chocolate. Pour onto a tray and leave to set. Count how many there are. Divide them onto two plates – one small, one large. Compare the number on each plate.	**Play dough:** Roll out the play dough. Children make door number plaques. *Who lives at the flat/house with the largest number?* They decorate the plaques with beads and small shells.	**Sand:** Bury some number cards (1 to 5). Each time a child finds a card, they build that many castles. *How many castles altogether?* They compare the number of castles they have each built. *Who has built more?*	**Cutting and sticking:** Children use cut-out pieces of paper to make a number. *Which number is largest?*
Language	Number names one to twenty, how many?, more, less, larger, smaller, further along, line, near, close, between				
At home	***Stair numbers*** **Old greetings cards, a pen** Write numbers on the back of some old greetings cards to number some stairs or paving stones. Call out some instructions to your child. *Stand on the stair that comes between six and eight. Stand on the stair that is two more than eight. Stand on the stair that is two less than ten.*				
Resources	Washing with large number cards (1 to 20) pegged to it, pegs, toys, a telephone, 2-digit numbers written on paper	Large number cards (1 to 20), raisins, chocolate, tray, plates	Washing line with number cards (1 to 20) pegged to it, large number cards (1 to 20), pegs, large building bricks, play dough, beads, shells	Large number cards (1 to 20), sandpit, buckets, scoops	Washing line with large number cards (1 to 20) pegged to it, pegs, paper, scissors, glue

- Sing a number song together.
- Count together from 1 to 50, using fingers to mark the units. Encourage the children to jump up and wave both hands in the air at multiples of 10.
- Say a number between 1 and 10. *Five.* The children hold up that number of fingers. Ask them to fold down one finger to show one less. *How many now? Stretch out that finger again. How many now?*
- Count together from 50 to 100. Encourage the children to count as fast as they can.
- Say a number rhyme together.

WARM UPS

DAY 1
- *Recognising a set of numbers more or less than a given number*

A washing line with large number cards (1 to 20) pegged to it, pegs

- Count quickly along the number line.
- Choose a child to unpeg the number 7. *Which number has he taken? Seven.*
- Point to the numbers before 7. *These numbers are all before seven. They are* ***less*** *than seven.*
- Count from 1 to 6. *These are all the numbers we say* ***before*** *we get to seven.*
- Point to the numbers after 7. *These numbers come after seven. They are all bigger than seven. They are* ***more*** *than seven.* Count on from seven. *Eight, nine, ten, ... These are the numbers we say* ***after*** *we have said seven.*
- Repeat, unpegging the 10.

DAY 2
- *Recognising a set of numbers more or less than a given number*

Large number cards (1 to 20)

- Give 20 children a number card each and stand them in order. They hold up their numbers.
- The other children count with you from 1 to 20, pointing to each number as they do so.
- Choose a child to point to 9. *What number is this? Nine.*
- Point to children holding numbers bigger than 9. *Hold your number cards high above your heads so they can still be seen.* Point to children holding numbers less than 9. *Kneel down but hold your number so it can still be seen.*
- Count from 10 to 20. *These are all the numbers we say* ***after*** *we have said nine. They are all bigger than nine. They are* ***more*** *than nine.*
- Choose another child to point to 9 again. *What number is this? Nine.* Count from 1 to 8. *These are all the numbers we say* ***before*** *we say nine. They are all smaller than nine. They are* ***less*** *than nine.*
- Repeat for the numbers more and less than 6.
- Repeat, starting with 12.

DAY 3 • *Recognising a set of numbers more or less than a given number*

Large number cards (1 to 20), a washing line with large number cards (1 to 20) pegged to it, pegs, large building bricks

- Give out the number cards, one to each pair of children. Ask several pairs to say their number.
- Choose two pairs. Point to the first pair. *Where is your number on the line? What number is it?* Encourage them to point to their number on the number line and say the number name. *Six.*
- Ask the second pair to find their number and say the number name. *Twelve.*
- Point to both their numbers on the line. *Whose number is further along the line? Whose number is larger?*
- Ask each pair to build a tower of bricks to match their number. *Whose tower is taller? Whose number is larger?*
- Repeat, using different pairs with different numbers. Stress that the numbers that are further along the line are larger.

DAY 4 • *Recognising numbers between given numbers*

Large number cards (1 to 20)

- Lay the numbers along the rug to make a number track. Choose a child to take the number 8. *What number is this? Eight.*
- Choose a child to take 14. *What number is this?* If necessary, count in whispers up to 14. *Fourteen.*
- *Which numbers come between eight and fourteen?* Ask children to point to the numbers in between. Count from 8. *Nine, ten, eleven, twelve, thirteen.*
- Point to the numbers 9 to 13. *These are the numbers we say when we count from eight to fourteen. They are **between** eight and fourteen.*
- Repeat with different children and the numbers 5 and 11. *Which numbers come between these?*

DAY 5 • *Recognising numbers between given numbers*

A washing line with large number cards (1 to 20) pegged to it, pegs

- Choose a child to point to 6 on the number line.
- Ask all children to show six fingers. Demonstrate, holding up six fingers. Agree that there are different ways of doing this, e.g. three fingers on each hand, or five fingers on one hand and one on the other.

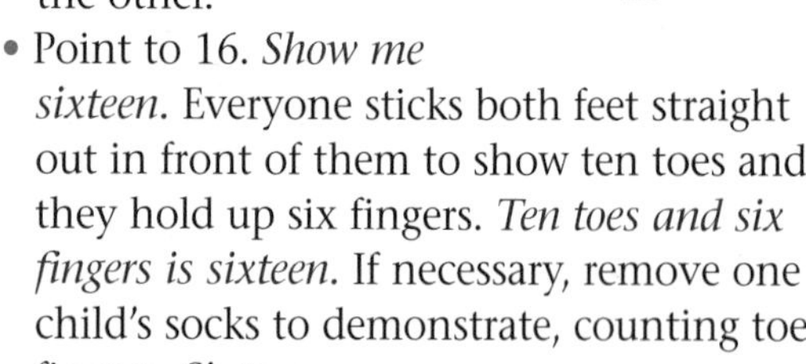

- Point to 16. *Show me sixteen.* Everyone sticks both feet straight out in front of them to show ten toes and they hold up six fingers. *Ten toes and six fingers is sixteen.* If necessary, remove one child's socks to demonstrate, counting toes and fingers. *Sixteen.*

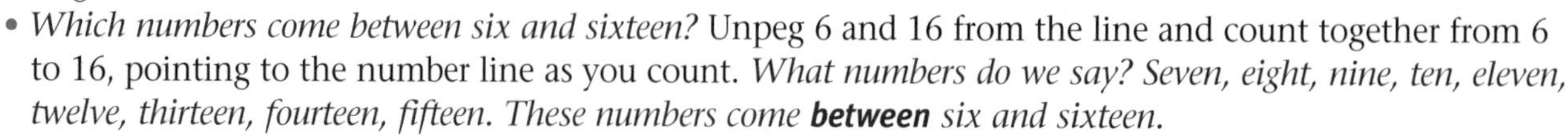

- *Which numbers come between six and sixteen?* Unpeg 6 and 16 from the line and count together from 6 to 16, pointing to the number line as you count. *What numbers do we say? Seven, eight, nine, ten, eleven, twelve, thirteen, fourteen, fifteen. These numbers come **between** six and sixteen.*
- Repeat for 4 and 14.

	DAY 1	DAY 2	DAY 3	DAY 4	DAY 5
Objective	**Removing a small number of objects from a larger number, counting back to find the remainder**				
Teacher-led activities *On the rug* (pages 104–105)	**Warm up:** Count to 50 as fast as possible. **Activity:** *How many cars on this tray? Nine.* Choose a child to unpeg 9 from the number line. *How many if I take away three cars and give them to the teddy?* Help children work this out, starting at 9 on the line and counting back 3. *Eight, seven, six.* Remove three cars and give them to the teddy. Count the cars left. *There are six.* Repeat, starting with eleven cars and counting back three.	**Warm up:** Sing a number song. **Activity:** Count nine cans into the basket. *How many cans left if I give away three? We can use the line to work out how many left. There are nine cans.* Point to 9 on the line. *We are taking away three cans.* Hold up three fingers. Count back 3 from 9 *Eight, seven, six.* Fold down one finger for each number. Remove three cans. Check the number left. Repeat with ten cans.	**Warm up:** Show fingers to match numbers to 10. Show one less, then one more. **Activity:** Lay large number cards (1 to 10) along the rug to make a track. Put a candle on each card, starting at 1. Point to the last card. *There are ten candles. How many if we take away three?* Help children count back in their heads, holding up three fingers, folding down one finger for each number, 9, 8, 7. *Take away three candles. Seven candles left.* Repeat with eight candles.	**Warm up:** Count from 50 to 100 using fingers. **Activity:** Lay large number cards (1 to 20) along the rug to make a track. Make a toy move along the track from 20 to 1, counting together 20, 19, 18, ... Choose a child to put the toy on 11. *Where will the toy get to if it moves back two spaces?* Children hold up two fingers and fold down one finger for each number, 10, 9. *The toy will be on nine.* Repeat with the toy on 15.	**Warm up:** Sing a number song. **Activity:** *How many biscuits?* Put them in a pile as you count them. Twelve biscuits. Choose three children. Use the puppet to give them each a biscuit. *How many biscuits in the pile now? We gave away three.* Hold up three fingers. *We had twelve.* Count back from 12, folding down one finger for each number, 11, 10, 9. *We have nine left.* Count to check. Repeat.
Teacher-initiated activities *Activity Book* (page 24)	**Easy:** Use number cards (4 to 10) arranged in order. Place one cube on each number to 10. Children take turns to take away three cubes. Before they take them away, they say how many will be left. If they are correct, they keep the cubes. **Medium:** Use a number track (4 to 20). Place a 1p coin on each number. Children take turns to remove three coins. Before they take them away, they say how many will be left. If they are correct they keep the coins. *Who has the most coins?* **Hard:** Shuffle number cards (4 to 25) and place them in a pile face down. Children take turns to take a card. They count back three from that number. If they are correct, they take a 1p coin. They replace the card on the bottom of the pile. *Who has the most coins?*				
Independent activities *Supported play*	**Construction:** Children each build a tall tower. *How many building bricks have you each used?* Remove two or three bricks from each tower. *How many bricks in each tower now?*	**Cooking:** Children cut bananas into pieces. Line up the pieces. *How many?* Eat one. *How many are there now?*	**Water:** Fill a small plastic bottle by counting spoons of squash into it. *How many spoons?* Children give several toys two spoons of squash each. After each toy, work out how many spoons of squash are left in the bottle.	**Sand:** Build ten sand castles. Knock down three. *How many sand castles are there?* Repeat twice. *How many are left?*	**Colouring:** Use a selection of candles. Children choose their favourite candle, look carefully at it, draw it and colour it in. *How many colours did you use? Suppose you used one less – how many then?*
Language	**Number names one to twenty, how many?, more, less, the number before, the number after, take away, count back**				
At home	***Down the snake*** **Counters, a coin, paper, a pen** Draw a snake with twenty segments and number them from 1 to 20. Place your counters on 20. In turn, toss the coin and move your counter accordingly: heads count back two spaces, tails count back three spaces. Encourage your child to say, before they move their counter, the number they think they will land on. The first to reach number 1 is the winner.				
Resources	A tray, 11 toy cars, washing line with large number cards (1 to 20) pegged to it, pegs, a teddy, building bricks	A shopping basket, ten cans, washing line with large number cards (1 to 20) pegged to it, pegs, bananas	Large number cards (1 to 10), ten candles, small plastic bottle, spoons, squash, water, toys	Large number cards (1 to 20), a soft toy, sandpit, buckets, scoop	30 biscuits, a puppet, candles, crayons or colouring pencils

- Count together from 1 to 50. Encourage the children to count as fast as they can.
- Sing a number song together.
- Say a number between 1 and 10. *Ten.* The children hold up that number of fingers. Ask them to fold down one finger to show one less. *How many now? Stretch out that finger again. How many now?*
- Count together from 50 to 100, using fingers to mark the units. Encourage the children to count quickly and jump up to wave both hands in the air at multiples of 10.
- Together sing a number song, which involves counting down.

WARM UPS

DAY 1

- *Removing a small number of objects from a larger number*
- *Counting back to find the remainder*

A tray, 11 toy cars, a washing line with large number cards (1 to 20) pegged to it, pegs, a teddy

- Spread out nine cars on the tray. *How many cars on this tray?* Encourage children to count, grouping the cars visually as you count them. *Nine cars.*
- Choose a child to unpeg the 9 card from the number line. *How many cars will there be if I take away three cars and give them to the teddy?* Help children to work this out. Point to the number line. Count back 3. *Eight, seven, six. There will be six cars left.*
- Remove three cars from the tray and give them to the teddy, counting back as you remove each one. *Eight, seven, six.*
- Count the cars that are left. *There are six cars left.*
- Peg the 9 card back on the number line and repeat, starting with eleven cars and counting back three.

DAY 2

- *Removing a small number of objects from a larger number*
- *Counting back to find the remainder*

A shopping basket, ten cans, a washing line with large number cards (1 to 20) pegged to it, pegs

- Count nine cans into the basket, counting each tin as you put it in. *There are nine cans in the basket.*
- *How many cans will be left if I give away three? We can use the number line to help us work out how many will be left. There are nine cans.* Point to the 9 card on the line. *We are taking away three.* Hold up three fingers. Count back 3 from 9. *Eight, seven, six.* Fold down one finger for each number spoken. *We will have six cans left if we take three away from the nine.*
- Remove three cans from the basket. Carefully count the number left. *There are six left.*
- Repeat, starting with ten cans and removing three.

DAY 3
- *Removing a small number of objects from a larger number*
- *Counting back to find the remainder*

Large number cards (1 to 10), ten candles

- Make a line with the number cards along the table.
- Show children the candles. Put one candle on each card, starting at 1.
- Point to the last card. *Ten. There are ten candles.*
- *How many will we have if we take three away?* Help children to count back in their heads, holding up three fingers, folding down one finger for each number spoken. *Nine, eight, seven. There will be seven left.*
- Take away three candles. *Look at the number. Seven. There are seven candles left.*
- Repeat, using eight candles and taking away three.

DAY 4
- *Removing a small number of objects from a larger number*
- *Counting back to find the remainder*

Large number cards (1 to 20), a soft toy

- Lay the numbers along the rug to make a number track. Make a toy move back along the track from 20 to 1, and count together. *Twenty, nineteen, eighteen, seventeen, ...*
- Choose a child to place the toy on 11. *Where will the toy get to if it moves two spaces back?* Encourage children to try this on their fingers, holding up two fingers and counting back from 11, folding down one finger with each number spoken. *Ten, nine. He will be on nine.*
- Move the toy back two spaces, counting back as you do so. *Ten, nine. The toy is on nine.*
- Repeat, starting with the toy on 15 and moving back three.

DAY 5
- *Removing a small number of objects from a larger number*
- *Counting back to find the remainder*

30 biscuits, a puppet

- Show children twelve biscuits. *How many biscuits?* Put them in a pile as you count them. *Twelve biscuits.*
- Use the puppet to give one biscuit to each of three children.
- *How many biscuits in the pile now? We gave away three.* Hold up three fingers. *We had twelve biscuits.* Count back from 12, folding down one finger for each number spoken. *Eleven, ten, nine. We have nine biscuits left.*

- Count the biscuits to check.
- Repeat until there are no biscuits left in the pile.
- Make sure that all the children have had a biscuit.

	DAY 1	DAY 2	DAY 3	DAY 4	DAY 5
Objective	Sorting 3-d shapes, recognising and naming cubes and cuboids, beginning to name pyramids and cones				
Teacher-led activities *On the rug* (pages 107–108)	**Warm up:** Sing the days of the week. **Activity:** *This is a cube.* Point out faces and corners. Count the faces, putting a sticker on each. *Six faces, all the same. How many corners?* Count the corners, putting a piece of Blu-tack on each. *Eight corners.* Give each pair a cuboid for them to count faces and corners. *Six faces and eight corners, the same as the cube. Not all the faces are the same shape.* Discuss cubes and cuboids.	**Warm up:** Count to 50 as fast as possible. **Activity:** Place the four shapes in a line. Talk about each shape. Look at the number of faces and corners. *Which two shapes are similar?* Point to the cube and cuboid. *They have six flat faces and eight corners.* Point to the pyramid and cone. *These are both 'pointy'.* Whilst children close their eyes, choose a child to remove a shape. *Which shape is missing?* Replace the shape and repeat.	**Warm up:** Say a number rhyme. **Activity:** Give each pair of children a 3-d shape. The puppet hides a shape. It describes the shape, focusing on the number of faces and corners and whether the faces are flat. If a pair think it is describing their shape, they wave it. The puppet shows its shape. Encourage children to name the cubes and cuboids and to try to name the pyramids and cones. Repeat several times.	**Warm up:** Count from 50 to 100 using fingers. **Activity:** Give each group of three children a 2 × 2 grid. They place a 3-d shape in each space. Place the large shapes in a bag. On a count of three, bring out a shape. *What shape is this?* Any group with that shape takes it off their grid. (Only **one** shape can be removed each time.) Replace the shape in the bag and repeat. The first to remove all their shapes shouts *Bingo*!	**Warm up:** Do bunny hops to match numbers up to 20. **Activity:** Put one set of four shapes in a line. Choose children to discuss each shape. Choose another child and Blu-tack a 3-d shape from the second set on her back. Turn her to show the class. Children describe the shape without using its name. She selects a matching shape from the line. *What is its name?* Discuss its properties. Repeat with another child.
Teacher-initiated activities *Activity Book* (pages 24–25)	**Easy:** Use a selection of 3-d shapes. Children sort the shapes into three sets, labelled 'cubes', 'cuboids' and 'other shapes'. **Medium:** Make a line of 3-d shapes: cube, cuboid, pyramid, cone. Children copy the pattern, naming the shapes as they lay them. *How many times can you repeat the pattern?* Talk about the properties of the shapes. **Hard:** Use nets of cubes and cuboids. Help children decorate their net, then fold it up to make a cube or cuboid. *How many faces does your shape have? What shape are they?*				
Independent activities *Supported play*	**Sand:** Bury different 3-d shapes in the sand. Children feel for them. Before they uncover a shape, they say what shape they think it is.	**Cooking:** Children make butter icing using the recipe in the Recipe Bank (page 119) and stick six plain biscuits (two square and four rectangular) together to make a cuboid.	**Play dough:** Children make spheres, cubes and cuboids and pyramids. Discuss how to can make the faces flat.	**Cutting and sticking:** Use nets of small cones made from plain card. Children decorate the cone before rolling it up and sticking it. *How many faces are there to decorate?*	**Painting:** Make a large cuboid from cardboard. Children paint each face a different colour. *How many colours?*
Language	**Cuboid, pyramid, cone, cube, corners, faces, curved, flat, square, rectangle, triangle, circle, same as**				
At home	***Building cuboids*** **Similar-sized cuboid building bricks** Give your child a pile of cuboid building bricks, all the same size if possible. Encourage them to make as many different cuboids as possible. Tell your child to remember how many different cuboids they made to tell the class.				
Resources	A large cube, a large cuboid, Blu-tack, stickers, small cuboids (one for each pair), 3-d shapes, sandpit	Four large 3-d shapes (cube, cuboid, pyramid, cone), butter icing mix, plain biscuits (square and rectangular)	Lots of 3-d shapes (cubes, cuboids, cones, pyramids), a puppet, raisins, play dough	A 2 × 2 grid on card (one for each group of three children), large and small 3-d shapes (cube, cuboid, cone, pyramid), a cloth bag, nets of cones, glue, scissors	Two sets of four large shapes (cube, cuboid, cone, pyramid) Blu-tack or sticky tape, cardboard, glue, scissors, paint, paintbrushes

- Sing the days of the week together. Encourage the children to remember the order by starting from days other than Monday.
- Count together from 1 to 50. Encourage the children to count as fast as they can.
- Together say a number rhyme, which involves counting down.
- Count together from 50 to 100, using fingers to mark the units. Encourage the children to count quickly and jump up to wave both hands in the air at multiples of 10.
- Make sure all the children have room to move. Say a number between 1 and 20. *Fourteen*. The children all do 14 bunny hops while counting together. Repeat for wing flaps, hand claps, etc.

WARM UPS

DAY 1

- *Recognising and naming cubes and cuboids*

A large cube, a large cuboid, Blu-tack, stickers, small cuboids (one for each pair)

- Show children the large cube. *This is a cube.* Point to each face. *This is a face. The faces are all the same. Each of the faces is square.*
- Count the faces, putting a sticker on each. *There are six square faces on a cube.*
- Point to a corner. *This is a corner.* Count the corners, putting a piece of Blu-tack on each. *There are eight corners.*
- Give each pair a cuboid. Hold up a large cuboid. Point to a square face on it. *This is a square face.* Point to a rectangular face. *This face is not a square. It is longer than a square. It is a rectangle.*
- Help children to count the faces on their cuboids – two squares and four rectangles. *There are six faces in all.*
- Help children to count the corners. *There are eight corners.*
- Show children the large cube. *This has six faces and eight corners.* Point to the large cuboid. *This has six faces and eight corners as well. But the shapes are not the same. This* (pointing to the cuboid) *is longer than this* (pointing to the cube).
- Point to the large cuboid again and encourage children to look at their cuboids. *Not all the faces are the same shape.* Describe how the cuboid differs from the cube.

DAY 2

- *Beginning to name pyramids and cones*

Four large 3-d shapes (cube, cuboid, pyramid, cone)

- Place the four shapes in a line.
- Show children the cube. Encourage them to remember its name. *This is a cube. How many faces has it?* Encourage children to remember. *It is a cube. It has six faces.* Show children a face. *The faces are all the same. What shape are they? They are all square.*
- Show children the cuboid. *This cuboid has six faces as well.* Show children the rectangular face. *This is not a square. It is a rectangle.* Talk about the faces and discuss how many faces the cuboid has.
- Show children the pyramid and look at the number of faces and corners. Discuss the shape of the faces. *This is a pyramid.*
- Show children the cone and look at the curved face and the circular flat face. Discuss the fact that there are no corners and that it will roll. *This is a cone.*
- Put the shapes back in a line. *Which two shapes are similar?* Point to the cube and the cuboid. *They both have six flat faces and eight corners.*
- *Which other two shapes are similar?* Point to the pyramid and the cone. *These are both 'pointy'.*
- Whilst children close their eyes, choose a child to remove a shape from the line. Children say what the missing shape is. *Look at the shape. Were you correct?* Replace the shape and repeat.

DAY 3 • *Recognising and naming cubes and cuboids*
• *Beginning to name pyramids and cones*

Lots of 3-d shapes (cubes, cuboids, cones, pyramids), a puppet, raisins

- Give each pair of children a 3-d shape. They study their shape carefully and ask each other questions about it. *How many faces does it have? How many square faces? Does it have any curved faces? Is it 'pointy'?*
- The puppet hides a shape. It describes the shape, focusing on the number of faces and corners and whether the faces are flat. *My shape has five faces. One of the faces is a square. It is a 'pointy' shape. It does not have any curved faces. My shape would not roll.*
- If a pair think he is describing their shape, they wave it. Encourage children to look carefully at their shape as the puppet is describing his shape. Is their shape the same?
- The puppet then shows its shape. Were they correct? Encourage children to name the cubes and cuboids and to try to name the pyramids and cones.
- Repeat several times. Give raisins as prizes.

DAY 4 • *Sorting 3-d shapes*

A 2 × 2 grid on card (one for each group of three children), 3-d shapes (cubes, cuboids, cones, pyramids), large 3-d shapes (cube, cuboids, cone, pyramid), a cloth bag

- Give each group of three children a 2 × 2 grid and four 3-d shapes (any combination of shapes). They place a 3-d shape in each space on their grid.
- Place the large shapes in the bag. On a count of three, bring out a shape. W*hat shape is this? Is it a cube, cuboid, pyramid or cone?*
- Any group with that shape takes it off their grid. (Stress that only ***one*** shape can be removed each time.)
- Replace the shape in the bag and repeat.
- The first group to take off all their shapes shouts *Bingo*! and wins.
- Play again, focusing on the properties of each shape.

DAY 5 • *Recognising the properties of 3-d shapes*

Two sets of four large shapes (cube, cuboid, cone, pyramid), Blu-tack or sticky tape

- Lay out one set of four shapes. Talk about each shape.
- Ask a child to select the cube. *Which shape is this? How many faces does it have? Six. Are the faces all the same? Yes. What shape are the faces? They are all squares. This is a cube.*
- Repeat for each shape, discussing the number of faces, whether they are flat or curved and what shapes they are. Name each shape.
- Choose a child and Blu-tack a shape from the second set on her back. Turn her to show the class.
- *What shape has she on her back?* Ask children to describe the shape to her without using its name. When she thinks she knows which shape is on her back, she selects a matching shape from the table.
- *Can we name this shape?* Remove the shape from her back. Discuss its properties.
- Repeat with another child.

	DAY 1	DAY 2	DAY 3	DAY 4	DAY 5
Objective	Recognising coins, solving simple addition and subtraction problems using money				
Teacher-led activities *On the rug* (pages 110–111)	**Warm up:** Count to 100 as fast as possible. **Activity:** Blu-tack the demonstration 1p coin to the board. *This is one penny.* Give a child a 1p coin. *This is one pence.* Blu-tack the demonstration 2p coin to the board. *This is two pence. Two one pence coins are the same as one two pence coin.* Give another child a 2p coin. Give the first child another 1p coin. *They have the same.* Repeat for two 10p and one 20p coin, then two £1 and one £2 coin.	**Warm up:** Say a number rhyme. **Activity:** Show the demonstration 5p coin. *This is five pence.* Choose a child. Give her a 5p coin. *You have five pence.* Talk about its properties. Give a different child five 1p coins. *These five one pence coins are the same as a five pence coin.* Point to both children. *You have the same amount.* Repeat for two 5p and one 10p. Give each pair 10p: either ten 1p coins, two 5p coins or one 10p. *Show me ten pence, five pence, ...*	**Warm up:** Show fingers to match numbers to 10. Show one less, then one more. **Activity:** *This teddy is in a jumble sale. It costs 7p.* Choose a child. Give her a 5p coin. *How much has she got? Five pence. This is the same as five one pence coins. How much is the teddy? Seven pence. Has she enough? No. How much more does she need?* Point to the 5p coin. Count on together, *6p, 7p,* holding up one finger for each number. *Two more pence.* Give her two 1p coins and sell her the teddy. Repeat with the 9p cat.	**Warm up:** Count from 40 to 80 using fingers. **Activity:** Blu-tack the demonstration 10p coin to the 10 card. *This is ten pence.* Give a child a 10p coin. Blu-tack the demonstration 1p to the 1 card. Give a child ten 1p coins. *This is ten pence. They have the same amount.* Point to the first child. *How much if you have a two pence coin as well?* Blu-tack the demonstration 2p to the 2 card. Use the number line to count on from 10. Repeat, adding a 5p to a 10p.	**Warm up:** In pairs, do jumps on alternate numbers in the count to 20. **Activity:** Blu-tack all the demonstration coins to the board. Whilst children close their eyes, choose a child and give her a real coin. Children find out the coin by asking her questions. *Is it round? Is it silver? Will it buy lots?* Help children listen to the answers and remove from the board the coins it cannot be. *If it is not silver we remove 5p, 10p, 20p and 50p.* Repeat.
Teacher-initiated activities *Activity Book* (pages 25–26)	**Easy:** Use real 1p, 2p, 5p, 10p, 20p, 50p, £1, £2 coins. Choose a child to take a coin. *Which coin is it? Can you find another set of coins that is the same as this amount?* Help the child to do this. If successful, they can 'buy' a small snack biscuit from you with their coins. **Medium:** Use biscuits, fruit and real 1p, 2p, 5p, 10p, 20p coins. Price each item, e.g. cake 10p, biscuit 5p, apple piece 2p. Each child chooses one item and uses two or more coins to pay for it. **Hard:** Use real 1p, 2p, 5p, 10p, 20p coins. Give one coin to each child. In pairs, children work out how much they have together. Write the matching sum. Give out different coins and ask children to pair differently.				
Independent activities *Supported play*	**Painting:** Children choose a coin. They choose a side and draw or paint a picture of it, looking at it very carefully.	**Cooking:** Children make shortbread using the recipe in the Recipe Bank (page 119). They cut it into different-sized pieces and 'sell' each piece for 5p or 10p, depending on the size.	**Playhouse:** Children use coins in role play, shopping in the playhouse.	**Cutting and sticking:** Stick cardboard coins in order from 1p to £2 along a line. Children stick equivalents below some coins, e.g. two 1p coins below the 2p coin.	**Jigsaws:** Children do a jigsaw. 'Pay' them 1p for every piece they do. *How much do they have at the end?* Can they swap their coins for an equivalent amount of different coins?
Language	**Coin names, how much?, how many?, cost, buy, sell, more, less, the same as, the same amount, penny, pence, pounds, money**				
At home	*Toy shop* **Five toys, sticky labels, coins (five 5ps, several 1ps), a pen** Using the sticky labels, price the toys at 5p, 6p, 7p, 8p and 9p. Ask your child to look at the price labels and place the correct coins by each toy. Explain that they should always begin with a 5p coin and add on the 1p coins to make the correct value. E.g. for 8p place a 5p, then three 1p coins. *Five pence, six pence, seven pence, eight pence.*				
Resources	Demonstration coins (1p, 2p, 10p, 20p, £1, £2) real coins (1p, 2p, 10p, 20p, £1, £2), Blu-tack, paint, paintbrushes	Demonstration coins (1p, 5p, 10p), real coins (1p, 5p, 10p), shortbread mix	A teddy (priced 7p), a cat (priced 9p), real coins (1p, 2p, 5p), playhouse items	Washing line with large number cards (1 to 20) pegged to it, pegs, Blu-tack, demonstration and real coins (1p, 2p, 5p 10p), cardboard coins, glue	Demonstration coins (all denominations), real coins (all denominations), jigsaws, Blu-tack, 1p coins

- Count together to 100. Encourage the children to count as fast as they can.
- Together say a number rhyme, which involves counting down.
- Say a number between 1 and 10. *Ten.* The children hold up that number of fingers. Ask them to fold down one finger to show one less. *How many now? Stretch out that finger again. How many now?*
- Count together from 40 to 80, using fingers to mark the units. Encourage the children to count quickly and jump up to wave both hands in the air at multiples of 10.
- Make sure all the children have room to move. Divide them into pairs. Say a number between 1 and 20. *Twelve.* Count together to 12. In pairs the children take turns to jump on alternate numbers in the count. Repeat for different numbers of jumps, foot stamps, hand claps, etc.

DAY 1

- *Recognising coins*

Demonstration coins (1p, 2p, 10p, 20p, £1, £2), real coins (1p, 2p, 10p, 20p, £1, £2), Blu-tack

- Blu-tack the demonstration 1p coin to the board. *This is one penny. It can't buy much!* Give the real 1p coin to a child. *You have one penny. You don't have very much money! You need lots of one pence coins to buy something.*
- Blu-tack the demonstration 2p coin to the board. This is two pennies. This does not buy very much either. Give the real 2p coin to a different child. *You do not have very much money either. But you have more than she does.* Point to the first child.
- Point to the 1p. *Two of these one penny coins are the same as one two pence coin.* Give the first child another 1p coin. Point to both children. *You have two pence and you have two pence. You both have the same amount of money.*
- Show the class. *They have the same. Two one penny coins and one two pence coin are the same. That's fair!*
- Repeat to show that two 10p coins are the same as one 20p coin.
- Repeat to show two £1 coins equal one £2 coin.

DAY 2

- *Recognising coins*

Demonstration coins (1p, 5p, 10p), real coins (1p, 5p, 10p)

- Show the demonstration 5p. *This is five pence. What colour is it? It is silver. Is it large? No, it is quite small. What shape is the five pence coin? It is round.*
- Choose a child. Give her a real 5p coin. *You have five pence. It will buy a small lollipop!*
- Choose another child. *I am going to give you the same amount of money. You would also be able to buy a small lollipop.* Give that child five 1p coins, counting these out. *One pence, two pence, three pence, four pence, five pence. This is five pence. I have given you five one pence coins. It is the same as one five pence coin.*
- Point to both children. *You have the same amount of money, one five pence and five one pence coins.*
- Repeat to show that two 5p coins are the same as one 10p coin.
- Give each pair of children 10p. You can either give them ten 1p coins, two 5p coins or one 10p coin. Each pair looks at their coins to check the amount.
- Ask the class to show different amounts of money, if they can. *Show me ten pence. Show me five pence. Show me two pence.*

DAY 3 • *Solving simple addition problems using money*

A teddy (priced 7p), a cat (priced 9p), real coins (1p, 2p, 5p)

- Show the teddy. This teddy is in a jumble sale. Point to the 7p price label. *This teddy costs 7p.*
- Choose a child. Give her a 5p coin. *How much has she? Five pence.*
- Point to the 5p coin. *This is the same as five one pence coins.* Count out five 1p coins to demonstrate.
- Point to the teddy. *How much is the teddy? Seven pence. Has she enough money? No. How much more does she need?* Point to her 5p coin. Count on together. *Six pence, seven pence.* Hold up one finger for each number spoken. *She needs two pence more.* Give her two 1p coins. *Now she has enough!*
- Point to the teddy. *He costs seven pence.* Let the child pay her 7p and give her the teddy.
- Repeat, choosing another child to buy the cat for 9p.

DAY 4 • *Solving simple addition problems using money*

A washing line with large number cards (1 to 20) pegged to it, pegs, Blu-tack, demonstration coins (1p, 2p, 5p, 10p), real coins (1p, 2p, 5p, 10p)

- Choose a child to find the 10 card on the number line. Blu-tack the demonstration 10p coin to the 10 card on the number line. *This is ten pence.*
- Blu-tack the demonstration 1p coin to the 1 card on the number line. *This is one pence.*
- Give a child one real 10p coin. *This is ten pence, it is the same as ten one pence coins.* Give a different child ten real 1p coins, counting them out. *She has ten pence. They are the same amount.*
- Point to the child with the 10p coin. *You have ten pence. How much will you have if I give you this coin as well?* Give her a real 2p coin. Blu-tack the large 2p coin to the 2 card on the number line. *This is two pence. So how much is ten pence and two pence?* Write '10p + 2p =' on the board and read it.
- Encourage children to count on from 10 using two fingers. *Eleven, twelve.* Demonstrate on the number line how to count on from 10. Write the answer, '12p'. *Ten pence and two pence more makes twelve pence.*
- Repeat, adding a 5p coin to a 10p coin.

DAY 5 • *Recognising coins*

Demonstration coins (all denominations), real coins (all denominations), Blu-tack

- Blu-tack all the demonstration coins to the board. Discuss the shape and size of each of the coins. *The brown coins don't buy very much. The silver coins buy more. The gold ones buy most.*
- Whilst children close their eyes, choose a child and give her a real coin. Children find out what coin she has by asking questions. *Is it round? Is it silver? Will it buy lots?*
- Help child listen to the answers, and then remove the coins it cannot be from the board. *If it is not silver, we can remove the 5p, 10p, 20p and 50p.*
- Repeat.

	DAY 1	DAY 2	DAY 3	DAY 4	DAY 5
Objective	Recognising the days of the week, ordering the days of the week, beginning to understand tomorrow and yesterday				
Teacher-led activities *On the rug* (pages 113–114)	**Warm up:** Count down from 20 to *Blast off!* **Activity:** Show 'Monday'. *This is Monday.* It is the first day in the week. Blu-tack 'Monday' on the left of the board and the 1 card below. Show 'Tuesday'. *This is Tuesday. This is the second day.* Blu-tack 'Tuesday' beside Monday and the 2 card below. Continue to Friday. *This is the last day before the weekend.* Stick 'Saturday' and 'Sunday' at the bottom with 6 and 7 cards. *This is the weekend.*	**Warm up:** Sing the days of the week. **Activity:** Draw a wavy line down the middle of the board. Label the left side 'weekdays' and the right side 'weekend'. Talk about what children do on weekdays/weekends. *Which days are weekdays? Which days are the weekend?* Blu-tack day labels on the correct side, saying the days of the week as you do so. *How many days are weekdays and how many are weekend days?*	**Warm up:** Sing a song about days of the week. **Activity:** *What is the day today? Wednesday. What day comes after Wednesday?* Chant the days of the week, up to Thursday. *Thursday comes after Wednesday. Tomorrow is Thursday. What day was it yesterday?* Chant the days of the week, stopping at Wednesday. Write 'Yesterday', 'Today' and 'Tomorrow' on the board and Blu-tack the matching day labels underneath.	**Warm up:** Chant the days of the week. Count up to 7 and back. **Activity:** *There are seven days in the week.* Chant the days in order. Choose seven children to stand in a line. Give each one a day label so the line reads Monday to Sunday. Discuss various activities and which day/days children do it on. Those days of the week kneel. *We like swimming. We swim on Tuesdays*, so the Tuesday child kneels.	**Warm up:** Make animal noises to match numbers to 20. **Activity:** Blu-tack the labels to the board. Point to 'Today'. *What day is it today? Yesterday was teddy's birthday.* Point to 'Yesterday'. *Teddy went to bed last night after his party.* Point to 'Tomorrow'. *What day is it tomorrow? It is the cat's birthday. After one night's sleep, cat has her birthday.* Discuss children's activities, yesterday, today and tomorrow.
Teacher-initiated activities *Activity Book* (page 26)	**Easy:** Children make individual 'weekday' and 'weekend' posters. Write something special for the weekdays and for the weekends for each child, for them to illustrate with a picture. **Medium:** Children make individual week calendars. Write the days of the week and write something special for each day for each child, for them to illustrate with a picture. **Hard:** Look at a calendar for the current month. Talk about how the days are marked. *Which day of the week are we on now?* Find the date. *What is the date tomorrow? What was the date yesterday?* Write in some events on the calendar. *On what days of the week do we write them?*				
Independent activities *Supported play*	**Painting:** Children paint a weekend picture. Use colours and paint shapes which show the 'weekend feeling', e.g. bright cheerful colours, swirly shapes.	**Cooking:** Children make refrigerator cake using the recipe in the Recipe Bank (page 119). *We will leave it until tomorrow to set. What day will we eat it?*	**Playhouse:** Make a chart for next week to go on the wall of the playhouse. Together, write all the things the toys must remember to do.	**Cutting and sticking:** Cut out day of the week labels and make a day of the week frieze. Children decorate it with the activities special to each day.	**Toys:** The children pretend it is their favourite day of the week. They make the toys do the things they like doing on that day.
Language	Time, how long?, week, weekday, weekend, tomorrow, yesterday, today, Monday, Tuesday, Wednesday, Thursday, Friday, Saturday, Sunday				
At home	*Day by day* **Paper, coloured pencils/crayons** Fold a piece of paper into three sections and write 'yesterday', 'today' and 'tomorrow' at the top of the sections. Read the headings to your child and talk about events that happened/will happen on each of these days. Encourage them to draw a picture in each section to show something relating to each day.				
Resources	Day labels (Monday to Sunday), Blu-tack, large number cards (1 to 7), paint, paintbrushes	Day labels (Monday to Sunday), Blu-tack, refrigerator cake mix	Day labels (Monday to Sunday), Blu-tack, materials to make a chart, toys	Day labels (Monday to Sunday), scissors, glue	Labels (Today, Tomorrow, Yesterday), Blu-tack, a teddy, a toy cat, toys

WARM UPS

- Count up to 20 then back to 0, shouting *Blast off!* together at the end.
- Sing the days of the week together. Encourage the children to remember the order by starting from days other than Monday.
- Together sing a song, which involves the days of the week.
- Chant the days of the week together. Count up to 7 and back to 1 several times.
- Choose a child to say an animal noise, e.g. quack. Say a number between 1 and 20. *Eleven.* Count as the children make the matching number of animal noises. Repeat for different numbers and animal noises.

DAY 1

- *Ordering the days of the week*

Day labels (Monday to Sunday), Blu-tack, large number cards (1 to 7)

- Show the Monday label. *This is Monday. It is the first day in the week.* Blu-tack the Monday label to the left-hand side of the board. *Monday.* Blu-tack the number 1 card below it.
- Show the Tuesday label. *This is Tuesday. This is the second day in the week.* Blu-tack the Tuesday label beside Monday and the number 2 card below it.
- Continue until Friday. *This is the last day of school before the weekend.*
- Blu-tack Saturday and Sunday in a separate row at the bottom, with number cards 6 and 7 below them. *These days are the days we do not come to school. This is the weekend.*

DAY 2

- *Ordering the days of the week*

Day labels (Monday to Sunday), Blu-tack

- Draw a wavy line down the middle of the board. Label the left-hand side 'Weekdays' and the right-hand side 'Weekend'.
- Point to the weekdays side. *What sort of things happen on weekdays? We go to school. Lots of people go to work. Shops and offices are open, ...* Talk about the things people do on weekdays.
- *Which days are weekdays? Monday is a weekday.* Blu-tack the day label for Monday on the board under 'Weekdays'. Discuss anything special that happens on Monday.
- Continue for the rest of the weekdays.
- *Which days are weekend days? Saturday is a weekend day.* Blu-tack Saturday on the board, under 'Weekend', discussing the things you do on Saturday. Repeat for Sunday.
- Recap, pointing out which days are weekend days and which are weekdays. Discuss how many days are weekdays and how many are weekend days.

DAY 3 • *Beginning to understand tomorrow and yesterday*

Day labels (Monday to Sunday), Blu tack

- *What is the day today? Wednesday.* Write 'Today' in the middle of the board. Discuss things that happen in school on a Wednesday.
- *What do you do on a Wednesday? Go to friends, visit grandparents, go swimming?*
- Blu-tack the Wednesday label on the board under 'Today'. Write or draw some of the Wednesday things under the label.
- *What day comes after Wednesday?* Chant the days of the week, to Thursday together. *Thursday comes after Wednesday. Tomorrow is Thursday.* Write 'Tomorrow' next to 'Today'. Blu-tack the Thursday label under 'Tomorrow'. Stress that tomorrow comes after one sleep.
- Write or draw some of the Thursday things under its label.
- *What day was it yesterday?* Chant the days of the week, stopping at Wednesday. *What did we say before Wednesday? Tuesday. Yesterday was Tuesday.* Write 'Yesterday' on the left-hand side of 'Today'. Blu-tack the Tuesday label under 'Yesterday'.
- *Does anyone do anything on a Tuesday? That was yesterday.* Draw or write some things below Tuesday.
- Point to the labels and talk about yesterday, today and tomorrow.

DAY 4 • *Ordering the days of the week*

Day labels (Monday to Sunday)

- *There are seven days in the week.* Chant the days in order together.
- Choose seven children to stand in a line. Give each child a day label so the line reads Monday, Tuesday, ... Sunday. Say the days in order, pointing to each day in the line as you say it.
- *Can anyone think of something that we like doing?* Discuss an activity. *Which day or days do you do this? Which days do we play/watch football? Which days do we go to the dance class?*

- For each, point to the appropriate day or days in the line. Those days of the week kneel down. *We like swimming. We swim on Tuesdays.* So the child holding Tuesday kneels down.

- Discuss many different activities.

DAY 5 • *Beginning to understand tomorrow and yesterday*

Labels (Today, Tomorrow, Yesterday), Blu-tack, a teddy, a cat

- Blu-tack the labels to the board in order. Discuss what day it is today. *Today is Friday.* Write 'Friday' under Today. *Today is Friday.*
- Point to the Yesterday label. *What day was it yesterday?* Write 'Thursday' under Yesterday.
- *Yesterday was teddy's birthday! Teddy went to bed last night after his birthday party. Yesterday he was happy!*
- Point to the Tomorrow label on the board. *What day is it tomorrow?* Write 'Saturday' under Tomorrow on the board.
- *Is it anyone's birthday tomorrow? It is the cat's. After one night's sleep, the cat has her birthday! The cat thinks she is lucky because her birthday is at the weekend.* Discuss what children will be doing tomorrow.
- Talk about yesterday and tomorrow. *Yesterday was before last night's sleep. Tomorrow comes after one sleep.*

	DAY 1	DAY 2	DAY 3	DAY 4	DAY 5
Objective	Counting to 100, recognising larger numbers, beginning to count in tens, estimating quantities				
Teacher-led activities *On the rug* (pages 116–117)	**Warm up:** Sing the days of the week. **Activity:** *How many grapes?* Take guesses and help children to write their estimates on the board. Pull off the grapes and place them on a plate, grouping them in twos, then tens, to count. *How many grapes?* Find the number on the 1 to 100 grid and mark it with a Post-it note. Count to that number starting at 1. Compare with the guesses.	**Warm up:** Count to 100 as fast as possible. **Activity:** Point to the numbers on a number grid. Teach children the rhyme 'One Potato, Two Potato'. Repeat a couple of times. Write a large '7' on the board. *Who can think of a number that is more than seven?* Find each number they suggest on the grid. *Is it more than seven? As we go down the grid, the numbers get bigger.*	**Warm up:** In pairs, do jumps on alternate numbers in the count to 20. **Activity:** Point to the numbers in the last column of the grid. *These end in a zero.* Point to the first number. *Which number is this? Ten.* Point to the second. *Which number is this? Twenty.* Count down the multiples. *These end '**-ty**' not '**teen**'.* Choose a child to stand and show ten fingers. Point to ten on the grid. Continue, choosing children to show ten fingers as you count multiples to 100.	**Warm up:** Sing a song about the days of the week. **Activity:** Blu-tack demonstration coins to the board – one 10p and one 1p. *This is ten pence. It is the same as ten one pence coins.* Give the teddy a 10p coin. *The teddy has ten pence.* Point to 10 on the grid. Give the teddy another 10p, and point to 20. *The teddy now has twenty pence.* Continue to 100, with children joining in. Count back in tens taking a coin from the teddy each time.	**Warm up:** Show fingers to match numbers to 10. Show one less, then one more. **Activity:** *This is a night sky picture.* Ask children to guess how many stars there are. Help them to write their guesses on the board. Discuss how to count the stars so that none are missed or counted twice. Group them visually in fives as you count together. Write the total, '30'. Compare guesses, finding the closest by looking at the grid. *Which guesses were closest?*
Teacher-initiated activities *Activity Book* (pages 26–27)	**Easy:** Use a number track (1 to 20). Children take turns to play. *Place a counter on a number. Say the number after it and the number before it.* If they are correct, they take a 10p coin. Continue until all the numbers on the track are covered. *Who has the most money?* **Medium:** Use a large 6 × 6 grid (1 to 36) with counters placed on 1. Spin a coin. Tails – move sideways one space (either direction), heads – move down or up one space. *Say the number you land on, and the number one more.* If children are correct, they take a 10p coin. Children have six turns each. The child with the most money wins. **Hard:** Children estimate the number of leaves on a branch. They write their estimates. They pull off the leaves and count them, grouping them in twos, then tens. Compare their estimates with the total.				
Independent activities *Supported play*	**Painting:** Children each paint a large number of splodges on a page. They count them, then ask someone else to guess how many.	**Cooking:** Children decorate a small pizza base with a variety of toppings. Estimate how many of each, then count. Bake as directed.	**Construction:** Make a large model using lots of different-coloured building bricks. *How many bricks altogether? Write your guess and then count.*	**Water:** Children estimate how many cups are needed to fill a teapot. They check by filling it and counting. Repeat for other containers.	**Dominoes:** Children guess how many dots on five dominoes selected at random. They count to check. Select another five. *How many dots?*
Language	**Number names one to one hundred, zero, more, less, how many?, before, after, count, penny, pence**				
At home	*Up to 100* **A packet of dried fruit/pasta/corn flakes, a tray** Let your child pour out the contents of a packet onto a tray and count the items as far as they can, up to 100, if possible. Help your child with the counting, putting the items in separate piles of ten and then counting the total in tens.				
Resources	About 35 grapes in a bunch, large number grid (1 to 100), Post-it notes, paint, paintbrushes	Large number grid (1 to 100), Post-it notes, pizza base, toppings	Large number grid (1 to 100), building bricks	Blu-tack, demonstration coins (1p, 10p), real coins (1p, 10p), a teddy, large number grid (1 to 100), cups, teapot, water, containers	Dark blue paper with 30 stars on it, large number grid (1 to 100), dominoes

- Sing the days of the week together. Encourage the children to remember the order by starting from days other than Monday.
- Count together to 100. Encourage the children to count as fast as they can. Point to each number on a 1 to 100 number grid as they count.
- Make sure all the children have room to move. Divide them into pairs. Say a number between 1 and 20. *Twelve.* Count together to 12. In pairs the children take turns to jump on alternate numbers in the count. Repeat for different numbers of jumps, foot stamps, hand claps, etc.
- Together sing a song, which involves the days of the week.
- Say a number between 1 and 10. *Ten.* The children hold up that number of fingers. Ask them to fold down one finger to show one less. *How many now? Stretch out that finger again. How many now?*

WARM UPS

DAY 1

- *Recognising larger numbers*
- *Beginning to count in tens*

About 35 grapes in a bunch, a large number grid (1 to 100), Post-it notes

- Show children the bunch of grapes. *How many grapes?* Encourage children to discuss then guess how many there are. Choose different children to write their guesses on the board. Remind them how to form the numerals, starting at the top.
- Pull off the grapes and place them on a plate, grouping them in twos, then tens, to count them. Demonstrate how grouping the grapes helps to count them. *How many altogether?* Write the total on the board.
- *How many grapes?* Find that number on the grid. Mark it with a Post-it note.
- Count to that number, starting at 1. Compare the total with the guesses, finding each guess on the grid and comparing it with the actual number of grapes.

DAY 2

- *Recognising larger numbers*

A large number grid (1 to 100), Post-it notes

- Teach children the rhyme, 'One Potato, Two Potato'. Do the hand movements. Repeat it a couple of times.
- Write a large '7' on the board. *Who can think of a number that is* **more** *than seven?*
- Look at the grid and find 7. Mark it with a Post-it note. *Which numbers are more than seven?* Stress that as we go down the grid, the numbers get bigger.
- Choose several children to suggest numbers that are more than 7. On the grid, find each number they suggest. Compare each number with 7 on the grid. *Is it more than seven?*

DAY 3

- *Beginning to count in tens*

A large number grid (1 to 100)

- Point to the numbers down the right-hand column of the grid. Point out that they all end in a zero.
- Point to the first number in that column. *What number is this? Ten.* Point to the second number. *What number is this? Twenty.* Count down the multiples, *Ten, twenty, thirty, ...* Stress that they end '***-ty***' not '**teen**'.
- Choose a child to stand up and show ten fingers. Point to 10 on the grid. *Farhana has ten fingers.*
- Choose another child to show another ten fingers. *Winston has ten fingers.* Point to Farhana and then Winston. *Ten, twenty. Twenty fingers.*
- Continue, choosing another child to show ten fingers each time as you count the multiples to 100.

DAY 4
- *Beginning to count in tens*

Blu-tack, demonstration coins (1p, 10p), real coins (1p, 10p), a teddy, a large number grid (1 to 100)

- Blu-tack a demonstration 10p coin to the board. *This is ten pence. Each ten pence coin is the same as ten one pence coins.* Blu-tack a demonstration 1p coin to the board. Show children ten real 1p coins and one real 10p coin. Stress that the 10p coin and the ten 1p coins are the same amount.
- Give the teddy a 10p coin. Point to 10 on the grid. *The teddy has ten pence.*
- Give the teddy another 10p coin. Point to 20 on the grid. *Now the teddy has twenty pence.*
- Give the teddy another 10p coin. *Now the teddy has ten* (holding up the teddy's first coin), *twenty* (holding up the teddy's second coin), *thirty* (holding up the teddy's third coin) *pence. The teddy has thirty pence.* Point to 30 on the grid. *The teddy has thirty pence.*
- Continue, asking children to join in as the teddy collects 40, 50, 60, 70, 80, 90 and 100 pence in 10p coins.
- Count back from 100 in multiples of 10, taking a 10p coin from the teddy each time.

DAY 5
- *Recognising larger numbers*
- *Estimating quantities*

Dark blue paper with 30 stars on it, a large number grid (1 to 100)

- Show children the stars on the paper. *This is a night sky picture. How many stars do you think there are?* Encourage children to discuss with each other how many there are. Help them to write their guesses on the board, talking about how to form each numeral.
- Discuss how to count the stars so that none are missed or counted twice. Group them visually as you count together. *One, two, three, four, five.* Pause and group the five stars visually. *Six, seven, eight, nine, ten.* Continue to find the total.
- Write the total, '30'. Find the number on the grid.
- Compare this total with children's guesses, finding the closest by checking on the grid. *Which guesses were closest?*

At home activities

On each weekly plan there is an 'At home' activity provided. It is intended that these are used to enable parents to share mathematical activities with their children and become more closely involved in their mathematical development.

The activity for each week can be photocopied from the appropriate weekly plan and sent home with the children or displayed on the parents' notice board. However, you may wish to provide a separate simple instruction sheet to explain the activity and how it is related to the mathematical topic that the children are doing in the class, nursery or playgroup. The following shows a suggested format for a letter, which you may like to send home to inform parents/carers what the child is working on and encouraging them to take part.

Dear Parent/Carer

Enjoying mathematics and becoming confident with numbers at an early age is an extremely important part of your child's development. You can help by sharing activities with your child – playing games, singing songs and talking about numbers. You don't need to be a mathematical genius to make a huge difference!

There are many ways in which you can help your child become fluent with numbers, and many situations in everyday life where they will see you using mathematics. Children's first ideas about numbers, time, length, weight, capacity, money, time and shape come from things they do at home. You can help their understanding by, for example, talking about numbers, using money to shop, measuring out ingredients, looking at numbers on houses, filling containers with water at bath time, playing 'I spy' for different shapes ...

Each week the children will learn about a different mathematical topic, using a wide variety of activities from the **Abacus Foundation** maths scheme. If you would like to help your child at home you might like to try the 'At home' activity related to each topic. The activity for each week will be displayed on the parents' notice board. Sharing these activities with your child will help make learning maths fun for both of you.

Please see me if you would like more ideas of mathematical activities, songs or rhymes to use at home.

Best wishes

The following are the basic recipes used throughout in cooking activities. Sometimes extra ingredients are added, e.g. sultanas or chocolate chips. Where necessary, these are noted within the activity details on the weekly plans. Please ensure that you are aware of any allergies or dietary requirements that children have when consuming the finished products.

SPONGE CAKE

Butter (100 g), sugar (100 g), self-raising flour (100 g), two eggs

In a large bowl, beat together the butter and sugar. Beat in the eggs, then fold in the flour. Pour the mixture into a greased 18–20 cm cake tin. Bake in a preheated oven, 325°F/160°C/Gas Mark 3 for 25 minutes.

BISCUITS

Butter (100 g), flour (200 g), one egg, water

In a large bowl make a 'crumble' with the butter (at room temperature) and flour. Add the egg yolk and water to mix. Roll out the dough on a floured surface until it is 0·5 cm thick. Cut into shapes as required. Bake in a preheated oven, 375°F/190°C/Gas Mark 5 for 10 minutes.

FLAPJACK

Soft brown sugar (110 g), butter (175 g), golden syrup, porridge oats (175 g)

In a saucepan gently heat the sugar, butter and a dessert-spoon of syrup until the butter has melted. Remove from the heat and stir in the oats. Pour into an 18-20 cm, lightly greased square baking tin and press out evenly. Bake in a preheated oven, 300°F/150°C/Gas Mark 2, for 40 to 45 minutes. Cool in the tin then cut into shapes.

SUGAR MICE

Two eggs, caster sugar (125 g), currants, liquorice strings

Whisk together the egg whites until stiff. Whisk in the sugar, a tablespoon at a time, until very thick. Spoon the mixture into a piping bag with a 1 cm plain nozzle. Line a baking sheet with non-stick paper and pipe the mixture into mouse shapes – wide at one end and tapering off to a point at the other. Place rolled and flattened pieces of mixture on the pointed end to form ears, and decorate with currants for the nose and eyes. Bake in a preheated oven, 225°F/110°C/Gas Mark $^{1}/_{4}$ for 2 hours. Allow to cool, then make a small hole in the tail end of each mouse with a skewer and attach a short length of liquorice string to make a tail.

CHEESE STRAWS

Plain flour (125 g), salt, butter (50 g), grated Cheddar cheese (75 g), one egg yolk, water

Sift the flour, and a pinch of salt into a bowl. Rub in the butter, then stir in the cheese, egg yolk and enough water to make a firm dough. Turn out onto a floured surface and knead lightly. Roll out into a large square about 5 mm thick, and cut into strips. Bake in a preheated oven, 400°F/200°C/Gas Mark 6 for 8 to 10 minutes.

MILKSHAKE

Milk (900 ml), vanilla ice cream (4 scoops), fruit (350 g)

Place the ingredients in a blender or food processor. Blend for 20 seconds then serve.

SPONGE BUNS

Butter (50 g), sugar (50 g), self-raising flour (50 g), one egg

In a large bowl, beat together the butter (at room temperature) and sugar. Beat in the egg, then fold in the flour. Divide the mixture between paper cake cases. Place on a baking tray and bake in a preheated oven, 375°F/190°C/Gas Mark 5, for 15 to 20 minutes.

PEPPERMINT CREAMS

Tin of condensed milk, peppermint essence, lemon juice, food colouring, icing sugar (400 g)

Empty the condensed milk into a large bowl. Add 4 drops of peppermint essence and 1 teaspoon of lemon juice to taste. Add a few drops of food colouring if you wish. Gradually add the icing sugar to the mixture, stirring continuously until it becomes dough-like. Roll out the mixture, cut it into shapes and leave to harden.

SHORTBREAD

Plain flour (175 g), caster sugar (85 g), butter (175 g), semolina (85 g)

In a large warmed bowl beat together the flour, sugar, butter (at room temperature) and semolina with a wooden spoon. Roll out the dough onto a sugared surface to fit a 28 cm x 18 cm lightly greased oblong baking tin. Press it out evenly and prick all over with a fork. Bake in a preheated oven, 300°F/150°C/Gas Mark 2 for 1 hour.

BUTTER ICING

Icing sugar (250 g), butter (125 g), milk (2 tbsp)

Beat together half the icing sugar with the butter until smooth. Beat in the rest of the icing sugar and the milk. Spread on cakes or biscuits as required.

REFRIGERATOR CAKE

Margarine (100 g), golden syrup (2 tbsp), sugar (1 tbsp), cocoa (2 tbsp), digestive biscuits (100 g)

In a saucepan melt the margarine, syrup, sugar and cocoa. Stir in the broken biscuits. Spread the mixture into a greased baking tray and place in the fridge for 1 hour to set.

BROWNIES

Butter (110 g), plain chocolate (110 g), caster sugar (225 g), two eggs, vanilla essence, plain flour (100 g), salt

In a large saucepan over a very low heat, melt the butter and chocolate. Remove from the heat and stir in the sugar. Add the eggs and a few drops of vanilla essence and beat well with a wooden spoon. Sift in the flour and a pinch of salt. Stir until mixed well. Spread the mixture into a greased 20 cm x 25 cm cake tin and bake in a preheated oven, 325°F/170°C/Gas Mark 3, for 30 to 35 minutes. Cool, then cut into shapes.

Curriculum matching chart

The grid shows how **Abacus Foundation** provides curriculum coverage for England, Scotland, Wales and Northern Ireland. It is expected that by the end of F2, children will have attained the goals in the areas shown and fully covered the objectives for each curriculum.

	Abacus Foundation F2																																						
	Term 1													Term 2														Term 3													
Week	1	2	3	4	5	6	7	8	9	10	11	12	13	1	2	3	4	5	6	7	8	9	10	11	12	13	1	2	3	4	5	6	7	8	9	10	11	12	13
Early Learning Goals (England & Wales)																																							
Say and use the number names in order in familiar contexts	●	●		●	●	●	●	●	●		●	●	●	●	●		●	●	●	●	●	●		●	●	●	●	●	●	●	●	●	●	●	●		●	●	●
Count reliably up to 10 everyday objects		●	●	●	●			●	●	●	●	●	●		●		●	●			●	●	●	●		●	●	●	●	●	●		●	●	●	●	●		●
Recognise numerals 1 to 9	●	●		●	●	●	●	●	●		●		●	●	●		●	●	●	●	●	●		●	●	●	●	●		●	●	●		●	●		●		●
In practical activities and discussion begin to use the vocabulary involved in adding and subtracting				●	●												●	●												●	●		●		●		●		
Use language such as 'more' or 'less' to compare two numbers								●			●								●	●	●												●	●			●		●
Find one more or one less than a number from 1 to 10	●			●	●				●					●			●	●				●			●		●			●	●			●	●		●		●
Begin to relate addition to combining two groups of objects and subtraction to 'taking away'				●	●												●	●												●	●				●		●		
Use language such as 'greater', 'smaller', 'heavier' or 'lighter' to compare quantities						●	●	●			●								●	●				●								●	●				●		
Talk about, recognise and recreate simple patterns			●							●		●											●		●											●		●	
Use language such as 'circle' or 'bigger' to describe the shape and size of solids and flat shapes			●							●	●												●	●												●	●		
Use everyday words to describe position																●				●									●							●			
Use developing mathematical ideas and methods to solve practical problems				●	●	●	●	●			●	●					●	●	●	●				●	●					●	●	●	●		●		●	●	●
A curriculum framework for children 3 to 5 (Scotland)																																							
Understand and use mathematical processes such as matching, sorting, grouping, counting and measuring	●	●	●	●	●	●	●	●	●	●	●	●	●	●	●	●	●	●	●	●	●	●	●	●	●	●	●	●	●	●	●	●	●	●	●	●	●		●
Apply these processes in solving mathematical problems	●	●		●	●			●	●		●	●	●	●	●		●	●			●	●		●		●	●	●		●	●			●	●		●		●
Identify and use numbers up to 10 during play experiences and counting games	●	●		●	●	●		●	●	●	●	●	●	●	●	●	●	●	●	●	●	●		●	●	●	●	●	●	●	●	●	●	●	●		●		●
Recognise familiar shapes during play activities			●							●													●													●			
Use mathematical language appropriate to the learning situations	●	●	●	●	●	●	●	●	●	●	●	●	●	●	●	●	●	●	●	●	●	●	●	●	●	●	●	●	●	●	●	●	●	●	●	●	●	●	●
Curricular Guidance for Pre-School Education (Northern Ireland)																																							
Space			●			●	●			●						●			●	●			●						●			●	●			●			
Size						●	●	●											●	●	●											●	●	●					●
Order and pattern	●	●	●						●	●	●	●	●	●	●						●	●	●	●	●	●	●	●						●	●	●	●	●	●
Number	●	●		●	●			●	●		●	●	●	●	●		●	●			●	●		●	●	●	●	●		●	●			●	●		●		●
Relationships	●	●	●	●	●	●	●	●	●	●	●	●	●	●	●	●	●	●	●	●	●	●	●	●	●	●	●	●	●	●	●	●	●	●	●	●	●	●	

This grid lists the Early Learning Goals for mathematics. By the end of F2 the children should have fully covered these objectives. Each box can be completed using a simple tick or your own coding system, e.g. colours or symbols to represent the children's level of attainment. This gives you a quick reference to each child's progress.

Early Learning Goal	Name																													
Say and use the number names in order in familiar contexts																														
Count reliably up to 10 everyday objects																														
Recognise numerals 1 to 9																														
In practical activities and discussion begin to use the vocabulary involved in adding and subtracting																														
Use language such as 'more' or 'less' to compare two numbers																														
Find one more or one less than a number from 1 to 10																														
Begin to relate addition to combining two groups of objects and subtraction to 'taking away'																														
Use language such as 'greater', 'smaller', 'heavier' or 'lighter' to compare quantities																														
Talk about, recognise and recreate simple patterns																														
Use language such as 'circle' or 'bigger' to describe the shape and size of solids and flat shapes																														
Use everyday words to describe position																														
Use developing mathematical ideas and methods to solve practical problems																														

Individual assessment grid

This grid shows the objectives covered in each week's teaching to enable you to track each child's individual progress. Space is provided to allow you to make notes about children's performance, including dates and contexts for the observations.

Name ....

Term 1		Term 2		Term 3	
Count to 10, and then to 20, count on from a given number, say the 'next' number to any given number		Count to 20 and then to 100, say the 'next' number to any given number		Count to 100, count on from a given number, say the 'next' number to any given number	
Numbers to 20: count up to 10 objects, begin to record numbers to mark the number in a set		Numbers to 20: count up to 20 objects, estimate, start to record numbers to mark the number in a set		Numbers to 20: count up to 20 objects, estimate, record numbers to mark the number in a set	
Sort 2-d shapes by shape, name squares and circles, begin to name other 2-d shapes		Use the language of position, and place things in given positions in relation to each other		Use the language of direction, move in given directions in relation to a starting point	
Add 1 to a number up to 10, find a total by counting on one when that object is hidden		Add 2 or 3 to a number up to 10, find a total by counting on when that object is hidden		Add by counting on, subtract by counting back, begin to know the number 1 more or 1 less	
Add by partitioning a set or by combining two sets		Understand addition as a combination of two sets, and relate this to counting on and the partitioning of a set		Understand addition as counting on and as the combination of two sets/partitioning of a set	
Compare the lengths of two or three objects, and use the language of length comparison		Compare the lengths of two/three objects, and begin to measure lengths using a non-standard unit		Begin to estimate a length/height, measure a length/height using a non-standard unit	
Compare tall and short and begin to understand the language associated with height		Compare heavy and light objects and begin to measure weights on scales using non-standard units		Compare the capacities of two containers, begin to understand the language of capacity	
Compare two numbers, compare two quantities, recognise who has less and who has more		Compare numbers up to 20, order numbers to 20		Recognise a set of numbers more or less than a given number, recognise the numbers between given numbers	
Count forwards and backwards to and from 10, recognise numbers to 10		Count forwards and backwards to/from 20, recognise numbers up to 15		Remove a small number of objects from a larger number, count back to find the remainder	
Sort 2-d shapes by shape, begin to name rectangles and triangles, rehearse naming squares and circles		Sort 3-d shapes by shape, recognise and name a cube, begin to recognise a cuboid		Sort 3-d shapes, recognise and name cubes and cuboids, begin to name pyramids and cones	
Recognise coins, count up to ten coins		Recognise coins, begin to match each coin to its appropriate number of 1p coins		Recognise coins, solve simple addition and subtraction problems using money	
Understand that we can measure time, recognise a minute as a unit of time, count the number of times something happens in one minute		Recognise the hours on an analogue clock, and read and set the time to the hour		Recognise the days of the week, order the days of the week, begin to understand today, tomorrow and yesterday	
Count to 20, recognise numbers to 20, count sounds and movements, estimate quantities		Count to 20, recognise numbers to 20, count sounds and movements, estimate quantities		Count to 100, recognise larger numbers, begin to count in tens, estimate quantities	

Notes